Antony Funnell is a Walkley award-winning journalist and broadcaster. He is the presenter of the *Future Tense* series on ABC Radio National and is a former host of *The Media Report*. Over the past two decades he has worked for many of Australia's leading news and current affairs programs, including *AM*, *PM* and *7.30 Report*.

The FUTURE

and #relatednonsense

Antony Funnell

ABC
Books

The ABC 'Wave' device is a trademark of the Australian Broadcasting Corporation and is used under licence by HarperCollins*Publishers* Australia.

First published in Australia in 2012
by HarperCollins*Publishers* Australia Pty Limited
ABN 36 009 913 517
harpercollins.com.au

HarperCollins*Publishers*
Level 13, 201 Elizabeth Street, Sydney NSW 2000, Australia
31 View Road, Glenfield, Auckland 0627, New Zealand
A 53, Sector 57, Noida, UP, India
77–85 Fulham Palace Road, London W6 8JB, United Kingdom
2 Bloor Street East, 20th floor, Toronto, Ontario M4W 1A8, Canada
10 East 53rd Street, New York NY 10022, USA

National Library of Australia Cataloguing-in-Publication entry:

Funnell, Antony.
  The Future and Related Nonsense: the insider's
  guide to where we are and where we're heading — the good, the bad and the
  bizarre! / Antony Funnell.
  ISBN: 978 0 7333 2991 3 (pbk.)
  Forecasting. Technological forecasting. Social prediction.
  Australian Broadcasting Corporation.
303.49

Cover design by Matt Stanton, HarperCollins Design Studio
Typeset in Sabon LT Roman by Kirby Jones

For my son Rupert and my brother Wayne.

CONTENTS

Preface

Part One: Hype, hope & headway

**Part Two: Challenges & opportunities
(which also look an awful lot like challenges)**

**Part Three: Is it just me, or is everything getting
a little odd?**

It seems rather quaint to pack sandwiches for the end of the world, but there you are.

Imagine it's the early 1920s and you're a member of a theosophical society called the Order of the Star of the East. You've just donated money to help build a neo-classical amphitheatre at Balmoral Beach in Sydney.* You're awaiting the Second Coming. It's the perfect spot for the Creator to appear. Or re-appear, as the case may be — lots of sunshine, fantastic views out over Sydney Heads, that kind of thing.

So you wait and you wait ... you eat your sandwiches and you wait ... you look keenly out to sea and you wait ... then you wait some more. You wait and you wait and you wait and finally ... nothing! Not a sausage! Eventually you fold up your crocheted tartan throw-over. You wait a tiny bit longer, just in case. Then you go home.

You're disappointed because the future didn't pan out the way you thought it would — and you'd made corned beef sandwiches!

So what do you do? Well, you could simply accept that your prediction was wrong, that it was built on a confection of

---

* Sounds bonkers, I know, but in the 1920s oriental mysticism had hundreds of thousands of followers across the Western world. The Order of the Star of the East was set up to follow the teachings of the new 'Messiah', Krishnamurti, a young Indian boy who was unfortunate enough to have been 'discovered' on a beach near Madras by an eccentric Englishman named Charles Leadbeater. The Order was dissolved in August 1929 when Krishnamurti renounced his messianic claim. He then disappeared into obscurity. In 1954 the *Sydney Morning Herald* found him living in the small Californian town of Ojai. As for the amphitheatre at Balmoral, it was demolished in the early 1950s to make way for a block of flats.

delusion and wishful thinking; there and then you could give up worrying about what might happen and pledge instead to live your life as best you could, remembering Einstein's dictum: 'A happy man is too satisfied with the present to dwell too much on the future.' Or, you could simply recalibrate and try again: 'When they said the Messiah was coming on Tuesday at 1.15 pm, perhaps I misheard. Maybe they meant next Tuesday. Better buy some more corned beef.'

Now, I'm going to digress for a moment and tell you about my favourite end-of-the-world forecast. It involves the Millerite movement in the United States, back in 1844. The Millerite leaders didn't just foresee the end of time, they even narrowed it down to a date — 22nd October.* Many of the faithful reportedly disposed of their worldly possessions in preparation — as you would. And, like the crowd at Balmoral Beach three-quarters of a century later, they then waited, and waited, prayed and then waited and waited again. Of course, the big day passed without incident, and for as long as the movement continued, followers of the Reverend William Miller henceforth referred to 22nd October curiously, and rather dispassionately, as the 'Great Disappointment'. Which must be one of the classic understatements of all time: You're expecting the Second Coming of Jesus Christ, son of the Creator of all things, Light of the World, one corner of the Holy Trinity, the progeny of God and yet God himself, and when he doesn't turn up, you're just 'disappointed'. I guess mid-nineteenth-century believers weren't that big on passion; guilt, fear, piety and anxiety, yes, but passion? Possibly not.

One of the great traits of humankind is our profound ability *not* to learn from our mistakes, but to keep on repeating

---

* Actually, 22nd October wasn't even the Millerites' first stab at a date. They'd originally calculated that Christ would come again sometime between 21st March 1843 and 21st March 1844. And after that there was also April 18th 1844. Out of interest, the modern day Seventh Day Adventist church grew out of the remnants of the 'Great Disappointment'.

them over and over again. In 2011, for instance, followers of a Californian prophet named Harold Camping also began clearing the decks for Armageddon. And they got quite a deal of attention for what they called the 'Rapture'. Camping reportedly spent tens of millions of dollars publicising his unique take on the end of days and it paid off, in one sense, because major news outlets across the world eagerly reported it all, including the BBC. Although, in fairness, the coverage was more mocking than reverential.

Anyway, this time the date was 21st May.

The fact that you're reading this book is as good a proof as any that the appointed day came and went without incident — another disappointment. But the wishful spirit of the faithful was not entirely conquered. As one of Camping's congregation told the *Los Angeles Times*: 'We obviously went too far, and that's something we need to learn from.'[1]

You've got to admire that kind of patient persistence.

And we shouldn't forget the Mayan calendar predictions — *National Geographic* identified six separate end-of-the-world myths for 2012, with a NASA scientist named David Morrison reportedly telling the journal: 'People are genuinely frightened. I've had two teenagers who were considering killing themselves, because they didn't want to be around when the world ends.'[2]

The future is like that. We love to anticipate it, to speculate about it and, like the Order of the Star of the East, to prognosticate about it, but it remains tantalisingly elusive. And although we often talk about it as if it were a thing, a place, a predetermined destination that we're all heading towards, it's actually a concept; and an extremely flexible one at that. And many of us don't like the idea that we shape it by our choices and actions.

Suffice to say, predicting the future is a fool's game. Only fools and marketing types, I often say; which doesn't seem to annoy the fools all that much, but does tend to send the marketing types into a bit of a tizz.

Short of God and Nostradamus, no one really has the power to definitively say what lies ahead (and sadly, at the time of going to print, I was still waiting for either of the aforementioned gentleman to respond to the long list of queries I'd sent via Ouija board). But that doesn't stop us giving it a try. Truth be told, we all obsess in one way or another about what's around the corner, what's just over the horizon.

US blogger Matt Novak describes himself as a 'paleofuturist'; an 'accidental expert', he says, on 'past visions of the future', visions he details and catalogues on a very popular website called the Paleofuture Blog. From comic strips to great works of literature, Novak scours public libraries and the backwaters of cyber space for the futuristic forecasts made by people in previous generations. He gets contributions sent to him from all over the world. Some of them, he says, are intriguing, to say the least.

'There's this article that I really love from the year 1900,' he tells me. 'It ran in *The Ladies' Home Journal,* about what the year 2000 was supposed to look like. It was by John Elfreth Watkins, who I believe was a mystery writer. He prefaced the whole article by saying "these are rather conservative predictions". Anyway, he predicted that there'd be no need for animals in the future, so we wouldn't have them. He said we'd only have horses in zoos. Which always gets a chuckle.'

Watkins also predicted that by 2000, humankind would have found a way to completely eradicate all flies and cockroaches, which plainly hasn't happened in my kitchen! But Novak says what surprises him most is the fact that even the really ambitious forecasters often get at least something right. And in the case of John Watkins, more than a few of his darts managed to hit the old pig bristle: 'Some of them were fairly spot-on. For instance, there was a prediction about how heat and cooling would be pumped into people's homes in the future,' says Novak. And from my cursory look, Watkins also did a pretty fair job of predicting radio, high-speed trains and tanks.

Another prophetic example I came across while digging around online was from the *New York Times* in 1982. The newspaper looked to the future and opined: 'There will be a shift away from conventional workplace and school socialization. Friends, peer groups and alliances will be determined electronically, creating classes of people based on interests and skills rather than age and social class.' Which, when you think about online social networking, isn't far off the mark.

Predicting the future might be a fool's game, but sometimes even fools get lucky, which is probably why we continue to do it.

In this book I'm going to both feed the human obsession for prediction and tut-tut it as well, which seems a thoroughly modern media thing to do. Someone once said to me that trying to understand the future is a lot like betting on a horse race: your best chance of getting it right is to study form — get a gauge of the horses, of the track and the techniques used by the various riders and trainers; which, for want of a better plan, seems to me like a fair enough strategy, so that's what we'll do.

This book has a heavy, though not exclusive, focus on technology, because technology is increasingly an indispensable part of our lives. But let me be clear about one thing: this is not a book about gadgets. This is not a technology tome. I'm interested in technology only in regard to the effect it has, or can have, on individuals and society. And another clarification: some of the people we'll meet have ideas that are so out there, they're likely to trigger what I call your Fukuyama reflex.

You've never heard of the Fukuyama reflex? Well, let me explain. The American philosopher Francis Fukuyama famously declared back in the early 1990s — after the end of the Cold War and the collapse of communism in Europe — that history, as we knew it, had ended. He wrote: 'What we may be witnessing is not just the end of the Cold War, or the passing of a particular period of post-war history, but the end of history as such: that is, the end point of mankind's ideological evolution and the universalisation of Western liberal democracy as the final form of human government.'

In hindsight that seems spectacularly ridiculous, but at the time it was such an outrageous statement that many serious journalists and commentators fell over themselves to repeat it. And because it was delivered with such confidence, they determined that it had to be true. It certainly caught the prevailing mood in the United States, where Americans were indulging in feelings of hegemonic self-satisfaction, having just stared down the Russian bear. If you listen really carefully you can still hear them laughing in the corridors of power in Moscow and Beijing and Kiev and almost any of the capitals of the former soviet republics that once made up the USSR. They're also still having a chuckle in Tehran. As I say, many people took Fukuyama's words very seriously. I, of course, thought it was nonsense. And with a smug smile on my face, I'm happy to report that my intuition has so far proven correct. Bit of a pity really for all those still toiling away under the heel of oppression, but that doesn't diminish my point. So, whenever you hear a statement that seems just too spectacular or incredible to be true, and you find yourself doing a little double-take — that's the Fukuyama reflex.*

I really should apologise in advance for any long-winded, pointless rambling on my part, any off-the-point, seemingly loosely connected mental meandering. And while I detest hyperbole, I reserve the right to employ it from time to time when it suits me. I also should warn you that while the spirit of this book is one of fascination and excitement about where we're heading, I won't be shying away from warts-and-all analysis when and where appropriate. In other words, if

---

* In fairness to Professor Fukuyama, the rest of the famous paragraph (the bit that's never quoted) went on to qualify the first part: 'The victory of liberalism has occurred primarily in the realm of ideas or consciousness and is as yet incomplete in the real or material world. But there are powerful reasons for believing that it is the ideal that will govern the material world in the long run.' Uh oh, there goes that reflex again!

you're the sort of person who's reluctant to take off your rose-coloured glasses, particularly when it comes to technology, then it's probably best you go straight to Chapter 12, where I deal with Klingons and space elevators.

Now, this is a book about the future, but it naturally reflects on our current times, as all genuine books about the future must. The author William Gibson once said: 'The future is already here, it's just not evenly distributed.' And that's the philosophy that underpins this inquiry.

In the last ten or so years, we've seen a remarkable transformation of society, but people have pretty much been left to themselves to navigate their way into the digital future. The pace of change has been so fast that I think many of us still feel somewhat disoriented. Nobody likes to admit to ignorance and so many of us have stopped questioning why we're being prodded and pulled in one direction or the other. Frightened of being labelled a Luddite, far too many people have allowed themselves to be swept along by those who make a business out of telling us what our future should be. And many others, just like the Millerites, have become cocooned in an unquestioning belief in the power of technology and its potential.

Douglas Rushkoff, the celebrated American media theorist, talks about subservience to technological fashion based on a fear of 'falling behind'. He exhorts people to be more assertive and selective about the various forms of social media they choose to engage with, for example. He maintains: 'You do have not just the right, but the ability to choose which of these things are going to benefit you, and which ones just don't really make sense for you.'

Well, I would go further than that and say you have not just a right, but a duty to be more assertive and more informed about technology and the future. Because, as we'll see in this book, the end result of acquiescence or indifference can, in the most extreme cases, end in disaster.

So, verily I say unto you, brothers and sisters, cast aside your digital rosary beads and look more closely at the world around you. Or better still, roll up your trouser legs and join me for a paddle through the shallow water at the edge of the future.

Be curious, be positive, and embrace your inner sceptic!

PART ONE

HYPE, HOPE & HEADWAY

In which we assess the motivations of those who seek
to guide us into the unknown; we hear about the desire of
a growing number of people to wrest back direct control
of their future; we learn about a new spirit of collaboration
in the cause of progress — and, just as importantly, its limits;
and we discover that the Western way isn't always the best
way when it comes to meeting the technological needs
of the developing world.

CHAPTER 1

COMMODITISING THE FUTURE

We know where you are. We know where you've been.
We can more or less know what you're thinking about.

Eric Schmidt, Executive Chairman and former CEO of Google[1]

Prophets of the future

Let's begin our journey with a critical look at those involved in the modern-day business of prediction. Or should that be the industry of the future?

The future can mean different things to different people and engender very different emotions. It can be a bad thing or a good thing, and how we envision it can change depending on the situation around us; that is, it's informed by the realities of the here and now. For some it can be a point of hope; for others a point of fear; for others still — like the Millerites — a point of both hope and fear and, ultimately, disappointment.

The fact that it acts as a repository for so much of our anxiety, emotion and desire also makes it a concept we crave to understand. And cravings desire to be fed. Who feeds them, how and why, is the focus of this chapter.

The future is a tale without a definitive conclusion, because it's impossible to know the end point of the story. So when most of us talk about the future, what we really mean is a point in time not actually very far off. The UK-based science fiction writer Charlie Stross takes a very practical approach to the issue: 'Attempting to extrapolate how the world will look exactly in say ten or twenty years is really rather difficult. However, one rule of thumb that is applicable is that the future looks just like the present ninety-five per cent of the time — and then you add five per cent unutterable weirdness on top.'

Predicting that five per cent is big business and in recent years it's become an industry in itself. A fact that no doubt would have pleased the late H. G. Wells who, in 1932, wrote: 'It seems an odd thing to me that though we have thousands and thousands of professors and hundreds of thousands of students of history working upon the records of the past, there is not a single person anywhere who makes a whole-time job of estimating the future consequences of new inventions and new devices. There is not a single Professor of Foresight in the world. But why shouldn't there be? All these new things, these new inventions and new powers, come crowding along; every one is fraught with consequences, and yet it is only after something has hit us hard that we set about dealing with it.'

Type the word 'futurist' into the search engine on your computer and within a micro-second you'll have literally millions of results. There are gazillions of people out there with the word somewhere in their job description (quite often a description they themselves have written up). They're the high-priests of the soon to be. And if you'll indulge me a little prediction of my own, you'll be hearing and seeing a lot more of them in coming years.

The actual term 'futurist' has been used by various people for decades. But in the past, it was always spoken of as an addendum. Somebody like Arthur C. Clarke was often referred to as a science fiction author 'and futurist'. But, until recently, I don't think anyone really thought of futurism as a genuine occupation. I mean, if you'd rocked up to immigration officials at an international airport prior to the year 2000 with the word 'futurist' scrawled on your arrival form, they'd have sent you to the back of the line with a reprimand for wasting their time and a warning against giving frivolous answers to serious questions. Not so today. Today futurism has taken on an air of respectability — at least in the West, that is; Customs and Immigration in China and Azerbaijan might have an entirely different viewpoint.

But in the Western world, the descriptor in question no longer automatically elicits either a giggle or a raised eyebrow. On the last day of 2010, the Australian Broadcasting Corporation's premier TV current affairs program *The 7.30 Report* marked the end of the year in a time-honoured tradition, by looking back at the major events of the past twelve months and speculating about the year ahead. Nothing unusual in that, except for the fact that on that particular occasion the 'expert' they chose to speak to was not an economist or an international affairs specialist, or even a social researcher, all normal guests for such occasions. No, on 31st December 2010 they chose a futurist. And futurists often turn up in the *New York Times* and *The Guardian* and all manner of other serious media outlets. They're definitely in demand.

These days futurists also give motivational presentations at senior-executive love-ins — they're the current corporate must-have* — and they're a firm favourite on the international conference circuit. Take a look at the speakers list for almost any major technology or 'ideas' summit and you're guaranteed to find a smattering of them. If smattering is the right collective noun, perhaps a 'seer' is more appropriate or a 'forecast' — a forecast of futurists?

Anyway, futurism is a growing industry, and while it isn't yet considered a profession in the strictest sense, there are now tertiary institutions running courses in future studies, there's

---

* Of course it all started with Time-and-Motion experts. Then in the 1980s and 90s the clever organisational thing to do was to engage a psychologist to tell you which of your staff were one type of personality and which were another. Though why that was helpful after you'd already employed them was never very clear to me. And now, in the short-pants stage of the new millennium, it's the futurist.

an Association of Professional Futurists, and there was even an international futurists convention held in Vancouver in 2011, organised by a group called the World Future Society.

Can you imagine the dinner conversation?

Futurist A: 'I think I'll have the Moroccan chicken with couscous.'

Futurist B: 'I knew you were going to order that.'

Futurist A: 'No you didn't.'

Futurist B: 'Yes, I did.'

Futurist A: 'You did not!'

Futurist B: 'Did so!'

Futurist A: 'Well, I knew you were going to say that.'

Futurist B: 'That's impossible.'

Futurist A: 'No it's not.'

But could futurism ever be recognised as a genuine discipline? And should it be? Anyone who went to university in the late seventies/early eighties would remember that there was still much discussion back then about whether psychology was actually a legitimate academic pursuit. That seems impossible to imagine today, because psychology now sits at the head table, it's part of the establishment. And it's just possible that futurism is heading in the same direction.

But who exactly are the prophets of the future?

Alex Pang is one of those who call themselves futurists. He's also an Associate Fellow at the Said Business School at Oxford University. Until a few years ago he was also involved with a California-based think-tank called The Institute for the Future. 'Part of the charm and in some ways a little bit of the frustration of the field, is that anyone can describe themselves as a futurist these days,' he says.

'It's not like being a lawyer or a doctor where you actually have exams and certification. However, I think we have to recognise that it's an expression of a very fundamental human desire. The Harvard psychologist Daniel Gilbert said that what sets humans apart from every other animal is that humans are the only ones who think about the future, who have a sense that the future can be different from the past. And so I think that if a diverse, sometimes kind of quirky constellation of personalities and ideas is the price you have to pay for human beings being like that, for human beings being able to think about the future and take it seriously, I think that's well worth paying,' he concludes. *

Of course, when you look at Pang's work it's clear he's an intelligent and thoughtful individual, but it has to be said that that 'quirky' side he mentioned can be difficult to intellectually accommodate if, like me, you're naturally given to scepticism. Some futurists I've come across practise 'visioning' and talk about being skilled in 'reading the air' and the importance of understanding what's 'in the ether'.

Not all futurists are that way, of course. People like Pang in the United States and Richard Watson in the UK — who wrote the 2010 book *Future Files: 5 Trends That Will Shape the Next 50 Years* — actually work with a lot more than just new-age language, they put intellectual rigour, research and experience into what they do. But there is still a point to be made that for every Richard Watson or Alex Pang, there's also an ether expert — a reader of the air. And, importantly, even the quirky ones can have serious influence, advising major corporations and even governments.

This chapter isn't meant to be an attack on people who call themselves 'futurists', far from it, but I think the growth of futurism and the nature of what it offers is instructive of a much wider point about our current attitude towards technology, and our relationship with it. It's interesting to examine exactly what it is that people who label themselves 'futurists' actually do. From

---

* Incidentally, a little while back Alex Pang wrote a whimsical blog post which he called: 'The Evil Futurists Guide to World Domination' and in it he poked fun at some of the less reputable in his field. Among his tips for all budding 'evil' futurists were: 'Be certain, not right'; 'Get prizes for being outrageous'; and 'Don't remember your failures. No one else will.' Does sound a lot like smoke and mirrors, doesn't it? And that's the point.

my observation, futurism tends to be highly industry specific and while there are futurists who focus on all manner of topics, from banking to climate change, it's in the communication/technology sector that they seem to have gathered in real strength. And it's not hard to understand why, given the incredible rate of technological development in recent years.

In an article he wrote for the *Harvard Business Review*, Umair Haque, the director of the Havas Media Lab and author of the book *The New Capitalist Manifesto*, mused about the fact that there were 20,000 new consumer technology products unveiled at the 2011 US Consumer Electronics Show — the biggest annual event of its kind anywhere in the world. He was quoting the figure from a post by Helen Walters, a former editor of innovation and design at *Businessweek*. Haque bemoaned what he called 'a vicious cycle of hypercommoditization — a global economy where there's a surfeit of faster, cheaper, bigger, harder, at the expense of a distinct lack of better'.

Now just think about that figure for a moment: 20,000 new consumer technology products on offer at just one trade show. Is it any wonder then that many people today feel as though they live in a state of constant change, of perpetual technological upgrade?

Feeding that beast means not only being competitive, but also trying to second-guess what technology users will purchase next. And that's the ground upon which many futurists peg their tent. Because there's big money to be made in accurate forecasting, and huge corporate dollars to be lost in getting it wrong: Motorola, IBM, even Nokia — it's not hard to draw up a list of companies that have rapidly slid from the very top of the game to secondary status by failing to keep abreast of changing times and tastes, while corporations like Apple and Google have leapt ahead in recent years in large part because of their flexibility and innovation.

For Brian David Johnson, staying ahead of the curve is everything. Mr Johnson is employed by one of the world's largest and best-known tech companies. 'Being a futurist at Intel might sound like science fiction, but it's actually pretty pragmatic,' he says. 'When we design the chips to go into your televisions, your computers, your phones, we need to do it about every five to ten years in advance. We need to have an understanding of what people will want to do with those devices five to ten years before they actually come out.'[4] As a matter of fact, Intel's current advertising slogan is 'Sponsors of Tomorrow'.

So the value-adding that futurists like Johnson offer technology companies centres around understanding tech usage, not necessarily technology itself. It's an important distinction and one that's easily overlooked.

Another Intel employee focused on the future is Australian-born Genevieve Bell, who heads up the company's User Experience Group: 'I think one of the big transitions that companies in the technology industry have really gone through in the last ten to fifteen years, is to start to have to build technology that really speaks to people,' she tells me during a visit Down Under, a visit that includes a field trip to several remote Indigenous communities in order to assess their technological needs and uses.[*]

'It's not enough that it be shiny or flashy and have blinky lights and be the coolest thing,' she says. 'It also has to do something people care about. And for me, getting that right, creating technology that matters, creating a company that thinks about where their technology might end up, and who cares about the consequences, is really important.'

Dr Bell has a background in cultural anthropology and, strictly speaking, she doesn't call herself a futurist. At least, I'm

---

[*] In 2009, Bell spent several months in Australia as one of the South Australian Government's 'Thinkers in Residence'. Australian-born and raised, but with an American accent, she confesses to a residual love of the stodgy, beige parcel of fat, salt and pastry that is the traditional Australian meat pie. You can take the girl out of the country … as they say.

pretty sure she doesn't. But the way she speaks about her role is typical of the sort of language used in the discourse of futurism and, more broadly, within the technology sector overall.

Futurists often portray their work as having two interconnected functions: to help their employer or client better determine future trends; and also to help assist in the design of products that are actually more useful to potential users. Or as Dr Bell puts it: 'build technology that really speaks to people'. Now it's the second of these that's particularly interesting, because it carries with it an altruistic tone. And yet, the idea of giving people technology that 'speaks' to them, doesn't necessarily mean technology they actually need, or is good for them. Sometimes it might mean that, but that's not essentially guaranteed. For instance, a new model smart phone, or tablet computer, might 'speak' to my personal needs in terms of functionality, portability and even desirability/social status, but do I really need it? I make the point as a reminder that futurists and technology consultants work to earn money — just like you or me. And that's regardless of whether they're engaged as permanent employees of a specific corporation or acting as freelance consultants. That's not to say that someone like Genevieve Bell is disingenuous when she talks about tailoring technology to people's needs — not at all. In fact, when you talk to her, she's clearly passionate about helping people, particularly the disadvantaged. But it is a reminder that futurists, even the most reputable of them, are not public servants, they're in business, and their master is a company, or several companies, not society.

So much of the language that surrounds our modern digital technologies and the future, particularly communications technology and social media, is dressed in a cloak of public good. And in such an environment, it can be extremely difficult for many people to tell the genuine from the deceptive. Let me give you another example, this time from Facebook's founder Mark Zuckerberg: 'When you give everyone a voice and give people power, the system usually ends up in a really good place. So, what we view our role as, is giving people that power.'

Surely no one with any critical faculties would believe Zuckerberg's primary motivation in building his company is the promotion of freedom of speech. You know, Truth, Justice and the American way!

And if facilitating free speech truly is Zuckerberg's primary motivation, he obviously never mentioned it to Adam Conner, Facebook's Associate Manager for Privacy and Global Public Policy back in 2011. Because, in response to questioning about whether the company had ambitions to try to enter the lucrative Chinese market, Conner made the telling remark: 'Maybe we will block content in some countries, but not others. We are occasionally held in uncomfortable positions because now we're allowing too much free speech in countries that haven't experienced it before.'[5]

So free speech is great as long as it suits the company's strategic plan and doesn't get in the way of making a profit. And that's the truth of it. Altruism might be the cloak, but the suit, socks and shoes all smell of revenue. As Bill Clinton's one time war strategist James Carville might have said: It's the business, stupid!

Of course, I'm not the first person to make this point. Back in 1998, Douglas Rushkoff wrote a blog post ever so subtly titled, 'Why Futurists Suck'. Rushkoff, a bestselling author on the relationship between people and technology, teaches at New York University. 'The act of futurism itself, as practiced by today's leading cyber pundits,' he wrote, 'is less predictive than it is propaganda. Think of the shady fortune teller who foresees "a terrible illness" in her client's future, just so she can sell some herbs and schedule a follow-up visit.' He went on to suggest that futurists 'use their authority and our timidity to shape a future that keeps them in business. Likewise, the companies and magazines selling us the future do so for their own gain'.[6]

It's such a good point that once again I feel a need to digress. It helps, I think, to make a comparison with auto mechanics. Odd, I know, but trust me on this one.

Hands up anyone who's ever taken their car for a regular mechanical check-up and *not* been forced to fork out money? Now I can't actually see how many arms have been raised, but I bet I could count the number on just one hand (pardon the pun). It's a great universal truth — when you take your car to the garage, there's always something that suddenly needs fixing: new brake pads, or a faulty alternator, or some dodgy electrical thingey that you didn't know you had. There's always something just about to give up the ghost that urgently needs replacing. In the end, most people, myself included, simply raise their eyebrows, grumble a bit, and open their wallets. After all, what do we know about cars and the way they work? We're entirely reliant on the mechanic to keep us motoring. And it's little different in the communications technology world. Everything is always up for replacement, and it's the manufacturers themselves who, more often than not, call the shots.

Now, I say 'little different' advisedly, because the really weird thing about the communications technology field is that many ordinary people actually embrace the need to replace. Apple has made an art form of all of this. No sooner have you bought one of their gadgets when suddenly it's been superseded. In fact, the team at Apple are so good at convincing people to throw out their old technology whenever the company tells them to, that in October 2010 there was a public backlash when newish CEO Tim Cook held an iPhone launch that failed to live up to expectations. In Pavlovian fashion, Apple devotees had sniffed the wind, read all the familiar signals and, when the launch day arrived, were ready and waiting to be dazzled by an entirely new model, having tweeted and blogged themselves into a euphoric frenzy. They'd even christened it the iPhone 5 in advance. But the new model never came. What they got instead was just an upgrade — a more sophisticated version of the iPhone 4.

Such was their disappointment that shares in the company actually dropped by almost five per cent.* The stock price only recovered when news of the death of Apple co-founder Steve Jobs broke later that same week.

Now I have to say, it's a pretty unusual world when people get angry at the fact that the expensive phone they own *hasn't* been superseded; when they're ready to 'lynch' company executives because they're *not* required to spend hundreds of dollars on a new model.

Strange days indeed.

So, where was I? Ah yes, business — it's all about money. A point you really shouldn't have to make in a capitalist society but, as I say, it's a pretty unusual world in which we live. Going back to my point about futurists and Facebook and the like — whether they're called technology companies or social media platforms it doesn't matter, essentially they're retailers and their profits are huge, even though they're often secretive about just how much money they actually make. In August 2011, *The Economist* estimated the then value of Facebook at around US$66.5 billion, while the *New York Times* in 2010 speculated that the personal wealth of its founder Mark Zuckerberg was, by their best guess, around the US$14 billion mark. *Forbes* magazine estimates that, including Zuckerberg, 'there are now six individuals who get the bulk of their fortune from Facebook'.[7] All of them, by the way, billionaires not millionaires.

But, of course, the two giants in the field are Apple and Google. Google's market value in January 2011 was put at not much under US$200 billion.[8] And its profit in 2010 was

---

* During a live blog of the iPhone 4S event one of *The Guardian*'s technology writers declared: 'If they don't have an iPhone 5 then people are going to lynch someone. All that just for this?' Mind you, old habits die hard. After the initial shock devotees, it seems, reverted to form, reportedly snapping up more than 4 million new iPhone 4S devices in the first three days after the launch.

estimated at approximately US$6.5 billion.[9] And Apple? Well, it's the real behemoth — its market value at the beginning of 2012 was somewhere around the US$343 billion mark. Suffice to say, if Apple and Google were countries, they'd be up there among the richest.

Serious money indeed. And you don't get that rich through altruism.

It's all about you — of course it is

When the US comedy duo Rhett and Link devised and performed an annoyingly hummable little routine called 'The Facebook Song', their YouTube video quickly went viral. They sang: 'There's an online world where I am keen of a little website dedicated to me. With pictures of me and a list of my friends and an unofficial record of the groups that I'm in.'[10]

The characters they portrayed were goofy, starry-eyed and naive. It was satire, naturally, but like all good satire it resonated with truth — 'dedicated to me'. Now, skip this next sentence if you're thin-skinned. There is a sort of narcissism about the way in which many of us view modern technology. Growing up in an era of seemingly endless choice, there is a widespread tendency to assume that the gadgets and platforms we embrace exist for no other reason than to serve our needs and desires. It's all there — in front of us — and so it's ours for the taking. Writing for the *New York Times* in 2010, technology correspondent Nick Bilton pondered what it meant to be a citizen and a user of technology in the online age. 'Now you are the starting point,' he exclaimed. 'Now the digital world follows you, not the other way around.'

On the surface of it, he's correct. Personalisation is what it's all about — tailoring things to suit you. And how do we know that? We know it because that's what everyone keeps telling us — futurists, technology journalists and the big social media companies. It's all about you, they say. It's about what you like, what you want — all you.

But personalisation in the digital world can be a deceptive concept. It's true that search engines and social media platforms quickly learn your habits and search preferences, and then feed you the sorts of information they anticipate you'll want to see, or recommend people they think you might want to 'friend', thereby saving you the hassle of having to dig around for things yourself. But their primary motivation for doing so isn't to selflessly serve your interests. They're businesses, don't forget. Their real motivation is to make money. Which is no bad thing, I hasten to add, as long as you understand that and companies are upfront about it.

And that's the problem. All that personalisation is actually designed to make it easier for businesses and marketers to more effectively target you with their online offerings. And so the more personal information companies like Facebook and Google can get you to put online, the more they have to offer to advertisers.

I'll let author and technology pioneer Jaron Lanier explain: 'A lot of companies, including the ones I'm currently doing research with — Microsoft and Google — what we do is we feed you these recommendations and there's a perverse incentive where if we can narrow the scope of things you see, because you keep on seeing the recommendations generated by the little computer model of you, then that's what creates the value in being able to sell somebody else access to you. Like a marketeer,' he says. 'But once you're living in this world of recommendations, you're guided into this cubby hole of this representation of you. So now we have you corralled and then we can charge for access to you. So there's a sense in which this idea of computers understanding you is part of a commercial game too.'

It's not such a surprising development really. Companies and organisations have been making extra money out of selling their customers' data for decades. I worked in the not-for-profit sector in the late 1990s and I can tell you for a fact that even charities at the time regularly bought lists of telephone numbers from each other — the phone numbers of people who were their donors or supporters. The difference today is that that exchange is done on a massive scale. And the data that Google or Facebook have to offer advertisers is incredibly granular — all the personal details you've ever listed on your Facebook page, birth date, friends, likes and dislikes, etc; or all of the things you like and dislike based on records of every single Google search you've done over the past year, two years, whatever. You can see why they're such profitable enterprises.

Yes, it's all about you — but only on their terms.

Even the personalisation options available to individualise the look of your Facebook page, none of that is what it's made out to be. Like most social media platforms, Facebook is actually heavy on uniformity. Take a good look and see for yourself. Far from being a place to fully express yourself, in reality, there's very little room for genuine personalisation in terms of content and style on a Facebook page. The layout, overall look and the functions are uniform. And there's a good reason for that. It's because standardisation helps the company get everyone's data into a comparable format. And why is that a good thing? Well, for the user there's no benefit, it actually means that he or she is forced to have a Facebook page that looks pretty much like everybody else's. But for Facebook, uniformity means everyone's data is easier to collate and sell — all the ducks are lined up.

Don't ask and we won't tell

There are lots of fascinating aspects to the digital and online technology explosion of recent years, but perhaps the most startling thing for me isn't the sheer scale of it all, but users' willingness to accept what's put before them without question.

Ponder this: How many people you know give much, if any, thought to the privacy policies of the various media platforms they use? Would they know, for instance, that Google keeps a record of every online site you visit (yes, even the one about German milk maids and bull whips) and that in 2010 the company's then CEO, Eric Schmidt, publicly, and chillingly, declared: 'We know where you are. We know where you've been. We can more or less know what you're thinking about.' Or that Facebook also keeps records of every photo, every comment and every link you make on their platform, and will continue to keep those records even after you've closed your account. This is of such concern that in Europe various privacy groups have threatened legal action against Facebook on the grounds that they believe the company is violating EU law by holding onto people's online data indefinitely.

One of the really annoying things about Facebook is that they've made a habit of constantly changing their terms of use without properly notifying or consulting users. And they're fond of using an 'opt out' approach every time they make an alteration. In other words, they make changes to functions or privacy provisions and automatically assume your acceptance unless you tell them otherwise; that is, unless you specifically notify them that you want to 'opt out'. In November 2011, the Chairman of the Federal Trade Commission (FTC) in the United States, Jon Leibowitz, criticised Facebook, saying: 'Facebook's innovation does not have to come at the expense of consumer privacy. Facebook is obliged to keep the promises about privacy that it makes to its hundreds of millions of users.'[11]

Chief among the privacy commitments the FTC found Facebook had broken was a commitment not to share people's personal information with advertisers. Under pressure from the FTC, the company agreed that, in future, it would obtain consent from its users before making changes to privacy settings.

Another question: How many people do you know who actively seek out information about how the digital platforms they use interact with government? Or which non-democratic governments certain technology and social media companies are willing and happy to do deals with? Even Google, whose unofficial motto is 'Don't be Evil', was at one stage quite happy to reach a working arrangement regarding censorship with the military-backed dictatorship in China in order to gain access to that nation's booming online market. And for the record, the company currently helps fund a Massachusetts-based technology firm called Recorded Future, which specialises in real-time data harvesting from websites. One of the firm's other major funders is In-Q-Tel — a technology investment organisation set up and owned by the CIA. Google is by no means alone in entering into such arrangements. And as recently as January 2012, Twitter was under fire from civil libertarians and groups like Reporters Without Borders after announcing plans to allow country-specific censorship of tweets if they were deemed to break local laws.

For me, the truly puzzling thing is that most of us don't ask questions when it comes to social and digital media and, more to the point, we don't even think to. But it's not like that when we deal with 'traditional' telecommunications companies and media conglomerates. With them, we're instinctively wary: Rupert Murdoch is a businessman — we know that, we recognise that; we all understand that his central focus is himself and his corporation. Indeed, many of us had a jaundiced view of the Murdoch empire even before the 2011 phone-hacking scandal that forced the closure of the *News of the World*.

Then there are the mobile-phone carriers. We all know they're as bad as each other, right? That's a given — they over-charge and under-deliver. Despite all their corporate marketing hype about 'customer service' and 'putting people first', we recognise that the primary motivation of traditional media and telecommunications organisations is profit. We understand that, because we're reminded of that fact every time we have a bill to pay, be it for connection fees, mobile-phone plans, newspaper subscriptions, etc.

In summary, we know from experience that companies like News Corporation and Time Warner work in the interests of their owners and/or their shareholders. But we seem to be far less wary when dealing with social networking sites and organisations like Google; and far more willing, I would suggest, to blindly trust.

'You know, those of us who are spending hours a day on Facebook are really living and interacting with people inside a marketing platform,' cautions Douglas Rushkoff. 'Those of us who are going on the world wide web are in a business space, as much as it is a social space.'

And adds Sydney blogger and journalist Elmo Keep: 'If you think that advertising is targeted now, it's nowhere near what can be done with 400 million people's information in terms of what they consume and what they like. You have to remember that all of these things, whether it's the various number of Google products, or Facebook, or MySpace, these things are businesses. They're data mining. They're going to be able to track the consuming habits, potentially, of an entire generation for as long as they like, and it's going to be the future of truly targeted advertising.'[12]

Perhaps one of the reasons we don't question the corporate underpinnings of what's offered to us in the new digital world is because so much of what's proffered online, even from the truly enormous players like Google and Facebook, appears to be free. There's no direct commercial charge attached to the use of their services. Therefore, one could speculate, there's a greater tendency for people to mistakenly view such platforms as public utilities, or at least commercially benign. And in turn, the absence of upfront charges then feeds our feelings of entitlement regarding the online world and, subsequently, our narcissism.

But it's not free, of course. It's far from free. Eli Pariser, author of the book *The Filter Bubble* and one of the co-founders of the highly successful online political activist organisation

Moveon.org, is highly critical of what he calls a lack of transparency on the part of social media companies about their intentions. Says Pariser: 'Hopefully we'll move past the point where companies can get away with the veneer of their services being free. That's not true. We hand over quite valuable personal data to them all the time, which they convert directly into money.'

A second possible reason for our unquestioning approach to digital platforms revolves, once again, around language. The very name News Corporation sounds ominous; it has the odour of lawyers and black suits all over it. No modern technology or social media firm has a name that isn't wacky, playful or silly — Dopplr, Blippy, Friendster, Zynga, Groupon, even LinkedIn — they sound more like cartoon characters than corporate brands. And the really big ones — Google and Facebook — certainly don't sound like the sorts of companies that might be recording your every move and pimping that data to other firms in order to fill their ever-expanding coffers. And the terminology they employ is also designed to reinforce the user's narcissism: with Facebook you have 'friends' and 'fans', while on Twitter you have 'followers'.

Another factor to take into account concerns the commercialisation and corporatisation of Western society. We live in a world where the commercial ethos is all pervasive: universities are no longer places of learning, they *sell* education, or 'career visions'; our clothes are covered in logos; buses and other forms of public transport have become moving billboards; and there's barely a sports stadium I know of that hasn't been renamed with a corporate moniker. To cap it all off, almost all Western countries use Gross Domestic Product (GDP) as the sole measure of national success and wellbeing, which is a bit like measuring the happiness of your family exclusively by the size of your pay packet, irrespective of whether Dad's a philandering drunk who's never home, or Mum's a long-term drug addict with a fascination for firearms. Out of interest, some European governments, including France, have now begun talking about the need to move beyond GDP as the yardstick of a nation's health and contentment. And in late 2010, the Government of India suggested it was planning to start factoring environmental costs into its GDP data.

If you think about it, it's not unusual to hear politicians in countries like Australia, the UK and the United States use the terms 'nation' and 'economy' interchangeably; or at least the latter in place of the former. It will be 'good for the economy' we are often told. The implication being that it will therefore be good for the nation. In Australia it's even got to the stage where the Federal Government now regularly uses the Productivity Commission — a body made up of economists — to advise on the appropriateness and/or viability of social and cultural policy.

In such a world, all interactions and services have become commercial activities, people have become 'consumers' and everything has become a commodity. Why then, you might ask, wouldn't we naturally accept that a marketing platform like Facebook should become the new town square?

And given all of the above, you could then argue that, in the embodiment of the futurist, the future has simply been commoditised, in line with everything else. And by commoditising the future, futurists make something of economic value out of little more than speculation, or an informed guess. In other words, they turn projections of what lies ahead into a product that can then be sold and bought in a corporate marketplace.

A deficit of sceptics

Of course, there are various agents in society whose job it is to help protect average citizens by equipping them with the information they need to better gauge when someone, or some company, is trying to deceive them. There are academics and there are journalists,* both of whom are meant to value

---

* By journalists, I mean columnists, opinion writers and commentators as well as straight news reporters.

objectivity, but both, unfortunately, have their own difficulties in dealing with the digital world.

The problem in the media sector is that ailing newspapers and broadcast news organisations are often compromised in their analysis of social and digital technology, because they see them not just as the legitimate targets of journalistic examination and investigation, but also as potential lifelines for their own troubled industry.

When the first iPad was released in 2010, the world's media went crazy in a burst of unseemly worship. It was only after a hurricane of tweets, posts and articles swept the globe, praising the tablet computer, and declaring it to be the greatest invention since Gutenberg's press, that more reasoned voices began pointing out some of the device's limitations. And not insignificant ones at that — like the fact that it came without two industry standards: a USB port and an SD card slot. Most people, I think, believed that these would be added in later models, but that's beside the point.

In fact, the world's major media outfits not only gushed over the iPad, they also fell over themselves for a seat on the bandwagon.

'*The Washington Post* Comes To iPad,' the venerable newspaper proudly declared on 8th November 2010. The journal with a wine-cellar full of Pulitzers and the disgruntled ghost of Nixon still pacing its corridors, managed to find enough space between the hard news of the day to advise its readers: 'Today *The Washington Post* introduced its new app for iPad, now available on the App Store. It combines *The Post*'s trusted reporting and analysis with innovative social media and sharing capabilities and award-winning multimedia to provide an immersive news experience for iPad users.'

Apple is an interesting case study because every product launch is now treated as news. Whenever Apple unveils a new line it automatically gets column inches or air time. The BBC, the *New York Post*, the *Sydney Morning Herald*, they all do it. I've never seen figures for Apple's PR expenditure, but I bet it's minimal. After all, why spend money on marketing when journalists are happy to do it for you?

And media academics are little different, I'm sad to say. Well, not all of them. I exaggerate, of course, but a great many do seem besotted by communications technology and are forever talking up the 'revolutionary' nature of new devices and digital platforms. 'Boosters' is a bit of an old-world term, but I think it pretty much hits the mark.

One who hasn't given over his critical faculties is Professor Graeme Turner, the director of the Centre for Critical and Cultural Studies at the University of Queensland. Turner argues that a kind of 'aspirational rhetoric' has built up among his colleagues. 'What happens is that people who are watching what's happening in the expansion of consumer choice and the multiplication of formats of delivery of media, there's a kind of excitement that moves away from looking at what's actually happening at the moment to immediately predicting the future,' he says, adding that many media academics then lose the distinction between what they hope will happen and what actually might happen based on existing evidence.

I came across a good example of this in 2009 when, at the end of a dramatic and bloody leadership crisis in Canberra, a well-known journalism academic declared: 'There is a new electorate in Australia and it's on Twitter.' She made the call based on just '7678 tweets' generated by just '2647 users'. A new electorate, based on just 2647 Twitter users in a country that had, at the time, more than 14 million eligible voters?* Come again?

She continued: 'In the same way political journalists have realised they can't afford not to be on the news gathering and

---

* According to the AEC (Australian Electoral Commission) there were 14,088,260 eligible voters for the 2010 federal election. And when you do the maths 2 647 works out to be about 0.01879 per cent of 14,088,260.

dissemination platform that is Twitter, politicians can no longer afford to ignore the electoral leverage of the Twittersphere.'

But the reality was that they actually did ignore it at the Australian Federal election of 2010. And social media, including Twitter, played a minuscule role in the UK election of that year as well, despite also being endlessly talked up by academics and the media in that country. But what was most interesting about that particular Canberra academic's article, and which perhaps supports Professor Turner's contention, was the fact that she made the above statements before then adding: 'I am in the process of doing deep analysis on the use of Twitter and the impacts of this usage on journalism.' So, a declaration about how important Twitter is, comes before you've done the 'deep analysis on the use of Twitter and the impacts of this usage'? To me that seems a lot like putting the cart before the horse.

Now, without being disloyal to my own profession, it's not hard for me to imagine journalists getting just a teeny, weeny bit carried away with what Professor Turner and others call 'digital optimism'. That is, an over-inflated view of the benefits of the internet and social media for our present and our future. I have to admit that for all our many virtues, we in the Fourth Estate can be such a shallow lot at times, given to hyperbole, sycophancy, incredulity, laziness, deceit, cunning and outright distortion (forgive me if I've left anything out). But it does surprise me that so many academics in the area of technology and media studies have also become social media boosters. Not all, by any stretch of the imagination, but an awful lot. So why, I ask Graeme Turner, have such a significant number of his colleagues put aside their natural scepticism, their natural critical academic instincts?

Professor Turner believes a major part of the cause is what he calls the 'strange alignment' that's occurred between the media and the academic community over the past decade or so. 'Suddenly people who used to be told by the media "We don't want your point of view, we're not interested because it's too academic", are actually being approached by the media and being asked for their point of view,' he says.

And that certainly tallies with my experience. Until the digital age, most journalists I mixed with spoke about media studies academics with a sort of contempt. 'Those who can, do; those who can't, teach' was the feeling. As unfair as that clearly was, the attitude only changed when those academics suddenly became useful interview talent for stories about new digital technologies and social media. So journalists suddenly got the breathless, gee-whiz quotes they needed about the revolutionary nature of new technology, and media academics suddenly got media attention — air time and column inches to increase their profile and public recognition.

But Professor Turner thinks it's not just an alignment built on reciprocity — an unstated case of you scratch my back, I'll scratch yours. He says both communities have an almost utopian attitude towards new media, but for different reasons. The media because, as I explained earlier, digital platforms offer a means to make money, or at least to redress the fall in revenues caused by the dramatic decline in traditional media advertising; and the academic community because of what Professor Turner describes as: 'a kind of idealism about what the media can be, a criticism of what the media is now and the sense that the new media provide opportunities that didn't exist before to make the media more democratic in terms of how it's produced and how it's consumed'.

And that perhaps explains why we hear endlessly from some media academics about the rise of 'citizen journalism', or Twitter as the new dominant news force, or even the 'democratic' and 'revolutionary' potential of platforms like Facebook and YouTube. Like the Millerites, many in academia and the media have become lost in their own sense of wanting. They've become fixated on a saviour.

Right then. Having now ensured that my personal future will never involve working for a university, Intel, Facebook, Google or *The Washington Post*, come with me as I explore the primacy of trust in the relationship between people and technology; and the dangerous waters into which that trust is leading us.

Better bring a snorkel!

CHAPTER 2

SUCH TRUSTING SOULS

It's not a brave new world; it's a bad new world

Howard Stringer, CEO, Sony Corporation, 2011

Age of trust, age of vulnerability

The enormous trust we place in new technologies, and technology companies, makes it difficult to fully subscribe to the idea that we live in cynical, distrustful times. I know it's long been a popular mantra in intellectual circles, but it doesn't hold up when you look at our modern relationship with all things tech. Trust is at the core of that relationship, particularly our engagement with the digital stuff.

The rapid speed of technological advance has happened largely without regulation and without government involvement — at least in the West, that is. As I said earlier, people have been left pretty much to themselves to navigate their way into the digital future. And, by and large, you'd have to say that most of us seem pretty unperturbed by the way things have progressed. Or at least that seems to be the case looking at the simple statistics. They all point to a society which has, by and large, embraced the digital age: e-commerce and e-banking continue to grow; social media platforms like Facebook and Twitter are still gaining in popularity (Facebook reportedly had somewhere around 800 million registered users in 2011); smart phones have ushered in a whole new world of information mobility; and more and more of the

tools we need for our everyday work have been digitised and/
or computerised.

And yet the reasons for greater public concern are clearly
already there, because incident after incident demonstrates that
our unquestioning use of technology is making us ever more
vulnerable.

In 2009, Google was forced to apologise after its Street View
cars, which roam the world taking photos for the Google Maps
service, were found to have hoovered up vast amounts of private
information from people's wi-fi-enabled home computers. The
data, which was collected in over thirty countries, reportedly
amounted to around 600 gigabytes' worth. And what's worse,
the inappropriate collection happened over a period of several
years. It wasn't just a one off.

Then in April 2011, both Apple and Google admitted that
the smart phones they produced were surreptitiously tracking the
movements of their users and then transmitting that information
back to a company database. Both firms responded to privacy
concerns by saying that the data being collected was necessary
to make the geolocation functions on their smart phones work
correctly, which to an extent is true, but it was the secretive
manner in which the companies went about their activities that
raised questions. Leading technology analyst Tim O'Reilly told
the *New York Times*: 'It [the actions of both companies] is more
symbolic than anything else. It is one more sign of how devices
are collecting data about us and potentially sharing it with others.
This is the future. We have to figure out how to deal with it.'[13]

In fairness, Apple later joined two other major companies —
Microsoft and Mozilla — in announcing they were including a
'do not track' feature in their browsers to allow customers with
concerns about privacy to ward off unwanted data searching
by advertisers and others. But tellingly, two other firms, Yahoo
and Google, declined to join.

Data in the digital world is what it's all about — it's
knowledge, money and power.

I mentioned Recorded Future earlier. Let me just go back to them for a minute. The company's main selling point is that its computers can literally sweep tens of millions of available sources of online material in real time, looking for patterns and connections that they then onsell to interested clients. And the sources of data they scan, according to Recorded Future's CEO and co-founder, Christopher Ahlberg, include anything that they can legally access — from Twitter messages to Facebook pages to company records to chat room conversations. So privacy isn't a consideration; if it's legal to snoop and harvest people's data, then it's all fair game.

And the clients for such a service? I ask Ahlberg directly.

'People in the workplace who need to analyse and take in information in a clever fashion,' he replies. 'So we think this could be in the hands of anybody: a marketing person who needs to know what markets to go after, when you find a gap in the product launch calendar; a sales guy who needs to find new business opportunities that might build up in the future; loads of different sorts of people. Now in the early days with the company, just to kind of do this in a targeted fashion, we've been focusing on people in quantum finance, you know, the sort of mathematically oriented people of Wall Street, and other like places, as well as government analysts who need to understand what's happening in the world geopolitically.'

And, of course, those 'government analysts' include the Central Intelligence Agency. It's interesting to note that the CIA also has its own data-harvesting unit called the Open Source Center, which scans anything and everything it can find looking for matters they deem untoward — including all forms of social media. According to *The Atlantic Monthly*, the centre was set up after September 11.

It can be a bit of a confusing area to get your head around, so let me give you an example of the sort of service Recorded Future might perform for a client, say the US Government, for want of a better example. Washington might publicly float a contentious idea, say raising taxes for the rich, which is always a hot topic in the United States. They could then hire Recorded Future to give them a sweep of all the millions and millions of things people are saying about that decision across America on blogs, in online comments on websites, tweets, Facebook pages, the lot. And the US Government could then use the breakdown of that data to help them better understand where public sentiment actually lies.

The approach is not that different from standard polling, except for the scale. Recorded Future can harvest massive amounts of data. And importantly, data from people themselves, unaffected by the sorts of biases you might get in a traditional questionnaire from poor question formulation, for instance. Of course, it's harder to determine how random your sample is, but I guess Recorded Future would counter by saying that the sheer volume of material they harvest rules out any potential skewing in one direction or the other.

But Recorded Future isn't the only company out there making money out of data mining, there are myriad such firms involved in the practice. So many in fact that they're now just part of the fabric of the online world. While I was combing the guest list for a technology conference recently I came across a speaker who described herself as a 'Lead Product Evangelist' for a company called Buzz Numbers. And her company role, she wrote, was to help 'corporations track and data mine online conversations about them, their competitors and industry issues across social media forums, blogs, website news and all online channels'.

Heads in the Cloud

Charles Dickens began *A Tale of Two Cities*, one of his most successful stories, with an assessment of the late eighteenth century, yet another period of incredible social and technological change: 'It was the best of times, it was the worst of times,' he wrote, 'it was the age of wisdom, it was the age of foolishness; it was the epoch of belief, it was the epoch of incredulity.' Not a bad summation of our own times, you might think. But if you wanted to truly adapt it to the twenty-first century, you'd have to add the line: 'It was the age of trust, it was the age of vulnerability.'

The sophistication and size of our digital world hides its fragility. Most of us, whether by choice or not, now have a digital life that sits alongside our real-world life: we correspond with people via email, text and social media, rather than by hand-written correspondence; family photos are now stored in digital form, as is our music; we make reservations at the theatre and search for houses online; we bank online; increasingly shop online and store accounts and other financial material on the hard drive of our computer. The many advantages of such a situation hardly need repeating, but what happens when there's a problem?

With so much of our world driven or powered by computers and so many of our personal and business affairs now conducted in a digital realm — and with so many eyes, both legal and illegal, trawling over our data — it's important to ask questions not just about our personal online security, but also about the security of our broader community and society, because the list of serious security and systems failures continues to mount.

Just a few examples:

In Iran in 2010, that country's nuclear program was sabotaged by a computer worm/virus named Stuxnet, which Fox News labelled a 'cyber missile' and the *New York Times* declared to have been the result of a joint US/Israeli intelligence initiative.

In May 2011, Chinese hackers were found to have broken into the Gmail accounts of hundreds of users, with White House and other senior government officials the primary targets. It's estimated the Pentagon alone faces around 6 million cyber attacks every day.

In November 2011, the UK's Foreign Minister, William Hague, spoke about an 'exponential rise' in similar threats to British political, military and civil facilities, and he warned: 'Countries that cannot maintain cyber security of their banking system, of the intellectual property of their companies, will be at a serious disadvantage in the world'.[14]

In the Australian Capital Territory, several months earlier, two computer mainframes at a prison facility failed for undisclosed reasons, and in so doing, shut down the centre's entire electronic security system, including surveillance cameras, perimeter security and door locks.

And, just for good measure, we know from the experiences of countries like Estonia and Georgia just how crippling cyber disruption can be to the social and economic wellbeing of an entire nation when that disruption is inflicted as a deliberate form of warfare, with both nations literally brought to a standstill in recent years by Russian cyber attacks.

Keeping ahead of the hackers and attackers is a costly business, and increasingly there are questions about the willingness of companies and financial institutions to keep pace with the measures needed to secure their operations. After a series of security breaches involving five Australian financial institutions — all of them highly profitable organisations — banking analyst Brian Johnson, from the leading Asian investment and brokerage group CLSA Asia–Pacific Markets, warned about the consequences of underinvestment in security: 'There's no doubt about it, the technology is certainly ageing. They [the banks] really have sweated the assets and perhaps underinvested. And we're now starting to see the price being paid for that, which is that relatively small kinds of physical failures in equipment can have quite devastating implications,' he said. 'All banks basically need to invest in their distribution platforms. As you know, the quantum of the investment that is required to basically improve this is actually quite substantial.'[15]

Jost Stollmann, the Chief Executive of Tyro Payments, a company that provides EFTPOS services said: 'One of the problems is that security is actually pretty tough and very difficult and it's getting worse — as you see payments moving into integrated spaces, into online and into mobile, we have cardholder data in many different places and there are more and more fronts of attack.' And he added ominously: 'The challenge is getting bigger. The marketing is well in advance of the security.'[16]

I was given my own personal window into our increasing vulnerability not so long ago when the computer network I'm linked to at work suddenly went down. It didn't fail because of any untoward activity, it just crashed for about half an hour or so because of a technical fault — not a disaster really, except that during that time my ability to function as an employee was completely diminished. And that's not meant as an exaggeration. Almost everything that makes a modern office run is digital: files, work notes, contact lists, diaries; everything is stored on a computer or mobile digital device. And when the computer isn't able to function, neither are you. Even our ability to communicate with others is increasingly reliant on computers: think email, computer-related switchboard systems and internet-based services like Skype, which are increasingly used to make phone calls.

The outage at my work was just an accident. In truth, it was so short that it wasn't really a big deal, but it did give me pause for thought. In my case there was quite literally nothing left for me to do. And despite the fact that, as a lazy person trapped inside a busy person's body, I often fantasise about enforced leisure, it really wasn't a good feeling at all.

Now, the natural response to vulnerability is to build resilience, to seek protection. But another truly curious thing about our twenty-first-century faith in technology is that we seem to be choosing to go exactly the other way. The digital world we're creating at such a rapid clip is anything but resilient. And yet we seem to trust it more and more.

There is a time in the early years of our lives when we simply trust everybody and everything. But that period doesn't last long: your best friend at kindy eats your chocolate muffin when you're not looking or someone fails to catch you when you hurl yourself off the playground swing. The specifics don't matter, what's important is that there comes a time when you realise that we're all competing beings and not everyone has your best interests at heart. From an early age we learn to become more discerning about those we trust.

And trust isn't a great lump of a thing that you spoon out equally. We trust some people more than others, naturally, and we trust different people with different things. It also graduates — the more you get to know someone, the more you trust them. Or the less you trust them, as the case may be.

Now, I feel pretty safe in saying that in our private lives, very few of us would ever knowingly give over everything we value to somebody else's care. That sort of trust is pretty rare. In the normal course of events, it just doesn't happen. In families? Forget it — brothers and sisters are vultures. Even in rock-steady marriages it's common for people to have joint ownership of possessions. It just makes sense. So that's how trust works in our private lives, correct? And in our work life we're even more cautious of the people we have dealings with, and rightly so.

Now, imagine this for a scenario. Imagine a big profit-driven multinational corporation rocking up in your city and building a truly enormous warehouse on the outskirts of town — the mother of all storage facilities. And imagine the corporation's representatives then going door to door trying to convince the city's inhabitants — businesses, government authorities and citizens alike — that a really smart thing to do would be for everyone in the city to place everything of value into the corporation's trust, for safekeeping (and for a small fee, of course). And when I say everything, I mean not just people's personal effects, but their financial records and also those of the businesses and government departments they work for.

Now even with the promise of the best security fencing system in the world and a state-of-the-art fire plan, I'm sure very few sensible, sane people would take up the offer. It just sounds like a truly dumb idea. But in the digital world the picture I've just painted isn't just a scenario, it's what many believe is the way of the future. And that giant warehouse already exists and it's having other storage facilities added to it every day.

Welcome to the world of cloud computing. Or simply 'the cloud' — a name that cleverly manages to sound both impressive and innocuous at the same time.

'Cloud Power is going to change the way we do business,' proclaimed a recent Microsoft advertisement, spruiking the corporation's cloud computing services. And yes, you guessed it — once again, it's all about you!

'It's going to give you the power to think big. And be small,' the ad promised, 'The power to grow. And shrink. And not suffer for either. The power to do more with less. The power to be liberal with your ideas and conservative with your cash.'

In actual fact, what's now being called cloud computing has been around in one form or other for quite some time, but it's only been in the last couple of years that the major technology and communications companies have begun redefining it as the future of commerce, and the future of our digital lives.

In its crudest form, cloud computing is simply a variant of outsourcing: instead of storing data on your own computer or an inhouse computer server (if you're an organisation or company), you opt to transfer things you would normally store on your hard drive to a giant server, or bank of servers, operated by a cloud-computing provider, the servers being the modern equivalents of giant warehouses.

So just to be crystal clear, if you sign up to a cloud-computing provider, all of the material you would normally save on your own computer — photos, word documents, etc — all of it is transferred instead to one of the provider's digital storage facilities and kept there. So your files are no longer kept on your PC. And when you want to use them again, the provider simply gives you access to the items when requested. As Katie Cincotta, a feature writer for the *Sydney Morning Herald*, enthused: 'Why work on your hard drive, when you can work in the cloud for free and leave everything stored in someone else's safe keeping?'[17]

Many people are already using cloud-based services and probably don't realise it. Google's Gmail is the most well known, and its strength — and selling point — has been the flexibility it offers: through the use of a centralised data storage utility, Gmail users are able to access their email accounts from any computer, anywhere in the world.

But email is one thing. What people are increasingly being encouraged to do is to use cloud computing for *everything* they do online.

The flipside to convenient access to data held in the cloud is that once you've given over all your data, you no longer have personal control of it. If it's not stored on your own computer's hard drive, you're completely reliant on the probity and professionalism of someone else. So the flexibility of the cloud comes at the cost of having to essentially give over your private correspondence and records to a complete stranger. A corporate stranger at that. And we're not just talking about inconsequential material either — in the technology column of the *Courier-Mail* I found the following advice: 'One way to keep an extra copy of important phone numbers is to add them to the "cloud" or, in other words, use an online service. Users can import details from their email program by saving and uploading a CSV file, or they can simply type the important details into the website.'[18]

Significant resources are going into pushing the message that cloud computing is the way ahead. Among those now heavily promoting the concept and currently building giant server facilities (or server farms, as they're sometimes called) are Microsoft and Google, as well as the likes of Amazon, Fujitsu and IBM. In fact, IBM has been spending a fortune buying full-page advertisements in international business magazines to preach the virtues of cloud computing, and in none too subtle language. 'Widely embraced by consumers and businesses alike, the emerging computing option known as cloud delivers everything from music and photos through a public cloud to business email and data storage through a private, corporate cloud,' one of IBM's advertisements reads. 'Now cloud is poised to create new business models across industries and move into areas that matter at a societal level, such as finance and defence.'

So the hopes are huge and so too is the potential profit to be made. The research group Forrester conservatively predicts that by 2020 the global market for cloud-related services could be as high as US$241 billion.

Those who evangelise the cloud speak of a time not too far off when cloud computing is just the norm; when everything that human beings own — everything that's currently held in digital form, that is — will automatically be stored in one of these giant servers, whether we're talking about family photos, personal emails or company records. Said Apple's co-founder Steve Jobs when he launched his company's iCloud service: 'We are demoting the PC and Mac to just a device like an iPhone. We're going to move the centre of your digital life into the cloud.'

And the promise, as promoted by Microsoft's marketing types, is that individuals, and particularly businesses, can then do 'more with less': that by using the cloud they can save on the costs of running their own servers and having to pay for IT staff and security procedures. In fact, companies like Samsung and Acer have already begun producing laptops to fit the new cloud-computing world: computers that have almost no memory capacity, because in a cloud-based universe there's no need for you to store anything on your own digital device.

But it's not just individuals and companies who are being seduced by the promises of the cloud-computing providers, tertiary institutions — the University of Canberra, for instance — are also rapidly moving their IT approach to a cloud-based model. And in the United States, the Federal Government has begun a major rationalisation of its own server facilities and a move towards cloud-based storage. The Obama Administration has adopted a 'cloud first' policy, dictating that whenever possible, government agencies should opt for a cloud service to meet their future IT needs. In February 2011, then Chief Information Officer Vivek Kundra produced a cloud-computing strategy that spoke of moving up to twenty-five per cent of the US Government's IT facilities over to cloud computing during the course of the strategy's first phase.

And on it goes. In June 2011, electronics giant Toshiba announced a partnership with Hewlett Packard to start promoting cloud computing as a means of delivering what they call 'smart community' services to the providers of public networks like power, gas and water. Their profit forecast was around US$11 billion by 2015. In that same month, the technology services firm Avanade released global research they claimed showed a marked growth in the uptake of cloud services: 'In terms of overall cloud computing adoption, the survey found seventy-four per cent of companies are using some form of cloud service today — a twenty-five per cent growth in adoption since Avanade's September 2009 survey.' And, the firm went on to claim that of those organisations that had not embraced the cloud, three-quarters said it was 'on the horizon'.[19]

So the move to the digital promised land is already underway. And if the take-up of cloud-computing options continues as it's begun, it's certain to be one of the greatest leaps of techno-faith that humankind has ever undertaken, because the possible ramifications are huge.

Think about this: if cloud computing does reach its full potential — or even for that matter, if it comes anywhere near it — the public, personal and corporate data of whole communities, even entire societies, could end up being housed in a small number of facilities owned and operated by an even smaller number of giant multinational corporations. And, as mentioned, the material stored in the cloud wouldn't just be archival documents and records, but the vital current data needed for society's day-to-day business and interaction. But if that sounds like a precarious situation, fear not, because IBM's advertising team are here to reassure you that it's a risk worth taking: 'If we do this right — if we build in reliability, security and privacy by design — our public and private cloud-based systems have the potential to bring new heights of intelligence to the way the world works.'

But that *if* has a very big question mark attached to it. Despite the headlong drive towards the cloud, there have been some very worrying developments indeed. In February 2011, Google was forced to admit that it had accidentally wiped the cloud-based Gmail accounts of more than 150,000 users — just gone, by accident. Then less than two months later, one of Amazon's giant server farms experienced an outage that shut down the server and several large online companies with it, including Foursquare, Reddit and HootSuite — all businesses that rely on Amazon's cloud-computing services for their basic operations.

But wait, that's not all: even more troubling still was what happened to the Japanese-based company Sony. In April of 2011, it became clear that the giant electronics and technology firm had experienced a massive security breach of its cloud-supported PlayStation Network. The breach saw the entire international network shut down for over a month and Sony management were later forced to admit that they had been powerless to prevent the personal information of somewhere up to 100 million PlayStation users being stolen by hackers — information that included both passwords and credit card details.

Perhaps most telling of all though, were the words of Sony's Chief Executive, Howard Stringer, who told the *Wall Street Journal* that maintaining security was a 'never-ending process' and that, in his opinion, it was impossible to guarantee the security of any web system. He ominously added: 'It's the beginning, unfortunately, or the shape of things to come. It's not a brave new world; it's a bad new world.'[20]

Let's be rational about this ...

Now, human beings like to think of themselves as rational entities. We like to imagine that when it really matters the logical, cautious side of our brain will kick in and prevent us from getting carried away with something that could potentially prejudice our own interests. So it would be nice to think that if, as I suspect, the promise of cloud computing quickly proves to be a monumental privacy and security nightmare, we rational human beings will have the presence of mind to stop and reconsider the direction in which we're heading.

But humans aren't like that at all. If we were, there would never have been a First World War, let alone a Second. And no one would ever drink, smoke or gamble. In fact, the truth is that we can be surprisingly credulous creatures and extremely given to group-think. And our willingness to believe — to trust — can often get us into spectacular trouble. So if you think the very idea of large sections of society completely giving over responsibility for the storage and security of their private, commercial and governmental data to a small cabal of private technology/communications companies is simply too out there to contemplate, just reflect for a moment on our past, because you don't have to dig too deeply to find some very costly examples of collective belief triumphing over rationality.

Does anyone remember the Y2K bug? We have group amnesia about it now, but across the world in the years immediately before the dawn of the new millennium, a significant number of people in the 'advanced', well-educated and sceptical West managed to convince themselves that the world was facing a computer-related Armageddon that would befall humankind the moment the clocks in our computers ticked over into the new century. And many of us also believed and trusted the IT gurus who told us that, without paying them ocean loads of money, we were all going to Hell in a handbasket: aeroplanes would fall out of the sky and whole countries were expected to plunge into Stone-Age darkness as vital utilities closed down. In a flight of panic, the Australian Government even evacuated its embassy staff in Moscow in advance of the impending catastrophe. I bet they won't mention that if they ever get around to writing an official history of the foreign service.

Of course, nothing even remotely dramatic happened in the end. And even in countries like Italy, which spent very little time, money and effort on Y2K preparations, the disruptions that did occur were so minor as to be negligible. But our groupthink and trust on that occasion cost us an estimated US$500 billion — the worldwide price tag for our mistaken belief. Collectively we had put our trust in a farce, and collectively we quickly chose never to mention it again.

Then there was the Global Financial Crisis. It's easy now to forget just how much trust all levels of society, in any number of countries, placed in the banking sector and the free market in the first decade of this century. We in the West convinced ourselves that we had entered a new age in which recession was vanquished and the world would now enjoy a future of endless economic growth. In America, the UK, Europe, Australia and Canada, ordinary wage earners accrued enormous levels of personal debt as they embraced the message from finance gurus, and even governments, that the good economic times would roll on forever. Indeed, in Britain in March 2007, the then Chancellor of the Exchequer, Gordon Brown, famously declared to the House of Commons: 'We will not return to boom and bust.' He was so proud of the line, and confident in it, that he repeated it over and over again, more than a hundred times in subsequent months, by some estimates. It was as if, one British MP later remarked, 'we had transcended the laws of economics'.

In the United States and Europe, they're still mopping up the mess that reality made when the financial roof fell in.

So, yes, we can be cynical and distrustful in some ways, but in others, we can be very trusting indeed; and as with the Y2K bug and the Global Financial Crisis, trusting in ways that can later come back to bite us pretty hard.

Now, many of us like to entertain the idea that no matter how bad things might get under our stewardship, future generations will one day have the answer. It's a common enough line of thought, and with the digital world it manifests itself in the notion that coming generations of people, those who've grown up with computers and other forms of modern communication technology, will quite naturally be better equipped to deal with the contradictions and difficulties of our digital existence. For those generations — the so-called 'digital natives' — it's often said understanding the complexities of digital life will be instinctive and intuitive.

Well, maybe, but maybe not.

'I was the first, I guess, but many of the more optimistic media and cyber theorists really thought that kids as "digital natives" would understand these technologies better than we do, because we're just digital immigrants,' Douglas Rushkoff tells me, after admitting he now has second thoughts about the whole concept. 'You look at the experience of any immigrant family and it's the kids who learn the language and really move around like natives and it's the adults who are kind of stuck behind and not knowing what to do and really easy to fool. But if you look at all the research, it turns out that kids are much worse at distinguishing between a valid and an invalid source of information online. They fall for scams, they understand the interfaces less. They understand the biases of these websites a lot less than adults do. And it seems, I guess, that's because they were raised in a world with computers as just a given circumstance, these things were just here. They tend to look at the things on computers as pre-existing conditions, just as, you know, the way things are, rather than as creations of people and businesses with agendas.'

In other words, they have no pre-digital anchor point from which to set a baseline. So their handling of the future is likely to be just as problematic as our handling of the present. Or perhaps even more so.

Sorry Gen Y, but now we have one more reason to look down on you!

CHAPTER 3

I AM NOT A LUDDITE

There is a tendency of people these days to fear falling behind, and to adopt whatever seems to be coming down the pike in order to not fall behind — especially people who are in business. They think, 'Oh, I've got to get a blog, I've got to get a Twitter account, I've got to have presence on Facebook' — you don't. You do have not just the right, but the ability to choose which of these things are going to benefit you, or your business, and which ones just don't really make sense for you.

Douglas Rushkoff, US media theorist

Bless me, Father ...

If you have kids, or can remember what it was like to have really short arms and legs and to be always looking up at people, you'll know that one of the great motivators of action is peer pressure. I'm not talking about being covetous. Preschoolers want what other kids have from an early age, but that's a different thing. They just want it because it's there. What I'm talking about is the desire to be like everyone else. Around about the age of eight or nine, children start wanting to dress like their friends, and to have the same stuff as everybody else in their class; suddenly, they want the same sports shoes and T-shirts and caps. Prior to that you could dress them in a lime and orange jumpsuit and they'd be happy. But once that desire to be like their peers kicks in, well, that's it. And the major reason is fear — fear of being different.

It's pretty dumb when you think about it, but what's even more stupid is the fact that we never really grow out of that stage. And the fact that we don't underpins the entire advertising and marketing industry. Now, when Steve Jobs died in 2011 he was correctly eulogised for his amazing success as a businessman and technology innovator, but what the obituary writers overlooked, or simply didn't appreciate, was his incredible skill at playing to people's need to conform, their fear of not being like everybody else.

Jobs built a cult around Apple, which he then expanded into a universal church. Significantly, he did it by not only making good, innovative equipment, but by making products that were designed from the outset to become must-have fashion accessories. While others made functional gadgets, Jobs made cool technology; people bought Apple products not just because of their usability, but because of their social status. The very popular New York blogger Jeff Jarvis speaks of a conversation he had with a senior US advertising executive named Rishad Tobaccowala, around about the time the first iPhone was released*. Tobaccowala remarked to Jarvis, 'When you hold an iPhone, you have a Zen experience of divinity.'

These days to have anything other than an iPhone or an iPod or an iPad, is to risk being seen as somehow second rate. I couldn't tell you the number of times I've come across people who've bought a new Apple product, not because they felt they needed it, but because they felt it was the thing to do; that they'd be socially or professionally embarrassed to be caught without one.

Now, on a much broader scale the same is also true of the digital world in general, and social media in particular. Don't get me wrong, social media can be incredibly useful and enjoyable, but there is this aura of obligation and expectation that surrounds it, and that can prove limiting, not liberating. Here's a quick anecdote to illustrate my point.

---

* I've also seen Tobaccowala variously described as both a 'renowned futurist' and a 'guru of the future'.

I'm standing in a swanky kitchenware shop, just browsing, wasting time, when I spot someone I know. Someone I once worked with, briefly, about six years ago. When I last saw her, she was pregnant for the first time. Now she's being led around the store by two young children. She recognises me and we exchange pleasantries. We talk for about ten minutes before she asks me about my work. I present an international radio program dealing with people and technology, I tell her, and that's when the apology starts. No, not an apology, more like a confession: *Bless me, Father, for I have sinned. I'm not on Facebook, I know that's pathetic, but I just haven't got around to it yet; I've never used Twitter, I know I should be using it, but I just don't have the time; I have no idea how eBay works — I don't even have a smart phone!*

I've heard the confession before, on numerous occasions, and each time from very intelligent, well-educated and resourceful individuals: people who fear that they're 'falling behind', as Douglas Rushkoff puts it; that the digital world is passing them by, that they're no longer keeping pace with the way the world is changing; no longer even certain of their place in the future. And the fearful don't fit a lazy demographic stereotype either: my friend is only in her mid thirties, she's not what you'd call a technology curmudgeon — someone fixed in her ways, resistant to change. In fact, she was a television producer before she went on maternity leave, so she's hardly tech shy either.

As we say goodbye, destined not to run into each other again for another half decade or so, I can't help thinking how my former work colleague will handle a future in which so much more of our lives is automated and digitised. And I wonder whether modern technology, for all the good it brings, is also contributing to the opening up of yet one more division within our society — a division between those whose lives are embedded with technology and those who struggle, or who are barely literate in its use. The change has happened so fast, that from politics to shopping to warfare, our societies are struggling to adapt to the digital age.

But perhaps the greatest challenge in the near future is going to be a very personal one, as each and every person negotiates the relationship they want to have — or not have — with technology: working out how to handle the disruption, the problems and the opportunities opened up in rapid time by the internet and new communications tools.

At one end of the scale are the digital fetishists. I met one twenty-something American not so long ago who called himself a 'digital minimalist' and who was convinced that he could basically rid his life of everything but his laptop, his mobile phone and his bed. Though he did admit that things might not be so simple should he ever marry and have children. And then there are those who don't necessarily fear falling off the digital treadmill, in fact they'd quite like to, and they'd like others to follow suit. Because modern technology, they perceive, is having a detrimental effect on their lives and the lives of those around them.

'I am not a Luddite,' the novelist Cate Kennedy told the *Sydney Morning Herald*'s literary editor back in April 2010 as she took aim at the internet and social media.[21] At the time she was just getting ready to take part in a discussion at the Sydney Writers' Festival entitled 'Can Literature Survive the Digital Age?' To Kennedy, what many see as the great strength of the internet — its ability to provide near instant access to a rich variety and abundance of information — is also a negative. 'We're de-contextualising, pasting bits of other people's work on our blogs and creating unoriginal mash-ups,' she bemoaned.

Kennedy's comments were drawn from her personal experience as a judge with the Vogel Awards for young novelists. 'Toxic to fiction' was the way in which she described the use of the internet by her juniors. 'They're not reading or thinking about the impact of the words on the page.'

My first thought, on reading the article, was how disappointing it was that someone as intelligent and creative as Kennedy obviously felt the need to defend her observations with a clarification like 'I am not a Luddite'. And my second thought was how entirely understandable it was, given the way so many discussions about the social and intellectual implications of living in a media-saturated world have tended to bog down into a kind of verbal trench warfare.

I was also reminded of a conversation with Dr Tim Carmody who wrote a piece for *The Atlantic Monthly* magazine on the polarisation of debate surrounding technology. 'Every time you turn around you see a story about how the internet is rotting our brains, or there's some new technology that is going to make some previously insoluble problem completely obsolete,' he said. 'And so you get these kind of apocalyptic scenarios and these kind of triumphalist messianic scenarios, rather than something that is a bit more nuanced.'

Now, Carmody may well be right, but in most instances, I think the problem isn't that there's been too much debate, but that there probably hasn't been enough *genuine* debate. Because, up until now, very few people have been game enough to question the techno-optimist line for fear of being branded, well, a Luddite. Still, I think that's begun to change. And from my observation, this next decade will likely see an increase in a more measured critique.

What's becoming increasingly apparent is that there are some very obvious downsides to the new technologies we've adopted in the last couple of years, just as there were with television in the latter decades of last century. In some instances, for example, the smart phones that are meant to connect us can lead to greater isolation — just think of the number of times you've seen two young people sitting together at a bus stop, or in a shopping mall, side by side, but separately thumbing away on their smart phones, not talking to each other, or interacting in any way. Human beings are group animals. We have a need for physicality, and to deny the importance of that physical dimension seems to me a recipe for future social dysfunction. So why then some pundits feel the need to shout down any suggestion that new technologies and social media might have negative as well as positive consequences is beyond my comprehension.

What, I think, is still well and truly up for discussion though, is whether our engagement with the internet and social media is having a far deeper effect on our mental and intellectual capacities. Whether in fact all that tweeting and texting is changing the very way we think.

Dead for a day

'Kim Kardashian is Dead.' So the headline read. And there was a photo of the deceased lying in a coffin, all dolled up and trying to look like a designer corpse: dead, but still delectable — perfect hair, perfect make-up, perfect cleavage.[22] I like to think of myself as someone in touch with contemporary fashion and popular culture, but I had no idea who the faux deceased actually was until I picked up that magazine. I mean, I knew she was an American celebrity, but famous for what? Silly me. You probably know this already, but as it turns out, Kardashian is one of those celebrities who's famous simply for being famous. Like Paris Hilton.

Anyway, Kim Kardashian was lying in a coffin pretending to be dead. I was curious, I have to admit, so I examined the fine print on the article/advertisement. It read: 'Kim sacrificed her digital life to give real life to millions of others affected by HIV/AIDS in Africa and India. That means no more Facebook or Twitter until we buy her life back. Visit Buylife.org or text "Kim" to **** to buy her life now.' So, Kim Kardashian was dead and the only way I could assist, according to the article, was by making a monetary pledge. A pledge that would help resurrect her digital existence. A momentary thought flashed through my skull: Should I help? After all, apart from having to lie in a coffin, which I imagine isn't much fun at all, the very future of her digital life was at risk — it said so, right there!

And then another thought occurred to me. If I did nothing and let twenty-four hours pass by, all would still be fine, because the Buylife campaign that she was taking part in was only for one day. Which, arguably, says a lot about the modern attention span: Kim Kardashian could only manage to be dead for twenty-four hours. Any longer than that and OMG! It would just be soooo boring!

Now it could be that Kardashian is the way she is simply because she's an airhead. But ponder this for a second — could her shallow scattiness also be the result of the high levels of stimulation and distraction that most of us are now exposed to in an increasingly digital world?

No, on second thoughts, don't ponder that, because I think I already know the answer to that question and it's not going to take us much further.

OK, forget Kim. Let's try another course.

A couple of years back the British scientist Baroness Susan Greenfield, a professor in synaptic pharmacology at Oxford University, made brains boil in certain sections of the online community by suggesting that social networking sites had a negative effect on children's grey matter. And in 2010, the technology writer Nicholas Carr's book *The Shallows: What the Internet is doing to our brains* became a *New York Times* bestseller, pursuing a similar theme.

'As with many people, I've been spending more and more time online and more and more time on my computers, getting all the benefits you get from that, but what I realised was that I was losing my ability to concentrate, to pay attention to one thing for a sustained amount of time,' said Carr during an interview to promote his work. 'I particularly noticed it when I'd sit down, for instance, to read a book, something that used to come naturally to me. After a paragraph or two, or a page or two, my mind wanted to behave the way it behaves when I'm online, you know, jumping from page to page, clicking on links, Googling, checking email, and I began to make a connection between my seeming state of permanent distractedness and my increasing use of the web.'

And Carr put that change into an historical perspective: 'I think every technology that we use to think with — going all the way back to maps and clocks and so forth — emphasises some ways of thinking and de-emphasises other ways. And what the net does by providing not only lots of interruptions and lots of distractions, but encouraging us to browse and surf and skim and multi-task, is it's encouraging us to be quite adept and quite good at juggling, and shifting our attention very, very quickly. But it's not giving us any opportunity, or encouragement, to engage in more attentive ways of thinking, the ways of thinking that allow us to be contemplative and to be reflective and introspective. So I think it's shifting the emphasis of our thought in a way that ultimately makes us more superficial thinkers.'[23]

Now, I can't really comment on that argument because, to be quite honest, the quote was so long I started to fidget and then I needed to check my Twitter account. But Carr's theory certainly seemed to resonate with young talkback callers to the youth-oriented radio station Triple J after he was interviewed on the current affairs program *Hack*. The show's presenter asked her audience of twenty- and thirty-somethings for their thoughts about Nicholas Carr's proposition, and about the contentious notion of 'internet addiction'. There was no shortage of responses.

Boy: 'Last night I had to write a book review and it honestly should have only taken me a couple of hours. By the time I'd actually logged on to start writing it, I'd already checked my Facebook, my Twitter, my blog, chatted to people about what I was writing and then eventually at four in the morning I wound up finishing it.'

Girl: 'You know, like, you sit down and work in a browser and then enter the website and then expect straightaway to sort of see the website pop up, and I think that because we spend so much of our time on the internet, we've sort of come to expect the same instant gratification in the rest of our lives. So it's kind of like that instant gratification is leaving us less patient because we're so used to having what we want straightaway. And then that in turn has probably, I know in my case, maybe made me less inclined to concentrate on a task, especially if it doesn't have a sort of outcome that I'm going to see straightaway.'

Boy # 2: 'I guess it's having mobile internet access, which I guess in the last sort of two years of having iPhone has really changed that, really stepped that up. Being able to access multiple windows in my browser at any time of the day, I can go back and forth between Facebook, between forums, between word games that I'm playing, whatever it is that I'm doing, but having that sort of ability to do that is definitely changing the way that my brain works. It's a wide but shallow system as opposed to, like, a book, where it's sort of deep.'

Of course, that's all anecdotal, but it is clear that even young technology users, people who've grown up with digital gadgets, are among those beginning to question the effect the digital age is having on the way we process information and perform mental tasks. And, as it turns out, many of those undertaking serious research in the area are, like Nicholas Carr, being drawn to the subject as much by personal experience as professional curiosity. That's certainly what Pulitzer Prize-winning *New York Times* journalist Matt Richtel found when he tagged along on a camping trip with a bunch of neuroscientists.

'They had a purpose prior to even inviting me,' Richtel tells me over the phone from his home in the United States. 'They were doing this on their own, which was to go and observe themselves in a setting disconnected from technology, to fuel and inform their research about what happens to the brain when we get away from our devices.'

So off they all went with their sleeping bags and their camping gear to a spot in the southern part of Utah. A place where there was no internet access and no mobile phone coverage. And once there they began to study each other and themselves. Says Richtel: 'There is an emerging body of research that is looking at what happens when we are connected all the time. Not only to look at behaviourally what is happening, and I think it's pretty obvious to us that behaviourally we are affected by the iniquity of our devices, but also neurologically. Underneath the hood of our skulls if you will, what is the impact of all this connectedness?'

Now, as it turns out, the group was initially fairly evenly divided between those who believed in the possibility that heavy technology usage could impact on an individual's ability to focus and be creative, and those who were more than a little sceptical of the idea. But, reports Matt Richtel, as the camping trip progressed they all, to a person, experienced what he calls the 'three-day effect'.

'That is where time starts to slow down a little bit, it's a little bit more lucid, you feel comfortable, maybe letting a moment pass without talking, you take in your surroundings more,' he explains. 'Now I imagine you're saying, "Well that sounds so obvious to me; isn't that what we all experience on vacation?" Yes, to an extent, but remember it's getting harder and harder to get away from our devices, and so it felt a little bit more revelatory to them, just because they don't feel it that often.'

So there they all are, a bunch of brain scientists and a prize-winning journalist doing a techno detox in the wilds of Utah, just shooting the breeze. And then they get onto the really good stuff. 'The thinking has been when you're sitting at a computer and you're doing email, or you've got instant messaging coming in, it's hard to focus on your task at hand. But here's the interesting twist. I'm listening to these two neuroscientists sitting in a boat by the river and they're talking about whether your ability to focus gets impinged not merely when you're multitasking, but by the anticipation that new email might come in,' says Richtel. 'And they have actually already begun to show in research that when you are imagining that your phone could ring, or that you could get an email or an instant message, then that also impinges your ability to focus. That's a pretty profound thought, because if you're carrying a device around all the time, if you're always connected, even when you're not using it, some precious part of your intellectual capacity could be absorbed in the anticipation of its use.'

As it turns out, researchers even have a name for that phenomenon. They call it Phantom Vibration Syndrome. And whether it's true or not, I've been told that some people have reported feeling the physical vibrations of a mobile phone going off in their pocket even when they're not carrying one.

Anyway, towards the end of my discussion with Matt Richtel out comes that familiar line: 'I'm not a Luddite.' Not that I thought he was. And he points out that his newspaper, the *New York Times*, has taken a fairly balanced approach towards reporting the technological changes we've seen in recent years. Then, in parting, he offers an analogy that I particularly like: 'Lots of food is good, it's nourishing, we need it obviously. Lots of technology is good, we need it to survive in modern life,' he says. 'But some food is junk food, and I think we're starting to discover that some technology is good for us and some amount of consumption is good for us, and some of it is the equivalent of obesity, and that's the tipping point that I think we find ourselves at.'

I'm still thinking about the healthy technology analogy when, back at my desk and hunting around online, I come across a pertinent comment on a Facebook page from somebody named Emma. The subject of discussion is 'internet addiction' and Emma's comment reads like a cross between a personal observation, a confession and a plea for help: 'I'm fully addicted to internet,' she writes. 'I cannot stay in hotels, or anywhere away from home, unless I have a connection. I feel quite anxious, desperate, and lost without it. I rarely use my phone to speak. Internet is my main form of communication. I've just booked a cruise and the first thing I checked was whether there's any internet connection/wi-fi on board!!!!'

Logging off is as good as a holiday

The first day of my first full-time job was like walking into a fog. I'm not trying to be poetic; I mean it really was like walking into a fog — a thick blue haze that covered the entire newsroom. I'd go home at night and my suit would stink of cigarettes. Everybody at that time smoked. Well almost everybody. A chief-of-staff I once knew even indulged in cigars, though only the little thin ones, and he was judicious about when and where he lit up. And for those too young to remember, there used to be smoking on planes too, and buses, on all forms of public transport. It wasn't that long ago that you could smoke pretty much whenever and wherever you wanted. And, of course, you still can in most developing countries (and France).* But within a short space of time, having a fag in Australia went from being commonplace to being decidedly antisocial.

Then along came the mobile phone. And instead of blue smoke, the air around us soon began to be filled with the noisy verbal flotsam of everybody else's life. I went to a local shop recently and saw a sign at the cash register that read: 'If you're using your mobile phone, please don't expect to be served.' Or words to that effect. The notice was a new addition and hardly a surprise given that only a week or so before I'd watched a frustrated shop assistant trying to deal with a customer who barely acknowledged her existence. The shopper was yabbering away on her smart phone and rudely thrust out a credit card when the attendant finally managed to catch her attention. It was just plain bad manners — the technology equivalent of eating with your mouth open.

In the city of Brisbane they're starting to fit out suburban trains with designated mobile phone-free carriages, designed to let commuters travel to and from their work without being

---

* One of the best advertisements against cigarettes are the little tiny smoking rooms you can still find in Asian airports. I went into one in Bangkok just for a look. The air was so dense it looked like a sauna, though it certainly didn't smell like one.

assailed by half-a-dozen people having very loud conversations, about very personal, but often very trivial, matters. Similar bans are popping up all over the place.

It's not the same as the prohibition on public smoking, of course. And to describe it as a backlash would definitely be going too far. But it's certainly evidence of a growing public awareness of the social disruptiveness of modern technology.

Then there's Bill Clinton — the ex-US president with an inventive fondness for cigars. Since leaving the Oval Office in 2000, Clinton's life has been one long series of paid speaking engagements. He talks about grand things, gets a round of applause, a decent-sized cheque for his efforts and then moves on to the next engagement. Having been the 'leader of the free world', you can imagine he's the sort of guy who likes people to pay attention when he's speaking. Now, I'm not in the old Arkansan's league when it comes to oratory, but I have given quite a few lectures and presentations over the years and I can tell you that the one thing worse than staring out at an auditorium full of inattentive students, is looking out and finding that half the gathering aren't even mentally in the same room — they're nose deep in their laptops or busy texting or tweeting away on their phones. So I confess to having indulged in a little smug smile back in November 2010 when I read the uproar among social media enthusiasts about a decision by Clinton's minders to slap a ban on the use of all electronic devices during a speech the former president delivered in Moscow. Childish, I know, but there you are.

You see, for me, the problem isn't the electronic devices themselves — they're great. The issue is how people use them and also how often they use them.

In early 2011, the British communications regulator Ofcom conducted research for its annual Communications Market Report.[24] The survey turned up a staggering increase in smart-phone uptake. Around a quarter of the adults surveyed reported owning a smart phone. For teenagers (from the ages of twelve to fifteen) it was nearly half. And more than fifty-nine per cent of all respondents said they'd purchased their device within the previous twelve-month period. I've since seen similar figures for the United States and Australia.

However, what really caught my eye with the Ofcom report were the admissions people made about their smart-phone behaviour. Confessions that were both enlightening and somewhat worrying: half the adults questioned for the survey, and two-thirds of the teenagers, said they used their phone while physically socialising with others (you know, texting while somebody's physically trying to talk to you, that kind of thing); and a quarter of the adults and a third of the teenagers said they also played with their devices during family mealtimes. I used to get a clip over the ear for having my elbows on the table!

But here's the truly disturbing thing — fifty per cent of the teenagers surveyed and around twenty-two per cent of the adults said they used their smart phone while on the toilet. On the loo!

Now, I'd like to think of that as a peculiarly British thing to do, but I have a sneaking suspicion that it might just be universal. Regardless, I think it's fair to say that when you get to the stage of making telephone calls from the toilet you're talking about a serious problem. But don't just take my word for it, ask the bog-callers themselves. In fact, when directly asked how they would categorise their own smart-phone usage, one in three adults surveyed, and sixty per cent of teenagers, described themselves as 'highly addicted'.

Disturbing stuff, but it doesn't have to be that way. And there is help at hand, as they say.

In Oakland, California, Sal Bednarz, a one-time engineer with Virgin Mobile, has been trying to help people cut back on their digital addiction by making it easier to go cold turkey. He runs a coffee house called the Actual Cafe. And on the front window of his establishment there's a motto: 'Not just another wi-fi shack'.

Bednarz has purposely designed his coffee shop to attract people like himself, people who use a lot of technology, but who are fearful of letting it dominate their lives. Says Bednarz: 'There are places that when you walk through the front door, what you see are rows and rows of people on laptops with headphones on, and cables everywhere, and it's quiet. There's no interaction. And they're the sort of places that if you go with a friend, and if you don't have your laptops with you, and you want to have a conversation, you feel self-conscious because you're the only ones talking in the place.'

So the Actual Cafe was intentionally created, says Bednarz, to try to counter that dynamic: 'I designed the cafe in a way that I thought would be only moderately conducive to laptop use. I didn't put in extra outlets for laptops. I put in a lot of communal seating and in the more prime spaces in the cafe, there aren't ways for you to get power and other things. So I wanted to try it out and just see what developed, to see what happened organically in the space after having said my piece and designed the cafe in a certain way.'

And to get people talking as well as typing, he also instituted a laptop-free weekends rule, which he says has also been well received by his customers: 'The name Actual Cafe comes from a conversation on this very topic. I was telling a friend that we're becoming more dependent on virtual socialising, and that it's becoming a substitute for the real thing in many cases, and that we, as human beings, need actual contact in order to stay healthy — real face-to-face interaction. This is a key value of the cafe.'

Now, around about the same time that Sal Bednarz instituted his weekend laptop curfew, Jennifer Rauch, who lives on the other side of the US in Brooklyn, was also beginning the process of weaning herself off all things digital.

'One of the techniques that I started doing was to go offline on one day a week, usually on Sundays, where I would just retrain myself not to carry my cellphone around, not to go on the internet or respond to emails,' she tells me. 'From there it sort of escalated. Part of it has to do with my role as a teacher and as a scholar. This is something that I've addressed in the classes that I teach as well as some of the research that I do. But my interest in it, at the most cerebral level, is as a human being.'

And by 'escalated' Rauch, who lectures in Journalism at Long Island University, means she decided to go entirely offline for six months. In late June 2010, she wrote on her blog: 'With three days to go before taking the red pill, it's probably a good time to sketch the contours of the Slow Media experiment that I'll be conducting until 2011. My main priority is to escape the gift/curse of constant communication and infinite information, in order to 1) free up time to spend on other things, such as analog or material forms of media, and 2) enable some contemplation about the role of digital media in my life.'

Now going digital cold turkey wasn't easy, and the experiences that led to her decision sound eerily familiar. Says Rauch: 'I love the internet and I love digital media. It's not necessarily an easy decision for me to push it out of my life. But at the end of the day, time is finite. And time that we choose to spend doing certain things is time that we spend not doing other things. I've found that over the past few years, the time that I've spent looking at screens, whether it's interacting with the internet or with cellphones, has increased bit by bit to the point now where other things have been crowded out. There's just been too many days where I wake up and I have my coffee and my breakfast, and I go on the internet to check my emails, and before I know it, six or eight hours have slipped past while I've been reading emails, sending emails, clicking on to links, checking my Facebook, just sort of trawling my way around the web.'

And how did it all turn out? Well in January 2011, Jennifer Rauch made a brief digital return to her blog to announce the result of her experiment: 'After six months of immersing myself in Slow Media, I'm back online now — though still not using a cellphone. Since starting the experiment, I have used payphones and Yellow Pages and typewriters ... penned piles of letters and postcards ... watched all my VHS tapes and listened to all my audiocassettes (along with some vinyl, until my record player broke) ... devoured a huge stack of newspapers and books ... deciphered many a printed map ... and taken photographs with disposable cameras, 35mm film and Polaroids. It was really fun. And honestly, life without digital media wasn't that hard, folks. You should try it. Maybe just for a day, or a weekend?'

All good teachers lead by experience, of course, but that's not to say that their students necessarily follow. Rauch set her pupils at Long Island University the task of emulating her Slow Media experiment for a day, just one day — no digital devices for twenty-four hours, though the students could still use any form of media, or any electronic gadget, that existed prior to 1990. As it transpired, only a few members of the class completed the assignment successfully. And only, Rauch informs me, with a lot of difficulty. Many others, she says, barely got past the starting line.

'They found they missed their little devices and were always wondering what they were missing out on; and missed the connection with their friends, their family, or whoever else they were used to having just a few clicks away. Some of my students didn't even take the assignment very seriously because they decided it was impossible to achieve and they doubted the desirability of even trying to get away from digital media for a day. They more or less admitted that they had done it for the morning, maybe half a day, but then suspense got the better of them, and they just decided that they couldn't do it.'

Which suddenly makes Kim Kardashian and her twenty-four-hour digital fast look very impressive indeed.

Digital entrepreneur and activist Clay Johnson believes our addiction to devices goes hand in hand with our ever increasing hunger for information. He draws a fascinating analogy between the way we consume information and our relationship with junk food. And he's now an advocate for what he calls the 'information diet'.

'When we talk about information overload, it places the blame on the wrong thing. We don't say that obese people are suffering from food overload, they are suffering from either eating too much food or too much bad food and not enough good food. I think the same thing is going on with information. We're not suffering from information overload, we're suffering from information over-consumption. Before going on an information diet, I found myself being a virtual symphony walking down the street with my phone beeping, playing little tunes for all these different services that were commanding my attention. And really a healthy information diet is about consuming quality information and developing habits and healthy choices.'

Johnson, who co-founded the company Blue State Digital and ran Barack Obama's digital and social media campaign back in 2008, says he hit on the 'information diet' idea when he realised that most people who undertook a technology fast, simply failed to break their addiction.

'When you decide that you are going to go on a social media vacation or just to unplug, all you're going to do is binge when you get back, or rush to your email at your earliest convenience, it is not going to actually create any permanent habitual change in your life.'

But he's in no doubt that for most people the message of moderation and self-control is going to prove enormously challenging. 'It is very difficult,' he tells me. 'It's also very difficult to be a vegan or a vegetarian, but these are the challenges that we have to face.'

Where are you, John Kinsella?

One person who doesn't lack determination, and passion too, is the internationally acclaimed poet John Kinsella. Kinsella divides his time between Perth in Western Australia and the UK, where he's a Fellow of Churchill College at Cambridge

University. You can call Kinsella a Luddite — or at least a neo-Luddite — without fear of offending him. In fact, he wears the badge with pride.

Such is his antipathy towards modern technology, that if there was actually such a thing as an anti-technology army, he'd no doubt be happy to accept its commission as commander-in-chief, except for the inconvenient fact that he's a pacifist, more interested in moral persuasion than physical protest.

'Technology isn't the deliverance of humanity,' he once declared in print, 'it is its damnation.'[25]

When I read that quote in an opinion piece he'd written for an online commentary site I knew I needed to speak to him. Because, for all my earlier talk about the need for a more genuine and balanced discussion around the effect technology is having on individuals and society, let's face it, it's always fun to hear from those at the extreme. And Kinsella, despite his attachment to one of the oldest establishment universities in the world, is an outright, self-declared anarchist. I also knew I had to get to him fast, because at the end of the article he announced his intention to turn his back on modern communications and go 'entirely offline and off computers and off grid'.

Unlike Jennifer Rauch, he wasn't just talking about a period of experimentation. John Kinsella was logging off for good, he defiantly explained. So I got his email address and in rapid time we made contact. As I discovered, Kinsella's rejection of technology wasn't exactly as I had expected. In my imagination I envisioned him as the sort of poet who, over decades, had filled vast numbers of yellowing notepads with beautiful copperplate script, a person with a long history of aversion to anything that wasn't made of tree pulp, or didn't have a pointy end loaded with ink. Wrong indeed. The truth is that Kinsella's rejection of modern technology is borne of familiarity, not ignorance. From his teenage years in the mid 1970s right through the eighties and nineties he was actually a bit of a computer geek and certainly an early adopter of technology, but his enthusiasm for the online world diminished over time as he perceived it becoming more about commercial imperatives and less about human advancement.

'I believe that we've got to an unnecessary level of materialist consumerist usage,' he tells me. 'Technology is said to make our lives more comfortable and more interesting and safer and more productive. Well I actually don't believe that's true. I believe that these kinds of enhanced technologies are actually depriving us of our liberty, are actually encroaching on our health, encroaching on our mental and physical freedom.'

Kinsella, like Nicholas Carr and Baroness Greenfield, and the others mentioned earlier, fears that an all-pervasive digital environment is starting to change not just the way we behave, but also the way we think — and detrimentally so. But what he said he feared every bit as much as that adaptation was the effect that various forms of modern technology were also having on our environment and its resources. And he was disdainful of what he described as attempts by technology companies to mask their wastefulness.

'Now you're getting the new generation of so-called "green" computers, but they're only relatively green,' he tells me. 'I mean if you actually look into them, the basic materials are still the same; they have a few differences, they may include less toxic materials, but in essence, they're still consuming and using a massive amount of material.

'The other thing about computers is that they are a faddish technology, in the sense that they are constantly upgrading, and constantly changing, and we constantly feel the need to improve our own technologies to do more things. So it's not like you go and buy a computer and you sit on it for thirty years,' he complains. 'In five years your computer really doesn't work very well, it doesn't actually function in the way it used to function. It's not adequate, if you like. And that's just basic consumerism. It doesn't make sense to me. You look at what we've got and you see it's being consumed for the sake of a faddish and fetishistic process.'

Now, that's a point that isn't John Kinsella's alone and it's one which we'll explore more fully in a forthcoming chapter on energy efficiency, so stay tuned. But I have to confess that as we talk, I can't help but think that the sort of life the noted poet continues to lead as an international literary identity, flying here and there to lecture and research, also holds some very obvious problems for a neo-Luddite, specifically where aeroplanes are concerned. It's a thought that gets louder in my head the longer we chat, so eventually I explicitly ask him about his extensive air travel and how he reconciles it with his beliefs.

The frank response I get is that he can't justify it at all, and so he's already begun taking steps to transform that part of his life as well. 'I lived in three countries for fifteen years. And I moved between those different institutions consistently,' he confides. 'One year I flew 900 hours, and I mean that's more than pilots are basically allowed to fly. That's how I led a life. And I thought, "I've got to give up flying. Here I am going around the world proselytising about this, and I am flying. I've got to stop." So I did. I haven't flown since, and I will never fly again. I'm not interested in destroying things like the Luddites did with the looms and so on, but I am interested in setting up an alternative example.'

So fewer trips it is. And by boat, not plane, when he absolutely has to.

I can happily report that John Kinsella is still writing poetry, 'proselytising' and, most importantly of all, is still offline. But exactly how he and his family are adjusting to the change, I have no idea — none whatsoever. You see, before going offline completely, the great poet gave me his postal address and we agreed to get in contact again at some future point for an update.

However, having wasted several stamps, I'm still waiting for a reply.

He may be a fantastic poet, but it seems he's not really a man of letters.

CHAPTER 4

RESETTING THE CLOCK

I think the benefits of particular technological advances are often overstated, and new technologies also tend to bring with them new inequalities, whose costs are often overlooked. But if you look at human history over long enough timescales, I think it's hard to make the argument that we would be better off turning back the clock.

Dr Duncan Watts, Principal Research Scientist, Yahoo Research[26]

The McLuhan switch

There's a great line in Shakespeare's Scottish tragedy where Macbeth, having driven a sword through everything he once held dear, questions whether it is possible to set a different course. To reverse the bloody path he has so far taken. He ponders for one brief moment before declaring: 'I am in blood, stepp'd in so far that, should I wade no more, returning were as tedious as go o'er.'

You can't turn back the hands of time, so the old saying goes. You can't undo what has already been done. The message from those I highlighted in the last chapter wasn't that modern technology was evil, or bad — John Kinsella being the exception — but that we have to be careful and judicious about how we use it; ensuring that we make it work for us and not the other way around.

It's about negotiation, says Tom Standage, the Digital Editor of *The Economist* and author of *The Victorian Internet*, a fascinating book about the development of the telegraph: 'It would be great if we could uninvent nuclear weapons, but unfortunately we can't. The point is that trying to uninvent things doesn't work — someone, somewhere will give them a try. So we have to have this negotiation between the technological possibilities and the political reality of how we are going to adopt technology and how we come to terms with what its impacts are.'

Still, it's hard not to imagine that there aren't just a few genuine Luddites out there. Those who'd like to take a sledgehammer to today's technology if they could. You know the type I'm talking about: anyone who once owned a One Hour Photo franchise, for example; or the boss of the company that had the patent for Liquid Paper.

And while many of us, in a frustrated moment of information overload, might occasionally wish that we could not only reset the clock, but turn the bloody thing off and throw it against the wall, it's actually hard to find anyone (credible or otherwise) who genuinely believes that it's possible to somehow go back, to 'uninvent' as Standage put it.

For the purposes of this book, I looked and looked and looked — and then I found someone. And it was a bit of an unexpected discovery.

Marshall McLuhan, the enigmatic Canadian media watcher, was famous for saying things that sounded profound, but were often extremely difficult to get a handle on. The phrase 'The medium is the message' is perhaps his most lasting legacy, along with the prescient term 'global village'. For anyone who doesn't know, McLuhan observed and theorised the growth of broadcast television in the 1950s, 60s and 70s. He documented its extraordinary take-up, its popularity and its power. How odd then, or at least curious, that he also believed it was possible to flick the switch and shut down the merry-go-round.

'Far from regarding technological change as inevitable,' proclaimed McLuhan, 'I insist that if we understand its components, we can turn it off any time we choose. Short of turning it off, there are lots of moderate controls conceivable.'

Even in his time that would have seemed a giant call, let alone in the age of the internet — the world that never sleeps. How exactly McLuhan believed we could turn off technological change isn't clear, and given that he's been dead for over thirty years, we'll never really know. Dead men tell no tales.

But then, as I was busy pondering the meaning of his words, looking for a deeper resonance, my attention was drawn to another of his opaque remarks and suddenly his pronouncements seemed to lose their intrigue.

The comment?

'I don't necessarily agree with everything I say.'

Enigmatic? Yes. Helpful? No.

In the previous chapter we heard from a variety of people who feel a need to jump off the treadmill, to find a balance in their lives between sanity and the future that technologists, commercial interests and the media keep telling them they should be aspiring to, and about which they feel increasingly uncomfortable. In short, Chapter Three was pretty much about frustration and the desire to find a better way of living.

The people we'll meet in this chapter have already largely determined what they need to do to live on their own terms, to retake control of their future. They're part of two counter-trends which advocate resetting the pace of life and reprioritising what's important for individuals and society. They're certainly future focused, but they borrow from the past. And neither is anti-technology or change.

I say counter-trends, but with a small 'c' — I really don't mean to infer that they're part of some great or noble revolution, just that their philosophy and actions question prevailing trends and wisdom. So here we go ...

Movement #1: The ultimate go-slow

In one sense we've already started on the first of these movements with Jennifer Rauch and her Slow Media experiment. But let me ask you this, what exactly is it we mean by the word 'slow'? In common parlance, slow has long been a pejorative term. To call somebody slow is to imply that they're dim-witted. If I describe a particular town or city as slow you understand the implication — that it lacks sophistication; that it's a bit of a backwater. In our fast-paced, immediate lives, slow is death, fast is the future. Speed is what we all want, be it traffic flow, internet connections or food service. Fast, faster and faster still.

And yet, we often forget that it's all relative: the lift in my office building is unbearably slow, everybody remarks on it. In the 1950s it would have been described as lightning fast. When it seemingly takes an age for my computer to log on and open up, I forget the fact that just fifteen years back — when the only connection I could get was dial-up — things were much, much slower. And it didn't seem unbearably frustrating at the time. We've become so used to doing things quickly that many of us don't question why we need to rush.

Carl Honore chuckles when he tells me about some of the 'absurd' examples he's come across: 'Near my house in London is a gym that now offers an evening course in Speed Yoga,' he says. 'It's for time-starved professionals who want to salute the sun, and bend their bodies into the lotus position. But they want to do it in twenty minutes instead of a whole hour. And I thought that Speed Yoga was the most ludicrous manifestation of this road-runner culture until a friend of mine in the United States got invited to a drive-thru funeral. The church places the coffin at the entrance, people pull up in their cars, wind down the window, throw flowers, say goodbye, and off they go.'

But his favourite tale involves a priest and a moment of spiritual clarity: 'I did a talk at a church in Vienna and afterwards the monsignor came up to me slightly sheepishly, and he said, "You know, when you were talking I suddenly realised how easy it is for all of us to get caught up in this speed approach," and he said to me, "I suddenly realised that I'd been praying too fast."' Honore chuckles again. 'If we've got to the stage where even monsignors are praying in fast forward, then we've really lost our bearing.'

When the Canadian author and blogger published his book *In Praise of Slowness: How a worldwide movement is challenging the cult of speed*, it quickly became a bestseller. It also became something of a bible for those who believe their lives can be just as rich and fulfilling without the need to do everything at a slightly manic pace.

Says Honore: 'A lot of people will know Slow Food, but that's just the tip of an enormous iceberg. There are movements for Slow Cities now: redesigning the urban landscape to encourage people to put on the brakes. You see this slow idea moving into the world of design, Slow Design; there is a Slow Technology movement. There's Slow Sex, Slow Parenting, Slow Education. Even in the fashion world, which defines itself by speed, there is a growing move towards what they call Slow Fashion.'

Slow Sex worries me, because after a certain age unless you do things with a certain vigour and pace, there's a danger of nodding off, which isn't going to impress anybody.

Now, in any given year I interview scores of people from a vast range of disciplines and professions, and recognising, or rediscovering, the benefits of not rushing is definitely a recurring theme. Geoff Hudson is one of those involved with the Slow Food movement's Australian chapter, one of 132 such organisations in the world. 'It really began in response to concern about the entry of fast food into Italy. And this was sort of a tongue-in-cheek naming to identify all those things that weren't fast food,' he says. 'The mantra, if you like, is good, clean and fair, and that relates to food and the production of food. So the good really relates to taste, that food should have good taste and good flavour and be a pleasurable experience to eat. Clean relates to the preparation of, or growing of food, the lack of chemicals. Intensive agriculture is not something that is encouraged — battery-raised chickens would be bad news. It's an endeavour to get back to some natural values in food. And fair relates to providing growers with a reasonable return for their efforts.'

Of course, we need to keep all of this in perspective. Those who would tag themselves as followers of a 'Slow' ideology are statistically a pretty small bunch by world standards, and there is a pretentiousness about Slow Food in particular that can be grating: trendy and expensive farmers' markets, that kind of thing. At its heart, it's actually a form of reaction — against consumerism, against supporting big corporations at the expense of small business, and against the disposability that Carl Honore spoke of. But it's also about appreciation — the idea that sometimes you might actually need to slow down to enjoy what you have in life.

The Australian novelist George Johnston once said that when you choose your means of transport, you choose the pace of your life, and even in the transport industry Slow Travel is now becoming a significant tourist trend. Sure, everybody wants to get to and from work in a speedy fashion, but the obsession with getting people to their destinations in record time and at a cut-price rate has turned the journey to and from holiday destinations into an endurance rather than an experience. One of those helping to promote the concept of Slow Travel, and making a comfortable living out of it as well, is a former British Rail employee named Mark Smith. Smith runs a very popular website called *The Man in Seat Sixty-One*.

According to Smith, the site's success came as a genuine shock. 'I've always taken the train to Europe. It's really easy and affordable and practical. It was just downright impossible to find anyone in the commercial world to tell you how to do it. So I thought, "Right, I'll put the information online myself,"' he says. What he soon discovered was that he'd inadvertently tapped into a rich seam of public disquiet: 'I didn't actually think anyone would ever read it. I certainly didn't think that a few years on it would be my full-time job and there'd be practically a million visitors a month looking at it.'

His company went on to be voted Best Travel Website in the 2008 *Guardian* and *Observer* Readers' Travel Awards and was also listed as one of *Timesonline*'s 100 best travel sites. And the reasons for the site's popularity, according to Mark Smith, are twofold. 'One is people are fed up with flying. They're fed up with the stress, the hassle, the delays, the airport check-ins,' he says. 'And secondly, they want to cut their carbon footprint. And most people say those two things in the same breath, as if they were flipsides to the same coin. No doubt for some people one is more important than the other, but they always seem to say them together — I'm fed up of flying and I want to cut my carbon footprint.'

But slow may not be the future for everyone. One of the criticisms of the slow movement overall, whether it's Slow Travel, Slow Food or even Slow Cities, is that, as popular as it's becoming, it's still very much a movement for the urban elites, the people with the money and time to escape the treadmill.

It's a criticism that Geoff Hudson rejects outright: 'I don't accept it at all. I think there are a lot of people in the Slow Food movement who you could, I guess, describe in that way. But there is also a very large number who have a genuine interest and concern about the direction in which we're heading with food. And it's quite frightening really when you get into the detail of commercial food and feed-lotting and all of that sort of thing. I think there are a lot of people within the movement who are committed to the good, clean and fair mantra.'

But Carl Honore's response to the criticism is to give a little ground: 'I think there are aspects or expressions of the slow movement that are only ever going to be within the reach or the grasp of the upper middle class and the affluent. I mean, if you're thinking of hand-gathered truffles from the Italian forests outside of Milan, not everybody is ever going to be able to afford that type of slow delicacy. But the other end of that

Slow Food spectrum is that anyone, on any income, can go into a supermarket and buy some dried pasta, a few tomatoes, a piece of garlic, go home and make a pasta for a family of four, sit around the table with the television switched off and have a conversation. And that costs a lot less than going to McDonald's to feed the same family. It's there for everyone, because ultimately, I think, slow is a state of mind. It's about how you use time and about how you approach every moment of the day. Do you arrive at every task thinking, "How can I do this as quickly as possible?" or do you arrive thinking, "How do I do this as well as possible?" and "How do I get the most out of it?"'

And it's not a bad way to avoid a heart attack one would have thought.

Movement #2: Rediscovering those grasping things at the ends of your arms

In Fritz Lang's 1927 sci-fi classic *Metropolis*, the future is an industrial nightmare in which ordinary workers are reduced to the status of robotic slaves, toiling away in blue-collar melancholy. If you were to remake that film today you'd have to make quite a few changes. Aside from the obvious ones — introducing sound and colour — you'd also need to have your depressed hordes engaged in something other than manual labour, because there are fewer and fewer people working on factory assembly lines these days. Let's face it, there aren't the jobs: factories have largely been automated. And even where manual labour is still required, everything's a lot less hands-on than it used to be. And that goes for society overall: we no longer make and fix, we buy and buy again.

When I lift the bonnet on my car there's not much to see, because the entire top of the engine is encased in a plastic cover. I'm a bit of an idiot when it comes to mechanics so I wouldn't be sure what to look for even if the cover wasn't there. I've owned the vehicle I drive for a couple of years now, and not once have I seen the bits that make it move, the engine block, spark plugs, none of it. It could be made out of chicken wire and bits of string for all I know. I've never really been into cars, so it doesn't overly concern me, which probably makes me a very modern person indeed, because almost no one mucks about with cars these days.

My first ever set of wheels was a second-hand Datsun 120Y. It was basically an oversized wind-up toy. And when I was at uni and it broke down (and I had very little money) there was always someone who could stick their head under the bonnet and work out what was wrong. It's a lot more difficult to do that sort of thing these days though, because the car of the twenty-first century is a device that's so complex it's best left to the experts. My current car is basically a computer with wheels attached. Actually, it's a collection of computers with wheels attached.

Another reason most people don't play around with cars these days is something I alluded to just before: most people don't play around with *anything* much anymore. When an object breaks, few people think to try to fix it; everything's too complicated and nothing's made to last at any rate — we've become a generation of consumers, not repairers. When something stops working, the natural thing to do is to simply throw it away and get a new one. And as a result, according to Matthew Crawford, most of us are now all thumbs and no fingers.

Crawford is the Carl Honore of the DIY movement and he bemoans what he sees as the devaluing of manual work and the loss of everyday skills. Something, he says, he first became aware of when he went to buy some second-hand tools and found out that most of the merchandise on offer was actually discarded equipment from local schools.

'I started looking into it and learned that shop class, as we call it in the States — where people learn auto mechanics, metal shop — has been pretty widely dismantled.'

Crawford, who studied physics, but says he couldn't get a job in his chosen field after graduating, fashioned his concerns into a best-selling book called *Shop Class as Soulcraft*. What I find persuasive about the argument Crawford makes in his book is his observation that we haven't just rushed to embrace new forms of technology in recent decades — 'enhanced' technologies, as John Kinsella would call them — we've actually traded-in our self-reliance in the process. In other words, we've allowed ourselves to become de-skilled to the point where most of us can't tell one end of a hammer from the other.* And central to his argument is the notion that what he calls 'futurism' has become wedded to what he calls 'virtualism'.

'Technology is always something that's handled by somebody else,' he says by way of explanation. 'It's almost a kind of weirdly pre-modern attitude where technology is this magical thing that relies on invisible powers, and I think that spirit of self-reliance is something that we need to cultivate. We've had this idea that somehow we're going to be gliding around in a pure information economy, and that hasn't quite turned out to be the case. It sometimes seems like the modern personality is getting reformed on the basis of passivity and dependence,' he says.

But society's 'passivity and dependence' represents a red flag to those who refuse to go quietly into the night. And such people form the core of our second counter-trend — the return of the DIY movement.

One of the movement's most colourful proponents is Mark Thomson, the self-appointed advanced research director of a self-built organisation called the Institute of Backyard Studies. He's a proud tinkerer with a desert-like dryness to his humour. Thomson is one of the flag wavers in Australia for what he describes as a pushback against 'mindless consumption'.

---

* TIP: The long wooden part is the handle — that's the bit you hold. The metal bit is the thing you use to hit the nail. And a nail is … Oh, never mind.

His institute, he tells me, is part of an informal 'shed-based network', poking fun at the age-old cliche that a man's best friend is his tool shed, while also drawing attention to the reality that most men these days are flat out fixing themselves a sandwich, let alone fixing a lawnmower.

'What we are trying to do is really tease out the unacknowledged creativity that goes on in small-scale culture around the place,' he tells me. 'Whether it's in a shed or in the backyard or out on the farm, or you name it, there's all sorts of interesting things going on where people are making things, inventing things, reviving things, and invariably involving a really interesting relationship between the hand and the brain. So we are about the stuff of small scale, beneath the official gaze, the small end of town.' And that approach is widely being called 'tinkering' — a tag that has also been recently resurrected from the past.

Thomson says one of the crucial aspects of tinkering is that it allows for failure in a way that our modern approach to manufacturing no longer does. In fact, Thomson describes failure as an essential component of any process of evolution.

'The expression "trial and error" does actually entail some error, and that has always been the culture of invention really,' he says, 'you have to make mistakes, and acknowledge that making a mistake is a problem, but what you learn from the mistake is the really critical thing in that process. And I think that's where tinkering, in particular, comes into an interesting kind of clash with the big end of town. Because the corporate world, the government world, are so risk-averse that they are obsessed with the elimination of risk, of error.'

The futurist Alex Pang is also a proponent of tinkering. He argues that tinkering has a powerful kind of emotional appeal that encourages a spirit of open-ended inquiry about the material world. 'It encourages a kind of empowerment, a sense that you don't just have to take things as they come. Even in today's apparently high-tech, slick, very pre-processed, very produced world, it is possible still to break open the covers, to get into the silicon, to get into the gears and to improve them. I think that's one of the other things that drives tinkerers, the sense that they often want to set themselves and their own personal material world apart from the kind of store-bought, commercial customisation technologies that most people have today.'

There is a depressing irony in the fact that many of the technology companies that now seek to standardise and package our world actually started from the DIY/tinkering environment that was the computer scene of the 1960s and 70s. Bill Gates was originally a 'hacker', after all. As was Apple's Steve Wozniak. But it's encouraging to find that those fighting against the rigid commercial conformity that Apple and Microsoft have helped create are also fighting to reclaim the 'hacker' mantle as well.

While it's true the term 'hacking' has a particularly negative connotation in the minds of many people these days, particularly after the 2011 *News of the World* scandal in Britain, it is a moniker that's actively being reappropriated by those who like to tinker. 'The original term, the original usage, is coming back,' says Steven Levy, the author of *Hackers: Heroes of the Computer Revolution*. 'Hacking has regained a bit of its glory. And people are talking about hacking in things other than computing. Something I call "the hands-on imperative" — get your hands on and change things — that's really an impetus that's behind the do-it-yourself movement.'

Originally written in the early 1980s, Levy's book profiled a host of rising young computer geeks who went on to become giants in the technology field. People like Bill Gates and Steve Jobs. It was re-released in 2010 with updated interviews. And one of the hidden gems for me was finding out that Gates now has fantasies about hacking the stuff of life — DNA. Says Levy: 'When I talked to Bill Gates he said, "You know, the big advances in computing have been made, we've changed the world and all that. But we're just beginning on things like biology." And if he were a teenager now, that's probably what he'd be interested in.'

Actually, there already is a burgeoning DIY field doing exactly that. It's called biohacking. And one of those involved is Kay Aull, a bioengineer and researcher by day, and a biohacker by night. 'I'm the kind of person who likes to take things apart and put things back together and what I've chosen to do that with is biology,' she says. 'For me biohacking is about the ability to understand the living things that go on around us. Biology, and genetic engineering in particular, is presented as this mysterious thing that happens in laboratories with white coats. And I think biohacking is about, hey this is just basic chemistry, anybody can understand that.'

Aull, who has a degree from the Massachusetts Institute of Technology and lives and works in Boston, says the biohacking community is pretty diverse, and she says it's taken off in recent years because the technology now exists to make simple experiments achievable: 'I think it's a response to having the tools for the first time to really do this kind of work. In the past biology has been about "stamp-collecting"; that's been the pejorative term. It's been about counting the number of legs on particular critters. But now we can actually go inside, see what they're really doing and even change that to do what we want to do. We've got sequencing data; we've got the ability to synthesise pieces of DNA; we've got the databases full of knowledge about biological systems and the ability to look those up on our home computers and even send those off to be synthesised.'

It's a hobby, insists Aull, but it's a hobby that allows people to have a better understanding and appreciation of how biology works. She says: 'Hacking is not good or bad. Hackers are not good or bad. If you want to use the technology in a constructive way, you can do that. And if you just want to blow things up, then that's an option too. But I would say that it's actually quite difficult to get yourself into trouble with biohacking, unless you're really trying to do that.'

A little further south in Brooklyn, New York, there's an old warehouse that's been converted into a biohacker's paradise. 'The world's first community lab' is how its operators describe it, 'a nursery for biotech entrepreneurs'.

The not-for-profit lab is called GenSpace and its president and Science Director is Dr Ellen Jorgensen. 'At first we started meeting in people's living rooms, where we would cover the living room in plastic and do an experiment and then we would dump it all in a bucket of bleach or whatever. And it just became really obvious that we needed a dedicated space of some kind. And the idea of the community lab evolved out of that.'

What impresses me about the facility is its openness and lack of pretension: it promotes itself as operating like a gym. You pay US$100 a month for membership and that entitles you to come in and do whatever you want — as long as it's legal. 'We have a mission to provide the space for people who want to be tinkerers or entrepreneurs, or artists exploring certain things in biology,' says Jorgensen, 'or students learning about stuff in a more hands-on, real atmosphere than the classroom. We want it to be a light-hearted thing. We want people to feel like they can tinker and play and be creative. If people want to express themselves, as long as they're not doing anything dangerous, I don't see why they should be held to whether or not it's going to make money, or whether or not it's going to be useful to society.'

I have to report that Dr Jorgensen has taken the precaution of establishing a close relationship with the FBI's Local Weapons of Mass Destruction Coordinator — yes, that's the person's real title. Post 9-11, I guess it pays to appreciate the local sensitivities when it comes to things like terrorism and home-made laboratories.

So, let's recap. Like the slow movement, the DIY/tinkering push isn't likely to force down the walls of consumer-driven capitalism any time soon, but it is a serious and substantive movement that reaches across a variety of fields and is about reasserting the control individuals have over their own lives. And while heavily focused on individual empowerment, neither movement is about toiling in isolation, they're both about encouraging cooperation and using technology when and where appropriate to do so. As Alex Pang says: 'Tinkerers these days are social animals, and their success depends in part on being able to tap into, often online, communities or people who share similar kinds of interests, or similar sorts of passion.'

One of the ways in which that sharing is maximised is through the use of an open-source approach. That is, where people make their ideas and research available free of charge to as many people as possible, with the hope that others will build on those ideas, rework them and improve them, for the benefit of all. It's a non-proprietary approach that has its roots in the software development sector, where many computer geeks work collaboratively to produce what's called open-source software. That's been going on for ages, but interestingly, what we've also started to see in recent years is a move towards 'open hardware': a parallel push for the collaborative approach of open source software to be applied to the physical side of manufacturing, so that enthusiasts can more easily share and tinker with the hardware for computers and other forms of electronics.

One company which specialises in open hardware is called Bug Labs and its founder is Peter Semmelhack. Semmelhack helped organise a conference on open hardware in New York in 2010. And his colleagues don't just provide people with gadgets, they provide people with the detailed knowledge and plans behind those gadgets: 'The promise is that if you have a device, you also receive with that device the schematics of all materials, the files that you need to modify that device in any way. And what we're doing now is we're trying to articulate the best ways to use those types of resources and bring the complexities down a notch, so that it doesn't take a Nokia or a Samsung to do these things, people can do them on a much smaller scale at a cost which is reasonable.'

And Semmelhack tells me that an interest in open-source design is now also coming from quite established companies, which have suddenly discovered there's a market for such products. Two of the firms he mentions are the US semi-conductor manufacturer Marvell, and Texas Instruments, both of which are decent-sized operations. Speaking to Semmelhack, I can't help but be reminded of another era, not so long ago actually, when kids made their own radios and things using a soldering iron and the bits and pieces bought from an electronics store. But let's not get bogged down in nostalgia; instead, let's remember that over the great sweep of history, many of the inventions that have shaped the future of humanity and the planet have been made by people mucking about in garages and bedrooms — Edison was an amateur to begin with, and so too were Messrs Gates, Jobs and Wozniak, to name just a few. And knowing that there are still people who haven't lost the need to tinker and explore, despite the corporate confines of patents and lawsuits, has to be good for our future prospects.

Now, having delivered an impromptu sermon, let me just briefly tell you about perhaps the most fascinating and unexpected domain in which the DIY ethos has taken hold — the field of space engineering and the manufacturing of satellites. There are now so many individuals and groups involved in DIY space projects that in 2010, the hobbyist magazine *Make* devoted an entire issue to what they labelled 'Space 2.0'.

According to Dale Dougherty, the general manager of Maker Media, which publishes *Make*, Space 2.0 is all about the open sourcing of exploration, allowing hobbyists and tinkerers to play a role in the space program, which sounds slightly ridiculous, I know, but it is actually happening, albeit in a small and uncoordinated way.

Because the costs associated with technology have come right down, it's now possible to build a small-scale satellite for around US$8000. And more and more groups have been getting involved, including a group of US teenagers, just out of high school, who in 2010 managed to launch a payload, including a camera and sensors, some 26,000 feet up into near-Earth orbit. Then there was a Danish DIY group who, in June 2011, launched a nine metre tall, homemade rocket from a barge off the coast of Denmark. The rocket cost 50,000 euros to make (about US$66,000) and it managed to climb to a height of eight kilometres before running out of puff. The team had hoped it would reach the sixteen kilometre mark, but were apparently delighted nonetheless. And, true to the DIY spirit, the construction plans for the rocket were all made open source.

The response from the professionals to all of this amateur space engineering isn't what you might expect. NASA, for one, actually encourages it, according to Dougherty: 'They would like to see a whole new era of involvement, framing it as massive participation, not just a few people getting involved in space. What they're excited about is that a lot of the technology that we can use today can be off the shelf. It doesn't need to be specialised. In effect, there's a change here, moving from NASA — which was a large, centrally controlled agency that decided what got into space, and what was worth exploring and experimenting on — into an era where it's more distributed and there's lots of different opportunities, whether they're private commercial opportunities, or individuals able to garner enough resources.'

Now DIY is good. That's one of the central premises of this chapter, but I have to confess to personally feeling just a little uneasy about the idea of do-it-yourself rocketry. As they say 'what goes up must come down'. And without being too alarmist, I also can't help remembering another expression from the dim, distant days of my childhood: 'It's all good fun until somebody loses an eye.'

CHAPTER 5

THE WISDOM OF THE CROWD — FACT AND FICTION

Science is the belief in the ignorance of the experts

Richard Feynman, Nobel Prize-winning American physicist

Collective individualism

I want to stay with the theme of cooperation and collaboration and further explore how it manifests itself in an epoch often celebrated — and derided — as being all about the self.

It probably wouldn't hurt to begin with a reality check.

The obsessive focus on the individual in the early twenty-first century is actually a paradox. While technology companies and their marketers continue to push the 'It's all about you' line, they also fall over themselves to encourage people to collaborate and to link to each other — to find 'fans', 'followers' or 'friends'. Perhaps we should call it *individual collectivism*, or maybe, better still, *collective individualism*. Anyway, there is an expectation in our modern world that you're not really pulling your weight unless you're truly individualistic, but also part of a social network at the same time. Or, at the very least, a member of some weird or obscure Facebook group: 'I Yell At Inanimate Objects,' for instance, or 'Students Against Backpacks With Wheels', which inexplicably had only ninety-nine members the last time I looked, and which really shouldn't be confused with 'Students Against Backpacks On Wheels', which had only thirty-two.

First off though, let me get the cynical thought that's whirling around inside my skull out and onto the table: Of course, the major reason marketers and technology companies want you to be as socially connected as possible is so that they can follow your links to others and then exploit your friends' data as well as yours. There, I've said it, and if you need reminding on that score you'd better go back to Chapter One.

There's an important distinction to be made between being social and being collaborative — one that's often overlooked. It may deflate some technology enthusiasts to hear this but it seems that, regardless of age, most people use Facebook as a purely social space, not as a tool of political empowerment or as a major new source of news. It's used for gossip and catching up — and planning what to do on Friday night, or after bridge, if you happen to be of an older demographic. It's not called 'social media' for nothing.

And that's especially true of the young. Facebook is to most teenagers today what the humble telephone was back in the 1970s. That's the truth of it. And the latest research seems to indicate that the majority of people's social connections on Facebook are a lot less adventurous and extensive than we're led to believe by the social media spruikers. The highly regarded Pew Research Center in the United States recently conducted a survey that questioned people about the diversity of their friendships on the social media site. What they found was that only around three per cent of Facebook friends were people the respondents had no prior connection with — in other words, people they had never met in real life. Ninety-seven per cent were already acquaintances.

On that score, Ethan Zuckerman, the director of the Center for Civic Media at MIT — and formerly of the Berkman Center for Internet and Society at Harvard — talks about what he calls 'imaginary cosmopolitanism': the idea that people think their online explorations and engagements are far more diverse than they actually are. Zuckerman explains it like this: 'I think there are moments in which being on the internet feels like we're living in the future, we're living in this wonderful place where at every turn I might click a link and find myself in China or in Cameroon. I might find myself engaged in conversation with someone halfway around the world. The truth is, most of the time, we don't. A lot of our interactions are with people we already know.'

And even our ability to access a diversity of opinion needs to be questioned. In 2008, I did an interview with Professor Henry Jenkins, the director of the Comparative Media Studies Program at MIT, about the types of clips that gain most prominence on the online video sharing site YouTube. 'I think a participatory culture is not necessarily a diverse culture,' he told me. 'If you look at the top 100 videos on YouTube in any given week, the vast majority of them are coming from white, middle-class males. It's not that minority content isn't produced, it isn't that it isn't circulated, but it circulates in a much lower level of visibility. The mechanisms of YouTube are those of majority rule, so that if we all vote the content up we want to see, it's going to be this content that speaks to the majority and there are not systems in place that ensure minority perspectives get heard or seen. So it may circulate there, but it may not reach anywhere near the level of public impact that videos that are produced by a bunch of high school guys goofing off receive.'

There's also evidence to suggest that most people's use of new technologies is far more limited and/or passive than you'd imagine. Having an iPhone loaded with apps doesn't necessarily mean you're going to use them all. From a personal perspective I have loads of programs on my laptop that I've never used and am unlikely to. So to judge my computer habits solely on the basis of the pre-installed programs I own, would be way off the mark.

'I like to watch', the fictitious Chauncey Gardiner from *Being There* liked to say and he's not alone. In March 2011, the director-general of the BBC, Mark Thompson, delivered a speech to the *Financial Times* Digital Media and Broadcasting Conference in which he conceded that the corporation's 2005 predictions for public engagement were wildly optimistic.

The BBC, he said, had projected that within five years at least half of all television viewers would be actively using 'time-shifted recording technology' to tailor their viewing choices, and 'user-generated content', the BBC thought, would be well and truly on the way to becoming 'mainstream' activity. But the reality in 2011, Mr Thompson pointed out, was far less dramatic. 'When it comes to user-generated content,' he told his audience, 'the old one-nine-ninety rule seems to apply: one per cent make, nine per cent comment, ninety per cent are content to consume and observe.'

Which is not to say that things won't change over time, a point made by Thompson himself, but if there is a change going on, it's happening a lot more slowly than was once imagined. I'm mindful of the words of the noted American geneticist Francis Collins, who once remarked: 'We tend to overestimate the short-term impact of technology and underestimate the long-term impact.'

Of course, I'm not just talking about television viewing habits. There's scant evidence to suggest that new technologies are making us more engaged in civic activities, despite the rhetoric we often hear to that effect from media academics and journalists. I'm sorry, but joining a Facebook protest group is a pretty low-level form of political or civic engagement; it's not like joining a political party or manning a barricade with a Molotov cocktail in each hand. Most of us aren't activists and never will be. The promise of greater direct public engagement is, at the moment, just that, a promise.

In summary then, most of us are couch potatoes who do more watching, listening and reading than taking part. And most of us use social media and the internet for pretty mundane things really — we're not out to change the world. And that's not necessarily a bad thing. In that sense, things are probably no different from the way they were twenty years ago, or the way they were for our parents.

What is different, however, is that for those who do choose to engage and collaborate, the tools available for doing so are far more sophisticated than they once were.

Which leads me to the concept of 'crowdsourcing'.

Two's company, three's a crowdsourced collaboration

My natural response to a term like 'crowdsourcing' is to turn and run — it just sounds like jargon. It's one of those ugly words that tries too hard. But I've included it in this book because I keep coming across really interesting and worthy projects that use it as their basis. I'll highlight a couple of examples shortly, but first some history.

Like many modern things, at its heart, crowdsourcing is actually a very old idea rebadged for the second millennium. It basically involves using digital tools to harness the wisdom and expertise of the group — the mob, the collective, the rabble, whatever you want to call them — ordinary people, as well as experts. It's the notion that the more minds at work on an issue, the greater the chance of a creative solution.

Wikipedia, the free online encyclopaedia — which is itself a crowdsourced initiative — defines the term like this: 'Crowdsourcing is the act of outsourcing tasks, traditionally performed by an employee or contractor, to an undefined, large group of people or community (a "crowd"), through an open call.'

Wikipedia is probably the best-known example of online crowdsourcing. It's the one that often gets cited because it's such a good exemplar: it's built on the volunteer work of large numbers of people, who remotely contribute specific chunks of information to the encyclopaedia, and then check and verify each other's content. Now, it's a not-for-profit operation, but crowdsourcing is increasingly being put to use in the commercial sector as well. One of the earliest examples of commercial crowdsourcing success — and again a bit of an exemplar — was Threadless.

The developers of Threadless made a fortune by using the internet to encourage people (the crowd) to create T-shirt designs. And they're still a very popular business. If you go to their website you can see how deceptively simple their strategy is. They take the designs (from the crowd), allow people (the crowd) to vote online for the ones they think are the most appealing, and then they produce and sell (to the crowd, of course) the ones that have proved most popular. The whole enterprise works because the company gets its design work and market research done largely for free, the successful designers get paid for their efforts, and everybody else gets a benefit out of either being able to showcase and test their homemade designs, or by being part of the company's creative decision-making process.

Jeff Howe, a former contributing editor for *Wired* magazine, was one of the first to employ the term back in 2006. He wrote: 'Technological advances in everything from product design software to digital video cameras are breaking down the cost barriers that once separated amateurs from professionals. Hobbyists, part-timers, and dabblers suddenly have a market for their efforts, as smart companies in industries as disparate as pharmaceuticals and television discover ways to tap the latent talent of the crowd. The labour isn't always free, but it costs a lot less than paying traditional employees. It's not outsourcing; it's crowdsourcing.'[27]

So, what defines the crowdsourcing approach is the scale of participation it allows and the speed of interaction that takes place between participants. And that seems to be the appeal to someone like Frank Farrall, a partner with the consultancy firm Deloitte Australia. Explains Farrall: 'In a large, complex organisation like Deloitte we are stronger going to market and assisting our clients if we have integrated teams with a wide variety of skills. So these [crowdsourcing] tools allow you to identify and bring together project teams that are more effective in helping clients.'[28]

Search the words 'crowdsourcing' and 'business' and up the articles and web pages pop:

10 Kickass crowdsourcing sites for your business
Crowdsourcing for a Billion Dollar Business
Crowdsourcing Directory: The Revolutionary Power of
the Crowd

Professor Thomas Malone, an organisational theorist and the director of the Center for Collective Intelligence at the Massachusetts Institute of Technology, explains the growing enthusiasm for the concept as a reaction against the age-old academic notion that crowds are ineffective when it comes to decision making; the idea that they're given more to emotion than to reason.

'There was a famous book called *The Madness of Crowds* and there was a lot of discussion of things like "group-think",' he says. 'Many people thought that whenever you had a bunch of people together, they became a kind of mob, and they weren't very smart, they were more stupid as a group than as individuals. That was the received wisdom. Probably the biggest thing that changed that was a book by James Surowiecki called *The Wisdom of Crowds,* about four or five years ago, in which he said, "Well gee, that's not really true. There are plenty of situations where crowds really do make surprisingly intelligent choices or decisions. And they're often better than almost all, or even all, the individuals in them."'

In 2011, the Government of Iceland used crowdsourcing to help legislators rewrite the country's constitution, employing a variety of social media tools including Facebook, Twitter and YouTube to elicit community input and involvement.

'I believe this is the first time a constitution is being drafted basically on the internet,' Thorvaldur Gylfason, a member of Iceland's Constitutional Council, told *The Guardian* newspaper.[29] 'The public sees the constitution come into being before their eyes. This is very different from old times where constitution makers sometimes found it better to find themselves a remote spot out of sight, out of touch,' he said. 'There's been a lot of goodwill for what we are trying to do. Their comments have been quite helpful and they have had a positive effect on the outcome.'*

But the crowdsourcing approach isn't just about the collaborative use of people's personal time, it can also be about designing mechanisms and systems that allow for group participation in other ways. I'll give you two examples of what I mean.

David Karoly, a professor of Meteorology in the School of Earth Sciences at the University of Melbourne, is involved in a global project which he describes as a 'citizen computing initiative'. It's called Climateprediction.net.

'It's seeking to harness the time on people's computers all around the world; background time, if you like, to run complex climate model simulations when people aren't actually using their computers — at night-time or when they're not being otherwise used,' Karoly tells me. 'It involves us trying to better estimate the uncertainties in climate model simulations, both for the current period and also projections into the future.'

The idea is that the more people who take part, the more collective computer capacity the project can then draw upon. It's similar to the approach long used by the organisation SETI (the Search for ExtraTerrestrial Intelligence), where home

---

* Citizens in the Icelandic capital, Reykjavik, also broke new political ground by being the first voters in the world to elect a clown as their mayor. No, I don't mean a bozo, or a buffoon — lots of cities have done that (London, for one, seems incapable of electing anyone else). I mean a genuine clown — a former stand-up comedian named Jon Gnarr.

computer processing power is used to analyse space data from scores of radio telescope users around the world. Explains Professor Karoly: 'This is the only way that we can get enough computer time to run a wide range of different uncertain parameters within the climate models. Each individual person is running a simulation with a certain set of parameters, and they're running it for a twenty-year period. The results are sent back to the University of Oxford, who are coordinating the project, and those results and data are compiled from different parts of the globe, to try to better understand the uncertainties in climate systems and how good, or in fact how poor, climate models are in some aspects.'

So far the project has managed to run more than 100,000 different climate model simulations for the equivalent of more than 160 years each. And according to Professor Karoly, trying to run the same models on a standard supercomputer just wouldn't be practical or feasible, even for a university like Oxford.

Now, my second example involves an initiative called Spot.Us. It was set up because of a concern about the diminution of quality reporting in the United States. As you'd be aware, the financial decline of American newspapers over the past decade has resulted in a reduced focus on serious news, and in particular, the sort of investigative journalism essential for a healthy community and democracy. The creator of Spot.Us, David Cohn, set up the venture in 2008 with initial funding from several bodies, including the philanthropic Knight Foundation.

'Spot.Us is community-funded reporting, and the idea is that we distribute the cost of hiring an investigative journalist to do a local story,' Cohn says. 'So if you have fifty people, for example, in Oakland, who want to investigate the Oakland Police Department, and are all willing to give fifteen or twenty dollars each, that's enough to then hire a journalist who will spend a month or two doing just that on their behalf. So really it's a marketplace where citizens and journalists can come to meet and figure out what stories really need professional reporting.'

As it turns out, Spot.Us actually did fund an investigation into the conduct of the Oakland Police Department in California, using fifty individual US$1000 contributions to make it happen. And other crowd-funded investigations have involved racism in the health care industry in the US and even a survey of forests in Sweden. Cohn told me he'd put in place strict individual funding limits in order to try to prevent the website being used by people or organisations with personal vendettas, as well as a provision to ensure all news generated from investigations funded by Spot.Us is made publicly available. 'The content is commissioned by the public so it's owned by the public,' he says. 'So we will give the content away via a creative commons licence to any publisher to re-use.'

There are now other projects that use the crowdsourcing approach to raise money for all sorts of initiatives; the best known is a US-based online service called Kickstarter. So it is a model that has been proven to work. But — and here's the caution — only in certain circumstances and jurisdictions. The United States, it should be pointed out, has a long history of corporate and individual philanthropy — it's worth tens of billions of dollars each year, but that's not necessarily the case in other countries. I note that a similar crowd-funded journalism project in Australia has floundered since its launch several years ago, perhaps because Australian giving habits tend to be smaller and largely focused on charities and aid organisations.

So in general terms, it's easy to see the attraction of the crowdsourcing approach, for both businesses and not-for-profit outfits. But all good ideas can run off the rails, of course. Or be corrupted at times, particularly when they become flavour of the month. Certainly MIT's Thomas Malone has begun to worry about whether the embrace of crowdsourcing might be going too far, particularly in the corporate sector. In a white paper entitled 'Harnessing Crowds: Mapping the Genome of Collective Intelligence' he wrote: 'There is the misconception that you can sprinkle crowd wisdom on something and things will turn out for the best. That is not true, it's not magic.'

Over the phone from Boston, I ask him to elaborate on that quote. He replies: 'At the time when Web 2.0 and all kinds of internet-based applications were enabling new kinds of crowd-based phenomena, I think a lot of people kind of went too far in the other direction, in saying, "Wow, it's wonderful if we just let everyone participate on the web, like in Wikipedia, everything will turn out great." So the point of my quote was that it's not magic. There are some things that work really well when done by crowds, and some that don't.'

And even Wikipedia, it seems, has some significant problems with its collaborative structure. In mid 2011, delegates from thirty-four countries met in Berlin for a tenth anniversary conference on the future of the online encyclopaedia. Those attending were told that the service has become heavily skewed towards a male-centric view of the world (more than eighty-five per cent of all Wikipedia editors are men), and that the vast majority of contributors come from wealthy Anglophone countries, in particular the United States, with only around twenty per cent of all volunteer editors based in developing countries.

Wikipedia aside, there are also questions now being raised about the sometimes fine line between collaboration and exploitation. That is, when does a company's or organisation's embrace of the crowdsourcing approach simply become a means of acquiring cheap or unpaid labour, under the guise of civic engagement?

In April 2011, unpaid contributors to the very popular and influential news and opinion site *The Huffington Post* launched a US$105 million law suit against the organisation after its socialite founder, Arianna Huffington, unexpectedly announced that she had sold the operation to AOL for a cool US$315 million.

Then there's the service called Mechanical Turk. Run by Amazon, Mechanical Turk provides an online marketplace for labour activity. Essentially, people are employed to perform small scale jobs — 'human intelligence tasks' they're called in the jargon — such as fact checking a piece of text or writing a product description. Those tasks are posted on the internet and then given over to the crowd. In return for performing the task, a small payment is made to the successful worker.

Though little known in the broader community, Mechanical Turk has been an incredible success in the online world. But in a 2006 profile article for the online arts and culture magazine *Salon*, journalist Katharine Mieszowski questioned whether Amazon's invention was a 'boon for the bored or a virtual sweatshop'. She wrote: 'There is something a little disturbing about a billionaire like Bezos [Jeff Bezos, the founder and CEO of Amazon]* dreaming up new ways to get ordinary folk to do work for him for pennies. Is a cut-rate pittance the logical result of tapping into a global workforce of people with a computer, an internet connection and an Amazon account? And, really, who are all these people working for a measly one cent?'[30]

Well, the answer to that rhetorical question is that many Mechanical Turk workers are from developing countries like India. And they, and even their colleagues in the developed world, are often paid rates that are well below US minimum standards.

So the crowdsourcing approach isn't going to work in every situation. As Thomas Malone says, 'it's not magic'. And the examples I've given show that it's just as susceptible to being corrupted by the unscrupulous as any other form of process.

---

* For the record, in 2006, the year Mieszowski wrote her article, Amazon reported fourth quarter revenue from its online retailing business of US$2.4 billion and a profit of US$22 million. And those figures were just for one quarter.

But after all, you don't blame the apple when you bite into it and find it's been eaten by a worm.

Still there is one last perspective I'd like to share with you, and it involves a caution from the technology pioneer, Jaron Lanier, who somewhat mischievously points out that many of those who promote the crowdsourcing concept actually don't use it themselves. 'You will not see an Apple product design crowdsourced,' says Lanier. 'It just doesn't happen. You will not see Google's search algorithm crowdsourced. You will not see Facebook's business strategy crowdsourced, because when we in Silicon Valley really do the stuff we care about, we know better. There is a degree to which we hold ourselves to higher standards than our customers, and I just wish our customers could be a little bit more aware of that sometimes. You know, there's the derogative term "designed by committee", which refers to what happens when you have a crowd attempt to do creative synthesis. It doesn't work; you get this sort of dull average. That's not to say there's no use for such things, but we shouldn't confuse that with a real voice, a real perspective, a real creativity,' he says.

No room for ambiguity there!

So Lanier doesn't think much of the concept, and he makes a good point about the major technology developers. But after careful consideration my regard for the crowdsourcing concept is undiminished — subject to the caveats I've already given, of course. Although, I have to say, Lanier's critique did get me thinking about why I find the concept so appealing. And what that is, I think, is the openness it tends to promote.

Everything these days is about transparency. From banks to governments to insurance companies; they all claim to be trying to make their operations more transparent. It's become one of those buzzwords that reek of spin — you claim to be 'transparent' in the same way that you also claim to be 'listening' to your customer base or to voters. But when you look around, there's very little genuine transparency to be found. Think of the last statement of fees you got from your bank, or the last time you heard a politician speak.

My favourite story about transparency involves the little-known declaration of 'Open Government' posted online in 2010. It read: 'The Australian Government now declares that, in order to promote greater participation in Australia's democracy, it is committed to open government based on a culture of engagement, built on better access to and use of government held information, and sustained by the innovative use of technology. Citizen collaboration in policy and service delivery design will enhance the processes of government and improve the outcomes sought.'

And it ended with this call to action: 'The possibilities for Open Government depend on the innovative use of new internet-based technologies. Agencies are to develop policies that support employee-initiated, innovative Government 2.0-based proposals.'[31]

All sounds good except for the fact that it was posted without fanfare onto just one government website, the one belonging to the Finance Department. There was no grand launch, no champagne and canapes, not even a press conference. And as far as I know, no government minister or senior official has ever publicly mentioned it since.

I don't want to get political, but I would also point out that the said declaration was drawn up under the prime ministership of Kevin Rudd, a leader who was deposed by his own ministry and caucus in large part because they claimed he was too autocratic, non-collaborative and far from transparent about the way he ran the government. And as if that wasn't enough, the declaration was posted on the very day before the 2010 election was called. A campaign, it has to be said, that was hardly noted for either its honesty or transparency.

So, that's a long-winded way of saying that genuine openness is to be applauded and encouraged, but it's hard to find.

One field where a new spirit of openness and collaboration is being put to good use is in the area of innovation. It's at the heart of what's being called the open science movement, a global attempt to use the internet and social media to break down the communication and research barriers that have built up within the scientific community over the past hundred years or so.

Open science

Australian author and science broadcaster Julian Cribb is a vocal enthusiast for the movement and he maintains that scientists were, on the whole, extremely cooperative and collaborative right up until the First World War. But he argues the imposition of military censorship, and the demand for new forms of weapons technology, made secrecy a default component of scientific activity. Then, after the Great War, the rise in popularity of commercial patents essentially ensured that the international scientific community became a patchwork of information and research silos.

Like the DIY/tinkering movement and the Slow movement, open science is an attitude as much as it is a practice. It too is a pushback against the commercial/industrial interests that increasingly dominate our world, and have every intention of dominating our future.

'The public has paid for this knowledge,' says Cribb, making a persuasive argument with regard to the huge amount of research conducted each year at state-funded universities and research institutes. 'They have paid for the university funding, they've paid for the salaries, they've paid for the equipment that did all this science, and they deserve to know what is going on and how it's going to affect their lives. So the opportunity is there with the new technologies to share it.'

Dan Gezelter shares Cribb's conviction. Gezelter, an Associate Professor of Chemistry at the University of Notre Dame in the United States, runs the Open Science Project devoted to opening up scientific procedures by giving away the information that's needed to fully understand them — lab protocols and source codes for simulations, that kind of thing. Says Gezelter: 'There's a wonderful site called Openwetware.org where various experimental groups can upload information about their protocols, and keep wikis on what they do. There is a huge number of people using open data sites. There are hundreds of astronomers contributing to the Worldwide Telescope, which has a really interesting tie-in with Flickr. And so there are lots of scientists looking for some way to share information about their experiments, their simulations,' he says. 'It's not a small number, it's actually quite a large number.'

And among them is Ashley Buckle from Monash University in Melbourne. Buckle's contribution to open science comes in the form of the MyTardis project, which sadly has nothing to do with Dr Who's famous time-travelling device, but has everything to do with a new data storage and management system. MyTardis basically involves a website that acts as a 'central repository' for scientists. It's all open source and the program is designed, according to Buckle, to make it easier for scientists in various parts of the world to reproduce experiments from other scientists, and to combine data from multiple experiments.

'Early on we realised that in any type of scientific experiment, there's only one way of really validating the experiment and that's to reproduce it. And in order to do that you need the raw data,' he explains. 'Up until we started the MyTardis project, for the type of experiments we're doing in protein crystallography, that raw data was never available. In the last couple of years some very high-profile studies on medically important proteins have emerged where there's possible inaccuracies, or over-interpretations, in that data. Now had the raw data been available, we could have gone back and validated it.'

Being totally honest, Dr Buckle completely lost me on the technical side of things the moment I heard the words 'protein crystallography'. However, I mention him because the MyTardis project is not only a good example of collaboration between scientists and their peers, but also between scientists and IT experts, with computer boffins actually working inside his research lab, helping to make sure the systems in place for sharing are up to date and effective.

But not every researcher is like Ashley Buckle. Toronto-based physicist Michael Nielsen reckons one of the problems, as he sees it, is that most established scientists, those at the peak of their discipline, continue to have a jaundiced and suspicious view of information technology. And because of that, he says, they've repeatedly missed opportunities for advancing the practice of science.

'If you actually look at what tools they've adopted, things like email, things like Skype, they're very conservative. They allow them to keep control of the conversation, and allow them to keep control of the collaboration. The tools that they use tend to be oriented towards very conventional ends,' Nielsen says. But he boldly predicts that the way in which science is conducted will change more over the next thirty years, 'than in the past 300'. A prediction he bases on generational change, which, to my mind, isn't entirely convincing. Having a closed mind can be a feature of youth, as well as old age.

Now I wouldn't want to fall into the same trap as those I've critiqued elsewhere in this book, those who get carried away with the promise of technology and the future, those who fail to properly calibrate for reality. The pressures on many scientists to tie their skills to commercial interests are only increasing, not diminishing. And we also shouldn't forget that despite all the sandstone and trenchers, most universities these days are also businesses as well as learning institutions, imbued with the same rivalries and profit imperatives as any corporation.

But that said, there is cause to be optimistic and Michael Nielsen leaves me with an anecdote of the sort of collaboration and openness that is possible. It involves a Cambridge-based mathematician named Timothy Gowers, and a little bit of crowdsourcing.

'What he did was he used his blog to post a problem he said he'd love to solve and that he had a few ideas about. But that's all he had, he just had a few ideas. Then he invited anybody who wanted to come along and contribute their thoughts on the problem,' Nielsen says. 'It took a little while, but once they got going there was this unstoppable momentum. Twenty-seven mathematicians ended up involved, collaborating online to solve what was a very difficult mathematical problem, and this success has spawned a whole range of similar projects, mostly being conducted at this point by mathematicians. But in each case, what they're doing is they're using blogs and wikis and other types of social media to try to attack these open problems.'

And a final thought, lest there be no misunderstanding. No one I've mentioned is arguing that all science should be free in the future, that there's something wrong with research companies making a profit out of their scientific labour, but as science writer Julian Cribb points out, in the current commercial climate things have sometimes got a little out of hand. Says Cribb: 'I think it's gone too far when you start patenting genes. Imagine if when we were discovering all the elements in the periodic table, you'd been able to patent gold, or you'd been able to patent iron. I mean that's ridiculous.'

Ridiculous indeed, but I'm sure all the patent lawyers out there would prefer to see them as 'missed opportunities'.

CHAPTER 6

OVERSTATE, OVERSELL

The internet is far too valuable to become an agent of
Washington's digital diplomats

Evgeny Morozov, author and Stanford University academic

A little protest in Johannesburg

I can tell you the exact moment when I realised just how
fantastically useful modern communication technology can
be. It was Tuesday, 27th March 2007, and I had just finished a
studio interview. I was gathering material for a radio program
about the ways in which exiled Zimbabweans use a mixture of
old and new technologies to feed outside information into the
heart of the Mugabe dictatorship; and to get inside information
about the regime and its abuses back out at the same time. The
person I'd been speaking to was Gerry Jackson, the director
of SW Radio Africa, based in London, and she had mentioned
towards the end of the interview a small but not insignificant
protest held outside the Zimbabwean diplomatic mission in
Johannesburg just a few days before. Returning to my desk,
I did a quick online search, just out of curiosity really, and
suddenly there it was — five or so minutes of the actual protest,
wobbly vision recorded using someone's mobile phone and
posted on a video-sharing site.

That I could so quickly and easily locate the vision and
audio from a small obscure political protest, staged in another
country, on a faraway continent, gave me genuine pause for

thought. It's a bit embarrassing to mention that when I began as a journalist in the mid 1980s, we were still using carbon paper and bashing away on old Remington typewriters. Sending stories from one place to another either meant dictating your item down the landline phone to a typist, or sending it via telex. There weren't even mobile phones at that point, let alone sites like YouTube. And although I had been part of the move from analogue to digital, from typewriters to the internet, it was really only at that moment in 2007, at my desk looking at the video of that protest in South Africa that the incredible reality of modern communications technology fully dawned on me.

The noted BBC journalist and broadcaster Nik Gowing, who lectures around the world on the changing information landscape, speaks of 'the new transparency' brought about by modern digital media. 'A new fragility and vulnerability of the political class,' he says. But while digital media's ability to catch out lying politicians and philandering public figures has been well documented, what's less clear is just how significant its impact will be on the future practice of politics and diplomacy — and specifically on the civic empowerment of individuals.

In a public lecture in Sydney in mid 2011 entitled 'The Internet: Prophesy and Reality', Professor James Curran, the director of the Goldsmiths Leverhulme Media Research Centre at the University of London, was deflating in his assessment of the web's role as an agent of positive international change.

'The idea that cyberspace is a free open space where people from different backgrounds and nations commune with each other and build a more deliberative tolerant and empowered world overlooks a number of things,' he told his audience. 'The world is unequal, uncomprehending in a literal sense, it is torn asunder by conflicting values and interests. It is subdivided by deeply embedded national and local cultures and some countries are ruled by authoritarian regimes. These different aspects of the real world penetrate cyberspace producing a ruined Tower of Babel with multiple languages, hate websites, nationalist discourse, censored speech and over-representation of the advantaged.'

A bleak portrait to be sure, but a weighty counterbalance nonetheless to the almost utopian picture of the internet so often portrayed in the popular press, and in technology and activist circles.

It's now become popular to ascribe transformative political power to the web and social media, to speak of their ability to radically change our future by enabling the empowerment of individuals and by forcing political structures to be more accountable. But how technology is actually shaping our political future is a lot more complicated than is sometimes portrayed.

The 'word-of-mouth revolution' just doesn't have the same ring to it

In January 2011, the henchmen of embattled Egyptian dictator, Hosni Mubarak, did a pretty simple and logical thing. Simple and logical, that is, if you're a bunch of rich, well-resourced, tyrannical thugs. Faced with a popular uprising of regime-threatening proportions, a grassroots, yet well–coordinated, threat to the status quo, the authorities in Cairo began cutting off people's access to social media. They turned off texting services first, then the internet, and then they closed down the mobile phone networks.

'For those of us who remember a time when there were only landlines, it wasn't so bad,' I heard one Egyptian-based journalist comment. 'But for those who have grown up with mobile phones and the internet, it was very difficult.'

The switch-off was effective in the sense that it frustrated the regime's opponents for a brief period of time, and gave Mubarak's supporters some respite, but the angry and determined protesters always had other ways to communicate and to organise, because social media wasn't the only thing that connected them. In fact, people in Cairo and the rest of the country had been using a variety of other means since the very beginning of the rebellion: television, leaflets, telephone and face-to-face contact.

Perhaps what was most remarkable about the switch-off wasn't the reaction from within Egypt, but the level of genuine surprise it generated in the West among those who had come to believe that the revolution was built on the back of social media. Online, there was a sense of indignation. It was almost as if Mubarak wasn't playing fair, that he wasn't playing by the rules: didn't he know that digital media can't be gotten around? Didn't he understand that you can't simply turn things off — that the internet is an unstoppable tool of grassroots democracy?

One New York-based blogger I came across immediately after the switch-off was crestfallen at the knowledge that the bad guys also knew a thing or two about communications technology: 'When something you have come to rely on is taken away from you, it is frightening,' Fred Wilson blogged. And remember, he wasn't in Cairo, he was in the relative security of NYC (muggings, car-jackings and indiscriminate shootings, notwithstanding). He went on to write: 'This week, when I read that Egypt's government was able to completely turn off the internet in the country, it stunned me. The internet was designed to be immune to such things.'

Well, no, it wasn't actually. And in fact, 'designed' is far too strong a word for the creation of the internet. 'Evolved', would probably be the politest way to put it. Presuming, of course, that you're hoping to avoid using expressions like 'cobbled together' or 'grew like black mould' or 'just kind of happened while I was out buying coffee'. But I digress. Our New York blogger went on to say: 'This past week has shown that the cyberutopian view is naive, and that those who are not interested in a better, safer, more open and free world will use technology to further their interests too.'[32]

Why anyone should assume that non-democratic governments are clueless when it comes to matters technological is baffling from an historical perspective. Lest we forget, one of the great developers, users and mis-users of technology in the last century was the KGB: think satellites, nuclear weapons and poison-tipped umbrellas. And today in China, the People's Republic is incredibly skilled not only at controlling communications technology, but also at using it against the very *people* who make up the republic — blocking access to the global internet when it suits them, and corrupting sites they don't like, etc. The Chinese, of course, don't do things by halves — think Great Wall, Great Leap Forward and great big humungous dam over the Yangtze — so the Communist authorities have been busy over the past decade building their own complementary internet of sorts, a place they can better control, filled with heavily monitored websites like Sohu and Sina and government-approved search engines like Baidu, which is currently the number one search platform in China with an estimated market share of over seventy per cent.

And, not to be outdone, the Iranian Government has now also floated the idea of creating an internet of its own, by employing the same tactics Beijing uses of blocking the sites it dislikes and promoting only platforms that suit its political ends. How it intends to do that given it doesn't quite have China's resources is unclear, but they certainly sound determined. Ali Aghamohammadi, a senior figure in Mahmoud Ahmadinejad's administration, was quoted by Iranian state-run media in mid 2011 as saying: 'Iran will soon create an internet that conforms to Islamic principles, to improve its communication and trade links with the world. We can describe it as a genuinely halal network aimed at Muslims on an ethical and moral level.'[33]

So, technology is simply a means to an end, not an end in itself — digital media isn't *inherently* democratic, it's simply a tool of communication. Still, the perception persists that social media is some kind of magical force driving ordinary people to extraordinary levels of connectedness and high-level social activity; that it has special transformative powers.

Appearing on CNN, Middle East-based activist Wael Ghonim was unequivocal in his praise of social media. 'This revolution started online, this revolution started on Facebook,' he told presenter Wolf Blitzer during the height of the so-called Arab Spring. 'This revolution started in June 2010 when hundreds of thousands of Egyptians started collaborating content, you know, like we would post a video on Facebook, it would be shared with 50,000 people on their wall within a few hours. I always said that if you want to liberate a society, just give them the internet; if you want to have a free society, just give them the internet.' Which sounds reasonably persuasive, until you realise that Ghonim had something of a vested interest in promoting the supremacy of online activism, given that he'd also worked as the head of marketing for Google in the Middle East and North Africa.

'Twitter revolution: how silent majority found its voice,' the headline read. These days, any instance of international unrest is immediately declared some form of social media revolution. Before Egypt, there was one in Moldova; one that didn't quite work out (but we don't talk about it anymore) in Iran in 2009; another that also wasn't so successful in Zimbabwe; and one in September 2007 that went absolutely nowhere in Burma. Oh, and let's not forget Tunisia. You could go on and on. And some people do. When I typed the words 'Twitter revolution' into the search engine on my PC over 101,000,000 results came up, and I'm sure there are even more there by now. Before Twitter, the buzz was all about camera phones and YouTube and their combined ability to reshape the global political world, and before that, it was the transformative political power of texting.

After the Tunisian uprising, which occurred only a matter of days before events turned angry in Egypt, Ethan Zuckerman from the Centre for Civic Media wrote: 'Pundits will likely start celebrating a "Twitter revolution" in Tunisia, even if they missed watching it unfold ... But any attempt to credit a massive political shift to a single factor — technological, economic, or otherwise — is simply untrue. Tunisians took to the streets due to decades of frustration, not in reaction to a Wikileaks cable, a denial-of-service attack, or a Facebook update.'[34]

In *The European* magazine, Vienna-based author and journalist Eberhard Lauth went further: 'It is good to have Twitter, even if you are not trying to stage a revolution, but the platform remains the stomping ground for a rather smug information elite that tend to overestimate their actions.' And referencing the Tunisian uprising directly, he then added: 'The regime could only be overthrown when people were willing to risk, or give, their lives for the cause of change. To describe a courageous coup as a Twitter-and-Facebook revolution is akin to a whitewashing of history.'[35]

Whitewashing, that is, in the sense that it downplays the role played by ordinary people — by human beings, not devices, including the journalists at Al Jazeera. For more than a decade, the Arab-language television service has been providing viewers in the Middle East with the images and information that the dictators of the region have long fought to suppress. As Stanford University's Evgeny Morozov said in an interview ahead of the release of his 2011 book, *The Net Delusion: The Dark Side of Internet Freedom*: 'The internet certainly helped spread information up to a point, but many of those protests were still organised either the old way through leaflets and through word of mouth, or the internet was used at the very final stage of maybe raising awareness of those protests.'

And others, including UCLA academic Ramesh Srinivasan, have since pointed out that there were actually very few social media users in Egypt at the time of the fall of Mubarak. Srinivasan also estimates that only around fifteen per cent of Egyptians had access to the internet during that period.

So, social media had its place, but not exactly the role it has now been given by the popular press. It's also instructive,

I think, to note how quickly people stopped talking about the revolutionary power of social media in Libya, once it all became too hard; once Colonel Gaddafi and his cohort dug their bloody heels in and it quickly became apparent that tweets alone weren't going to dislodge either him or his regime.

What would Comrade Beria think?

But does it really matter if we sometimes get a little carried away? While, as Eberhard Lauth pointed out, the fashion for ascribing such transformational power to social media does tend to underplay the human dimension of political struggle, there's also a far greater issue at stake concerning people's personal safety. Evgeny Morozov argues that encouraging people in politically sensitive situations to share information on platforms like Twitter, YouTube or Flickr can increase the risk of their detection and persecution. He notes that during the 2009 civil protests in Iran, for example, the secret police actually made use of Twitter to anticipate and very effectively prepare for the outbreak of protest activity.

It makes sense when you think about it. The very networks that social media create are also its weakness: to nefarious administrations they offer an unprecedented opportunity to track and monitor the thoughts and actions of their enemies. Imagine what someone like Lavrenti Beria would have made of Facebook. For Stalin's brutal and effective enforcer the social networking platform would have seemed like a wet dream: all those activists posting details about themselves and linking to their friends. You can almost hear him saying, 'Why spend hours torturing people to get information when it's all there online!' before deciding to torture a few hundred political prisoners anyway, just for the sport of it.

Says Peter Eckersley from the rights advocacy group Electronic Frontier Foundation: 'It's interesting that Facebook has become the focus of so much of this story about social media and uprisings in the Middle East, because Facebook is a platform, a whole technological infrastructure that was designed to explicitly encourage promiscuous sharing of personal information about people. You know, "put your life out there and publish things about your life" is the design philosophy behind that entire website. Clearly that's very cool, people like it. It's not clear that that's the design you want, and the design philosophy you want, if you're trying to organise an uprising against a violent government.'

And he adds: 'It can in fact be very dangerous to be sharing too much information with an authoritarian regime that will use that information against you. And in some ways it's alarming that Facebook has become the home of so many of these protests. It may be great if the protesters win and win quickly, but if you see a situation degenerate into prolonged violence it could turn out to be terrible for the people who were organising the protests to have been using Facebook for that purpose. Because at some point, people from the regime will find a way to get all their social graph information and all the things they've said, back out of that website. This is just one of the paradoxes of technology in this moment.'[36]

And sometimes those regimes will track you down and punish you even when you're not plotting to overthrow the government. In fact, sometimes it happens when you're on the same side.

In 2010, a young social media user named Cheng Jianping was given a one-year-all-expenses-paid holiday at the Shibali River Women's Labour Camp in Henan province, courtesy of China's police state. She was sent there in November of that year after tweeting a rather innocuous comment that included the words: 'Charge, angry youth'. The target of her exhortation was the Japanese Pavilion at the Shanghai Expo, and when she sent her tweet, China was being swept by a wave of anti-Japanese feeling. In fact, as it turned out, it was essentially a re-tweet and so Cheng was just echoing the words of someone else.

They would never publicly admit to this, but Chinese authorities often allow people to use the internet and social media to make threats and comments against foreign companies and governments. But only, it has to be said, when it suits them. And on this particular occasion it didn't suit them at all, probably because they'd suddenly decided it was time to mend fences with the government in Tokyo.

What a pity nobody told Cheng.

So Cheng Jianping was rounded up and gaoled. It's not exactly clear what the actual charge was; but her real crime was obvious: bad timing!

There are technologies that can be used to help mask an activist's online activity, the digital equivalent of invisible ink. The most well known of the lot is the strangely named TOR, which initially stood for The Onion Router. The weird name comes from the fact that the program allows users to encrypt their messages in a multi-layered manner — like the layers of an onion, is the idea. I can't really give you a more detailed account of how it works, because, quite frankly, I haven't got a clue. Suffice to say that it does, apparently. But the truly disturbing thing is that few people who engage in potentially dangerous political activity actually use TOR or any other type of masking tool. Even, it seems, in countries with really oppressive regimes. According to a 2010 study by the Berkman Center for Internet and Society, less than three per cent of internet users in authoritarian countries make use of circumvention technology to try to bypass censorship.

And even the US Government — 'Land of the Free and Home of the Brave' — is ambivalent about encouraging the use of such tools. They do so up to a point, but they do so cautiously. And the reason is entirely logical: it's because they realise that such applications can also be used to circumvent *their* authority. What's good for the goose isn't good for the gander, if the gander happens to be wearing red, white and blue. But, of course, nothing's ever guaranteed in life and, as it turns out, even using a system like TOR doesn't necessarily ensure your safety.

The executive director of TOR is a man named Andrew Lewman. He describes his organisation as a non-profit body 'dedicated to the research and development of tools and technologies for online privacy and anonymity'. But what I discovered when I made contact with him was that his company isn't only happy to offer its services to those trying to avoid government control, sometimes TOR is also content to work with governments as well: 'We do work with law enforcement to help them understand what TOR is, and is not, what our software should look like on a computer and what you should find and not find, depending on the particular investigation,' Lewman tells me. 'Their law enforcement people are very concerned about what information they give out when they go to do online stings, and in many cases the criminals are more sophisticated than the law enforcement is.'

Now by 'criminals' Lewman means drug-traffickers, paedophiles, mafia types and terrorists, not political protesters. But then again, what's a terrorist? There are many US politicians who maintain that Wikileaks is a terrorist organisation. And, don't forget, some of the more hawkish ones even called for its founder Julian Assange to be executed for treason against the United States — despite the fact that he's never been an American citizen.*

Just as disturbing, for those worried about the integrity of the internet, is the fact that the United States has also shown a tendency in recent times to pressure online businesses into doing its bidding. In 2010, pressure from the Obama administration saw Visa, MasterCard, PayPal and Amazon suddenly sever all commercial contact with, and support to, the Wikileaks organisation.

---

* In my view they just made the wrong call — a charge against him for being annoyingly smug and narcissistic, now there's an indictment we could all get behind.

Alright, I hear you say, so even the United States can get a little heavy-handed when it suits them, but at least the American Government isn't interested in doing a Mubarak and closing down the internet when things get a little uncomfortable.

Well, think again.

Enter former vice-presidential candidate Joe Lieberman; the man who would have been second-in-charge of the free world, and a heartbeat away from the Oval Office, as they say, if it wasn't for all those famous 'hanging chads' back in Florida during the election of 2000. In 2010 Senator Lieberman was the co-author of Bill S.3480 — also known as the 'Protecting Cyberspace as a National Asset Act (PCNAA)' bill. In the United States, it is more commonly known as the 'Internet Kill-switch' Bill.

To the best of my knowledge, Bill S.3480 is still winding its way through Congress — or stuck somewhere in some Committee Chairman's in-tray or something — but if it ever were to be passed, it would effectively give the American president the power, in certain circumstances, to shut down the internet right across the United States. Exactly what Hosni Mubarak tried to do and for which the United States roundly condemned him. Senator Lieberman's reasoning, when introducing the proposed legislation, was decidedly Cold War in its logic. 'Right now in China, the government can disconnect parts of its internet in a case of war,' he said. 'We need to have that here too.'

And just for good measure his Bill also contains a provision that would eliminate the possibility of judicial review should the president ever be tempted, or feel compelled in some way, to shut down the Ferris wheel.

It's a truly scary thought, because closing down the web in the US, or big bits of it, wouldn't just be a point of curiosity or academic concern, as the Egyptian shutdown was for the Western world, turning off the web in America would literally mean shutting down a major chunk of the rest of the world's online activity as well, because so many of the big internet players — Google, Facebook, eBay and the rest — all operate out of North America.

Oh, to live in such dangerous and interconnected times.

21st Century Statecraft

Lyndon Johnson once said of Gerald Ford that he couldn't 'fart and chew gum at the same time.'* And that pretty much sums up the way in which most democratic governments deal with the internet. They don't know whether they're Arthur or Martha when it comes to online policy and regulation: they like to play up the free-speech angle, but then they also take measures to rein it in when it suits them. The Open Net Initiative — the result of a partnership between four leading universities, Oxford, Cambridge, Harvard and Toronto — posted the results of its first 'global internet filtering study' in 2007 in which they surveyed content across 120 internet service providers in forty-one countries. The study found evidence that twenty-five of those forty-one either blocked or filtered internet content as part of a system of 'state mandated net filtering'. And among a roll call of the usual baddies were a couple of democratic surprises, including India and South Korea.

Now, democratic governments also get themselves into a muddle of confusion about the dealings they could and should have with the big technology companies, and even how and when to use the internet and social media themselves. Maybe confusion isn't the correct word. It's probably more accurate to say that they become inconsistent. Exploring some of those inconsistencies is what I want to do next.

When Hillary Clinton first took command of the State Department, she pretty quickly began talking about the internet

---

* Journalists at the time replaced the word 'fart' with 'walk'. And if you know your history, you'll also know that Johnson had more than just a potty mouth, he also used to conduct briefings with senior officials while on the toilet in the Oval Office. Puts a whole new perspective on the presidency, doesn't it?

in an interesting way. The Bush administration had largely ignored the web, but the new Democrat team made much show of embracing it. And Clinton caught many by surprise when she immediately appointed her own senior technology adviser.

'When this adviser came in, who was a veteran of the Obama campaign, he instituted a program that he began calling "21st Century Statecraft",' says Nancy Scola, the associate editor of the blog *TechPresident*, which focuses on politics and technology. And, says Scola, Hillary Clinton picked up on the term and began running with it right away. 'Within a few days of it being floated by the State Department, she was out using the term in commencement speeches she was giving across the country.'

Thankfully for those not keen on the language of modern politics, Clinton's usage of the phrase soon scaled back, but not the intent behind the proposition. So what exactly did Hillary Clinton mean by the term? Well it was always kind of woolly, but in one of her early speeches she declared: 'We understand that 21st Century Statecraft cannot just be government to government, it must be government to people, and people to people. So we want to engage civil society, women, youth, political activists and others as we pursue our agenda.'

So 21st Century Statecraft is technology, meets diplomacy, meets US political power. Scola interprets the policy as having two parts: 'The first one is what we talk about a lot, this use of Twitter or Facebook to go into countries and give people a voice. Those who previously didn't have a voice. So the State Department will go into Mexico, for example, or into South Africa, and try to connect people to some of these social tools, and create conversations around what the United States is doing out in the world.

'The second thing that didn't get a lot of attention, that's not as headline friendly as all the Twitter and Facebook stuff,' Scola adds, 'is that the State Department is really trying to use the development money that they already have on hand to give people tools so that they can figure out ways to empower themselves. The idea of 21st Century Statecraft, really most simply stated, is that by giving people a chance to participate in conversations with one another, they're going to see more options than they ever saw before. They're going to see more potential in the world, and the thinking is that what has pushed so many people into militant organisations, terrorist organisations, organisations that have traditionally opposed the United States, is a sense that they don't really have many other options in the world.'

On the surface of it, such aims may sound laudable, but as Hillary Clinton made clear, the policy is only about promoting empowerment that fits within what Clinton calls 'our agenda'. And creating conversations 'around what the United States is doing in the world' sounds dangerously like propaganda to my ears. Nancy Scola tells me that the State Department's online activities are still to be tested in the courts, where she says they might yet run into trouble.

'The United States has in place a particular law called the *Smith–Mundt Act*. It was put into place to restrict the United States' ability, through the State Department, to spread propaganda, particularly in the United States,' Scola says. 'So the State Department was considered to have sort of suspect political loyalty when the United States Congress funded the State Department to do outreach all around the world. They said, "Hey, listen, this has to stop at the United States border. You can't be spreading domestic propaganda." Now that law becomes questionable, if not obsolete, in an age where everything can be posted on the internet and read from anywhere around the world.'

Carne Ross, the former British Foreign Office official and founder of the non-government organisation Independent Diplomat, is one of those who views the new US approach with suspicion. 'I hate to sound overly sceptical,' he says, 'but I don't think it represents any real change at all, and I've heard a lot from Washington about Government 2.0 and all the rest of it.

It's just using a different means, the internet, to communicate the same message. The way that policy is formulated is still very much in the way that it was in the twentieth century, which is small groups of officials decide what is best for the US in Burma, in Afghanistan, or China, or wherever. It is not a broadly participative exercise. That has not changed in any way.'

Ross is an interesting figure. Having served the UK as a diplomat, he grew disillusioned with the British position on the invasion of Iraq and left the Foreign Office in 2004 after contradicting his own government's official position on the existence of 'weapons of mass destruction' in Iraq while giving evidence to an inquiry. His organisation is an independent consultancy that employs a team of experienced former diplomats and helps democratic organisations and governments in the developing world to better organise their diplomatic skills and representation. Diplomats for hire, so to speak, but only, Carne Ross is quick to say, clients who are 'committed to democracy, human rights, the rule of law'.

Like Evgeny Morozov, Ross believes it's important to always view the internet as a multi-headed beast: 'I think we've got to develop a different model of politics, and not look at technology as itself a new model,' he tells me. 'One has to look at the phenomenon of internet democracy and what the internet does for politics in a very, very critical way. It is not, per se, a good thing, it is a neutral technology that can be used for ill as well as for good.'

The sovereigns of our digital lives

When you think about it, it's a strange and unexpected thing that the internet has developed with so little official government regulation; in the West, I mean, and the rest of the democratic world. When other forms of communication came along they were pretty quickly regulated: the postal service, newspapers, radio, TV; all of them. There are still ownership restrictions in many countries relating to media concentration involving TV and print, for example, and viewing classifications for television, but there's none of that with the net. Perhaps that's chiefly the result of speed — the meteoric rise of the web from being a geek's toy to a vital piece of infrastructure. Regardless of the reason, the end result is that the owners of the big social media and technology companies have quickly become among the richest and freest corporate identities in the world; indeed, in the history of the world. And for the most part, they're beholden to no one.

Now whether online corporations should be subjected to the same sorts of regulations as newspapers and television stations is one issue, and a contentious one at that, but one area where you'd hope there'd be consensus is over the dealings such companies have with authoritarian governments and brutal dictatorships. In the very recent past, Google, Yahoo, Microsoft and the UK's Vodafone have all faced public criticism for compromising in their dealings with oppressive regimes in the Middle East and Asia in order to secure particular business interests. But public criticism is all they've faced. There was no American Government sanction for Facebook when it was actively helping Beijing with its censorship; likewise, Vodafone received no penalty from UK authorities for working with Mubarak's thugs during the uprising in Egypt. Self-regulation rules.

The Global Network Initiative (GNI) is an organisation whose primary role is to give advice to communications companies on how to operate in non-democratic countries without selling their soul. It sees itself as a sort of corporate moral compass, if you like. GNI's membership is made up of companies, academic institutions and various civil society organisations, including human rights groups. Rebecca MacKinnon, one of the organisation's co-founders, says the most significant problem she faces with the big players is getting them to realise there's actually a problem with their behaviour in the first place.

'Because many of these companies are being feted in the media as being a force for democracy, and because they're growing like gangbusters, I think perhaps they're getting a bit arrogant and developing a bit of a God complex,' she says. 'They're somewhat in denial about the fact that there are actually real risks involved and that accountability is part of obtaining and maintaining their customers' and users' trust over the long run. You know, they are sovereigns of our digital lives in many ways. I think it's reasonable to expect that companies accept a certain amount of accountability in the way they govern our digital lives.'[37]

Very hard to argue with, of course, and nice in theory, but is a continuing reliance on self-regulation ever likely to be genuinely effective? Joseph Menn is largely supportive of what the Global Network Initiative seeks to do, but he says he sees many potholes on the highway ahead. Menn reports on business for the *Financial Times* and he has a particular focus on new technology. He's also the author of a book on internet crime called *Fatal System Error.*

Says Menn: 'The Global Network Initiative is an interesting example of how companies are grappling, I think publicly and responsibly, with their new duties — duties which they did not expect. In the old, easier days, you just complied with whatever the local laws were and you were fine. But if those laws are quite vague and put the onus on the company to do self-censorship and to turn over information on protesters and that sort of thing, it gets very hard to sort through.'

And he makes the not insubstantial point that for all its efforts so far, GNI still only has three of the major tech companies onboard: Microsoft, Yahoo and Google. 'There's this glaring absence of the Facebooks and the Twitters and the second and third wave of these Web 2.0 companies,' he says. 'So that initiative still has a long way to go. It's very complicated and there are lives at stake.'

University of California law professor Anupam Chander is one of those who takes a much tougher line. He believes that it's now time for more stick than carrot. 'The first thing you'd say is they cannot act as a surveillance arm of these repressive governments. So you cannot be using Facebook, for example, as a way to disclose who all the friends are of the dissidents in a particular case. So everyone who follows a particular dissident tweeter should not then be turned over to the government by Twitter, or a similar company, because the government simply requests that information,' he says.

And Chander also argues for the introduction of binding obligations on technology and communications companies, citing the successful example of anti-corruption legislation introduced in the United States in the 1970s, which made it illegal for American businesses to pay bribes when they operate overseas. 'The companies protested,' says Chander. 'They said, "This will harm our competitiveness in the long run because other companies from Europe or Asia might step in and take our business." But what we did was we sought to work with our partners across the world, the OECD countries, the Latin American countries, and we convinced them that an anti-corruption rule was best for their corporations as well. And so we began with a home-grown rule saying no corrupt payments around the world, and we have internationalised that obligation through treaties.'[38]

Just how willing or confident democratic governments, including the United States, are likely to be in pushing the big online players to act with greater global responsibility in the future is yet to be seen. India, Brazil and South Africa have each called for a new global body to control the internet, but it's a call that hasn't gained traction. In the United States, as mentioned earlier, the FTC has put some pressure on Facebook to be more accountable with its privacy policies, while in Europe there are privacy provisions for the internet that are much stronger than in the US or Australia, but not so strong as to make any great difference to the way companies like Google or Facebook operate.

And finally, there have been flashes of impatience from some world leaders. At a special G8 gathering of communication technology heads and world leaders in May 2011, French President Nicolas Sarkozy warned those present: 'The world you represent is not a parallel universe where legal and moral rules, and more generally, all the basic principles that govern society in democratic countries, do not apply. You can't be exempt from minimum rules.'[39]

But it's worth pointing out that at the same two-day summit, the 'sovereigns of our digital age', as Rebecca MacKinnon likes to call them, showed just how resistant to change they're likely to be. Said Facebook's founder Mark Zuckerberg: 'People tell me on the one hand, "It's great you played such a big role in the Arab Spring, but it's also kind of scary because you enable all this sharing and collect information on people." But it's hard to have one without the other. You can't isolate some things you like about the internet and control other things that you don't.'[40]

Well, you can't, I guess, if you don't try. But that's not to say the big technology companies are going to have an entirely easy run of it in the future.

Simon Davies, the UK-based Director General of Privacy International, says he takes solace in the recent growth of grassroots activism around the issue of privacy.

'What we are increasingly seeing are young people who are privacy evangelists, and they create hubs of awareness, hubs of activism. You see this, for example, on the fast-moving cool sites such as 4chan, where there are thousands of advocates. And for these young people, privacy invasion isn't cool, unless you're invading the privacy of the bad guys.'

The 'bad guys', of course, being our digital 'sovereigns'.

'I'm not entirely sure that the young activists see a large corporation as anything more than a juicy challenge,' says

Davies. 'Yes, it is difficult for them to imagine bringing down a Google or a Facebook, but what they can do is destabilise confidence or destabilise the value of particular bits of technology, and in particularly apps. We live in a world of applications, but those apps are incredibly vulnerable to attack and to reputational damage brought on by these young activists. Take for example, Europe versus Facebook, an Austrian-based organisation that publishes the raw data about how badly Facebook handles privacy. That's become an evangelist organisation that really is difficult to reckon with because all they're doing is publishing information that tells the truth about the way the company handles people's privacy. You've got evangelists out there like that, you've got activists who are on the case, doing what the regulators in fact don't do, should do but don't do.'

CHAPTER 7

HORSES FOR COURSES

*What we anticipate seldom occurs; what we least expect
generally happens*

Benjamin Disraeli, 19th century British Prime Minister

A thing for your toes

In recent times Zimbabwe and the Victoria Falls Hotel have had
a strange converse relationship. When the country seemed on
the up, in the years immediately following the end of civil war
and the birth of the new nation, the hotel was on the decline.
And now, with Zimbabwe more basket case than breadbasket,
the elegant old Edwardian edifice is once again grand. I checked
it out online the other day and it's a hell of a lot more regal
looking than it was when I was there in 1993, when President
Robert Mugabe's megalomania and mismanagement were still
internationally acceptable — or at least not much commented
upon in polite diplomatic circles: 'Pity about that little square
moustache thingy,' they'd say over a decent single malt at the
British High Commission, 'Still, I'd have thought it was more
Chaplinesque than "let's invade Poland".'

Anyway, today the hotel is all chandeliers, designer decor
and enough over-starched white damask to send an origami
convention into a frenzy.

You're going to have to stay with me on this one, because
I mention Zimbabwe only by way of making a point about
perceptions and misconceptions, the subject of this chapter.

Now, we've already examined the enormous trust we place in our technology and those who provide it, but there's also the trust we have that everybody else in the world thinks as we do and wants what we want in order to make for a better future.

Back during my 1993 visit to Victoria Falls I happened to find myself in a small dusty store, a shop that sold everything from toothpaste to arts and crafts. In one corner there were shelves full of hippos carved out of soapstone, wooden giraffes of all sizes, and sundry other artefacts. And in among the carvings was a curious-looking object, about six or seven centimetres long with little finger-like extensions. It was dark in colour, and as I picked it up and gave it a thorough examination, my imagination roamed over its infinite possibilities: perhaps it was for ceremonial occasions; or maybe it was part of a traditional African headdress, to hold one's hair in place; or maybe, I mused, just maybe, it was used in some kind of exotic religious ritual. Still pondering its purpose, I took the mysterious object to the front of the shop and shared my theories with the woman behind the counter.

She looked at me as if I were an idiot.

'It's for your toes,' she explained dryly. 'It's for painting your toenails. It keeps your toes apart while you're putting the nail polish on.'

We in the West have been making ill-informed assumptions about places like Africa for aeons. We've also been making ill-informed assumptions about ourselves for just as long, but let's not go down that dark path. Much time and effort has been expended in telling Africans — and everybody else in the developing world for that matter — that their future lies in putting aside their own ways and following the 'modern' path instead. 'Modern' naturally equating with the current Western way of doing things.

Now, let's not get all 'black armband' about history, because it's important to remember that people in Africa and Asia were busy enslaving and colonising each other long before the Dutch arrived in Cape Town or the British grabbed Hong Kong. Which is not to excuse anyone's behaviour, it's just a fact. And truth be told, sometimes following the 'modern' way has been a really good idea indeed: think Western medicine, universal suffrage and human rights, for example. But sometimes it's been a mistake: think fast food, baby-milk formula and factories that turn into sweatshops.

European and American colonialists traversed the globe replicating what they knew best: conditions at home. They adopted a one-size-fits-all approach. What was good in Britain or France, or even the US, was good for the empire. And that approach still lingers in our attitudes towards technology and its usage in the developing world: we assume that people in different places will want to use the same technologies we've adopted in exactly the same ways; and that, by and large, the use of those technologies will result in the same outcomes. But, as we'll see in this chapter, that's not necessarily the case. Technology has helped to dramatically change the texture and tone of the developing world, but what's been truly fascinating about that change, particularly in more recent times, has been the fact that it's often occurred in a manner we in the West have not anticipated.

To illustrate what I mean, let's start in one of the remotest places on Earth, the highlands of Papua New Guinea. PNG is a relatively small country in terms of geographic size. However, because of its mountainous topography, and barely existent transport and communications infrastructure, its leaders have struggled for decades to advance the nation's economy, and to bring a sense of unity to its disparate people. It is estimated there are something like 800 or so indigenous languages; and unlike most of the world, it's still predominantly rural, with only around twenty per cent of the population living in urban areas. But over the past few years the nation has undergone a startling technological transformation and Jonathan Ritchie from Australia's Alfred Deakin Research Centre has watched it happen firsthand. 'Mobile phones just seem to have taken off. I've seen it off and on over visits to PNG since about the middle of 2008, and I think this year they're expecting to have something like eighty per cent of the country covered,' he says. 'This is all in a very, very short time, since the opening up of the mobile phone business in about 2007.'

Another academic surprised by the nature of the take-up is Amanda Watson, from the Queensland University of Technology. She's been specifically studying mobile telephony trends in Papua New Guinea, and her research has focused not on the highlands, but on two villages in Sumkar District in Madang Province. 'For these people it's almost magical to be able to hear the voice of their loved ones, some of whom they might not have spoken to for years,' she tells me. 'They might have a son who's away working in a city like Port Moresby, or they might have a child who's away attending high school. So people are reconnecting with family members.'

But, it isn't just the scale and speed of PNG's mobile phone adoption that's important to note, because such rapid uptake, while impressive, is hardly unique. In the decade between 1999 and 2010, it's estimated that the number of mobile phone subscribers in India rose from 1.2 million to approximately 600 million — that's roughly half the population. What's noteworthy about Papua New Guinea's embrace of the mobile is the fact that, in the process of adoption, whole generations of technology have been bypassed. Says Watson: 'In Orora village, which is on Karkar Island, the people there have no television, no computers, no internet, no electricity. Only about a third of the people in the village have a working radio receiver, and yet now they have full mobile phone reception throughout the village.'

So, Papua New Guinea hasn't followed the communications technology pathway that one might have assumed to be logical and natural. Instead, many villages have literally gone from the garamut — the traditional wooden drum — to the mobile phone in one giant leap. And according to Amanda Watson and Jonathan Ritchie, the types of phones the majority of Papuans are buying aren't the glitzy top-of-the-range models that we in the West all desire. They're the basic, cost-effective versions, some of them with a built-in torch in place of a camera. Explains Ritchie: 'One of the interesting things about the mobile phone roll-out in PNG has been the supply of comparatively low-cost handsets that do what they are needed to do and no more. So sending picture messages, or phones as videos, that's perhaps further away for many people. People use them as utilitarian devices, for a purpose.'

Horses for courses, as they say.

And with television it's a similar story. It might be popular in Western media circles to deride the 'idiot box' as an old-fashioned, increasingly outdated medium, but in the developing world it's growing in popularity at a breathtaking pace. In 2010, one of the World Bank's then senior economists, Charles Kenny, declared television — not the internet — the world's 'truly global ICT [Information Communication Technology]'. Kenny conducted research into the health of the TV industry worldwide and his findings appeared in the prestigious journal *Foreign Policy* in an article entitled 'Revolution in a Box'.

'In Australia and England and the US it's true that the internet is the ICT of the moment, the communications technology of the twenty-first century,' he tells me. 'But in many parts of the developing world, access to the internet is really pretty minor — less than ten per cent of the population have access. And that's not going to change any time soon, because using the internet successfully really does take a fairly high level of quality education, which is sadly lacking in many parts of the developing world.

'On the other hand,' he adds, 'TV is spreading really rapidly. Over the last ten years or so it's gone from about half of the households in the developing world up to nearly two-thirds of the households, and it's more amenable for use by people who are illiterate, or have a limited education. And so if you're looking for a communications technology that's really going to make a difference in the short term in developing countries, it's probably the TV rather than the internet.'

Strange then, you might think, that we so rarely ever hear television mentioned in that way. In fact, if you listened only to media academics and technology journalists, you could very easily form the impression that it's the internet, rather than TV, that's fast approaching global ubiquity.

And here's a little gem of information which may or may not come in handy the next time you're trying to bore people into submission at a dinner party: one of, if not *the* most, rapidly expanding television genres in the world is actually the much maligned soap opera.

Yes, the soaps!

In Britain, Australia and the United States, soap opera has been in a long-term death spiral. Or to put it in soap speak: the genre's been lying in hospital, drifting in and out of consciousness, unable to work out whether the people gathered around the bed are friends, or whether they're secretly plotting to turn off the life-support system the moment they get a chance.

But in contrast, in Asia, the Middle East, South America and Africa, soap opera is booming — even the American variety. Arvind Singhal, a professor of Communication at the University of Texas, estimates the global daily audience for the US soap *The Bold and the Beautiful* at somewhere around the 400 million mark. And in a place like India, the home-grown soap operas are more popular still.

In fact, such is the genre's incredible appeal in the developing world that aid and development organisations have even begun using them as a means of promoting tolerance and social cohesion.

When I was talking with Professor Singhal he cited a family drama called *Soul City*, which screened in South Africa, and which deliberately carried an underlying message about the harm caused by domestic violence. That program, he says, is now universally recognised as having helped change community attitudes. Although, it has to be said, the evidence does seem largely anecdotal.

But the example I love most actually comes from the South Pacific, from the tiny nation of Vanuatu. There in 2005, local performers from Wan Smolbag Theatre* were asked to get involved in a community awareness program centred around the risk of HIV infection and the need to treat those living with AIDS in a respectful manner. The end result was a wildly successful TV soap opera with the gloriously corny title of *Love Patrol*. Set in and around a police station, the program quickly became a hit not just in Vanuatu, but in nearby Fiji, Papua New Guinea and other parts of the Pacific.

'We've done a lot of street surveys and focus groups all over the Pacific,' Wan Smolbag's Jo Dorras tells me, 'and we've had people say things like "I'd never go to a workshop, they bore me to death, but I love watching *Love Patrol*." And people saying they'd never seen a condom demonstration until they saw it on *Love Patrol*. So we do have some suggestions that people learned something through it.'

Ah, the power of trash telly!

Now if we can only find a way to put *Neighbours* to the cause of global peace and nuclear disarmament, what a wonderful world it could be.

A little bit of consultation and a bit less blind faith

While there are international development agencies actively funding projects that produce television programs with an education or community-welfare focus, such initiatives are dwarfed in comparison to the hundreds of millions of Western dollars spent each year on schemes that promote the spread

---

* *Wan Smolbag* is pidgin for *One Small Bag*, but I haven't the foggiest why you'd want to name a theatre company after an item of apparel. And I forgot to ask.

of the internet in developing communities. Often pushed, and partially funded, it should be pointed out, by technology companies with clearly vested interests — companies like Microsoft. But while they're popular with donors and such projects tend to get good Western media coverage, their success rate has been patchy. Remember, as Charles Kenny points out, after years of promoting such projects, the fact remains that only around ten per cent of the population of the developing world have access to the web.

Richard Heeks, from the Centre for Development Informatics at the University of Manchester, argues that incorrect assumptions about the communications needs of the developing world have led to almost a decade of poorly directed assistance. Heeks contributed to the United Nation's 2010 *Information Economy Report* and he says the promoters of such projects often fail to ask questions about what people in poor communities actually want, and about the sorts of technologies they themselves see as beneficial to their own future. And he uses the 'telecentre' as a case in point.

A telecentre is a public facility, a communal space decked out with internet-connected PCs. Heeks says the development community became convinced that such facilities were the best model to use in developing countries. The somewhat patronising idea being that the poor are more communal than we rich people and therefore feel more comfortable sharing resources. So, IT people would fly into a village, build a telecentre in an accessible location, perhaps in a local government building, and then fly out again. Bob's your uncle. The only problem was that they didn't work: they weren't well used and they were often subject to damage caused by anti-social behaviour. Swinburne University's Ellie Rennie tells me an almost identical story about the failure of telecentre facilities in remote Indigenous communities in Australia's Central Desert, communal resources, which no one took ownership of and which consequently fell into disuse and decay. But for more than a decade they were the flavour of the month. 'They completely misunderstood the world's poor,' says Heeks.

And that wasn't the only wrong call that was made. 'I think if we look back to the late 1990s, the biggest mistake made by governments, by companies, by development agencies,' he says, 'was they completely missed the mobile revolution. So what I'm arguing now is, OK, we've accepted that the poor are consumers of mobile telephony. Let's not make the same mistake for the next ten years.' And if you think about PNG and the mobile phone explosion I described earlier, it's easy to grasp his point. Still, habits are hard to break. Much of the international aid effort related to technology remains focused on promoting the use of the internet and also expanding broadband access, something Charles Kenny describes as the international development sector's 'latest cause celebre'. And the poster boy for that cause is the OLPC: the One Laptop Per Child initiative, run by a not-for-profit organisation of the same name, with some serious corporate backing.

'We aim to provide each child with a rugged, low-cost, low-power, connected laptop,' declares the organisation's website. 'To this end, we have designed hardware, content and software for collaborative, joyful, and self-empowered learning. With access to this type of tool, children are engaged in their own education, and learn, share, and create together. They become connected to each other, to the world and to a brighter future.'

When you look at the photos on the OLPC website — a series of shots of dirt-poor children grasping shiny new laptops — it's not hard to see the appeal, particularly to a Western audience. Now, I don't mean that to sound cynical, but if internet levels in the developing world are as low as previously stated, and many poor people have no, or limited, access to education, then prioritising laptops above literacy does seem questionable. A bit like purchasing a car when you haven't got a driver's licence or buying a cow for somebody who doesn't live on a farm — only you can't barbecue a laptop.

And I'm pleased to say I'm not the only stone-cold, flint-hearted, pitiless soul who thinks that way. Bonn-based journalist and author Cyrus Farivar is the host of the science and technology program *Spectrum* on Deutsche Welle Radio, and he's spent several years examining the role the internet plays as a catalyst for political, economic and communications-related change in four countries: Estonia, Iran, Senegal and South Korea. Farivar has particular concerns about the way in which we in the West link human advancement to internet connectivity.

'Oftentimes people talk about the internet as if it's an actor, or as if it's an agent of change,' he says. 'I'm sure most people have heard of this concept of the Great Firewall of China, this pervasive filtration and censorship system. There's this kind of implicit assumption that if that were to be removed, Chinese society would be dramatically different, that if only we could bring unfiltered internet access to China, or Russia, or Iran, or Cuba, or places like that, then we would have dramatic political change. You see the same argument for economic development as well. Especially in places like sub-Saharan Africa — most notably in the One Laptop Per Child project — the presumption is that if only people had better access to computers, better access to the internet, then they could develop themselves and make more money and raise their standard of living. The reality is that the internet is more complicated, and more interesting, than that.'

And he adds: 'When we look at countries where internet access is much higher, education levels and literacy levels are quite high. But if you can't read, you can't use the internet. Or at least you can't use it very well. Sure, online there are videos and audio and things like that, but a lot of what we interact with on the web is text.'

So a sense of perspective is the overall message. And for development organisations, it's engaging with local communities to understand *their* genuine needs and desires before spending hundreds of millions of dollars pushing specific technology 'solutions'.

That said, there are those who are beginning to question the entire box and dice; to wonder about the very efficacy of technology aid. And one of them is Kentaro Toyama, a researcher in the School of Information at the University of California, Berkeley.

You could hardly accuse Toyama of being a Luddite: he has a degree in computer science from Harvard, and back in 2005 he co-founded Microsoft Research India. As he tells it, he was once a firm believer that Information Communication Technology (ICT) could change the world simply by its very existence, by its very take-up. A belief that's so prevalent in technology circles that it even has its own appallingly jargonistic name: it's called 'techno-determinism'.

Technology, according to the techno-determinists, makes a difference simply by its presence, by its very existence. Here's what Richard Heeks from the University of Manchester tells me when I specifically ask him about it: 'We have often argued that you need so many other things to be put in place other than a technology. You need skills, you need political change, you need regulations to change, you need mindsets to change, and so on. I think all of that is undoubtedly important, but I do get signs of organic change when ICTs arrive in a community, that the communities themselves start to find new ways of doing development as a result of ICTs coming into those communities.' As long as they're not housed in a telecentre, I say with a wink.

But for Toyama, the former Microsoft manager, what was once belief has now turned to deep scepticism. Toyama caused waves in 2010 when he penned an article for *The Boston Review* entitled 'Can Technology End Poverty?' Simply put, he believes technology only really changes people's lives when the recipients of that technology specifically and consciously want to use it to achieve change, and only if they already have the capacities to follow through on such a goal.

In all other situations, he argues, the adoption of technology largely just amplifies existing behaviour: 'I used to lead a research group in Bangalore for Microsoft,' he tells me, 'and what we did was to spend our time trying to understand how technology impacts very poor communities both in rural villages as well as in urban slums. I was certainly optimistic, in the sense that I felt that we could use these powerful technologies in some way that would really help and impact very poor communities. But over time, what I kept finding was that even in our successful projects, the impact of the technology depended entirely on the people who were either manipulating the technology from the outside, or using the technology from the inside. In both cases, what we found was that you needed well-intentioned, competent people using the technology in order for the technology itself to have a positive impact.'

In layman's language: Toyama says people who are given new technologies simply use them to enhance or extend the sorts of activities they're already engaged in. So, for example, those in a village engaged in business will use the computers they're given access to for commerce, but those who aren't interested, for whatever reason, in intellectually improving their lives, will simply use their PCs for entertainment and little more. Which is neither good nor bad in itself, but could lead to a gigantic waste of development resources.

And, if you follow Toyama's logic — that technology doesn't change behaviour, it merely amplifies it — then it's not hard to imagine that at its worst, a blind devotion to the power of technology as a tool of international development could actually lead to a widening, not a tightening, of the information and wealth divide between rich and poor. So what's the Toyama solution?

'I have two overall recommendations for this line of work,' he replies. 'First of all, if you're not tied to using the technology, consider seriously whether it's the technology that will help, or whether it's some investment in human capacity that will pay off more. Then if you are invested in using the technology, it's to ensure that the technology is applied to an existing social institution that's already having a positive impact. So one way to think about it is that the technology is in support of a working system.'

Literacy before laptops? Perhaps I should also add — people before PCs.

An old bus, some wire and a metal box

Time now to take a brief look at two successful examples of technology assistance at work. Examples where the use of techno-aid has genuinely 'made a difference', as they like to say in the international development sector. The ones I've chosen to mention have succeeded precisely because they're focused on that human dimension that Kentaro Toyama speaks of and also because they're creative in their approach; in both cases, blending a mixture of new and old technologies to achieve a result. What I also like about them is that they're comparatively low cost, they don't need a Microsoft or some giant humanitarian apparatus behind them in order to succeed.

The first involves the inspiration of a technology entrepreneur named Rose Shuman. A few years ago, California-based Shuman looked at the internet, the vast bounty of potential information available online, and then looked at the impoverished of India and wondered how she could help the poor make the most of the new information age. Her solution was to combine both high-tech and low-tech in a single service, which she called the Question Box.

The idea is ingeniously simple. The device is basically a metal box that's stuck on a wall in the middle of a village. It has two buttons on it, a green one and a red one. When someone in the village has a query and they want it investigated online—say the weather forecast for the region — they simply walk up to the box, press the green button and they're immediately connected to an operator who speaks their local dialect and can search the web for the answer to their question. Then, when the villager is finished, he or she simply uses the red button to disconnect. 'It's a portal for rural villages and urban slums to the world of the internet. A way that just about everyone can access,' explains Rose Shuman.

And according to Shuman, the system not only helps overcome problems with literacy, but also any language bias associated with the web. 'Something funny about the development of the internet,' she says, 'has been that if you read English or Spanish or Chinese, or a handful of other languages, you can pretty much find whatever you want. But if you read, say Gujarati, and you want local information that pertains to your state, you actually have a pretty small set of sites you can go to, even if you can get a computer and go online. And I think, for that reason, India has actually had a very slow uptake on the internet. Few people know this, but right now, India's got about 1.2 billion people in it, and there are really only about 80 million regular users of the internet in the entire country, which is less than one per cent. And there are many people, the poor of the poor, who have no access to either a mobile phone or a computer.'

What intrigues me about Rose Shuman's project is that, from a social equity point of view, the Question Box sets up benefits for a whole community, regardless of wealth or literacy levels. It's been underway in different parts of India since 2007 and in 2009, Shuman and her colleagues set up a similar operation in Uganda in cooperation with the Grameen Foundation, the institution that pioneered the idea of micro-finance.

And what have villagers been using it for? Well, Shuman says the deceptively simple machine has been put to use for educational purposes and also by small-scale farmers who now have a means of checking the actual market prices for their produce and thereby eliminating the need for costly middlemen.

'I think that it's generally a good idea, or a sort of universal design ideal, that technologies should be subordinate to human instincts, and to human logic,' she tells me, echoing Kentaro Toyama. 'And the most successful technologies, I think, cut across what country you live in, and are really about making technologies analogous to something that's already in your life.'

And that's also the philosophy adopted by Jerry Watkins, who helped develop DakNet, another internet-focused initiative, which has also been deployed in India. Instead of using a metal communications box to bridge the gap between villagers and the internet, DakNet uses an old bus to overcome the shortage of fixed-line connections in many rural parts of the subcontinent.

Watkins is a senior lecturer in design at Australia's Swinburne University. 'What happens with DakNet is that a wi-fi transmitter and receiver is fitted to the local bus. The bus drives along its normal route, goes through a number of villages, and what it's doing while it's stopping at the bus stop in each village is simply picking up and delivering information via wi-fi from publicly accessible computers in each village,' Watkins tells me. 'So it drives its route, does its wi-fi pick-up and delivery, and once it gets back into town, it simply uploads all its stored data onto the internet once it's at the city bus station. So in this way, the rural community is getting access to a very affordable internet connection, it's just not always on.'

Simple as that.

And echoing many of the other voices in this chapter, Watkins is critical of the approach he sees taken by the major providers of technology assistance in the developing world. 'There's a presumption about what people are going to use the internet for,' he says. 'One of the presumptions is that by delivering email and delivering fax and SMS, that's automatically going to benefit people. But what we found in looking at rural areas in many countries in South and Southeast Asia, is that generally villagers are quite busy people; they don't really have time to drop what they're doing and go and do a training course to understand how to use email. They don't necessarily want to use SMS because they're living in extended families in the village; everyone they want to speak to is living around them. So the kind of basic communications services that it's assumed rural areas require, actually we have to question that.'

It's not rocket science, after all. It's just about listening to people and acknowledging the fact that they might have different needs — horses for courses.

PART TWO

CHALLENGES & OPPORTUNITIES

(WHICH ALSO LOOK AN AWFUL LOT LIKE CHALLENGES)

Where we examine some of the interesting ways in which modern technology is being used to transform our day-to-day existence, whether we like it or not; we look at everyone's favourite subject, money; we question what it means to be 'efficient' and to strive for greater 'sustainability'; we explore the age of tracking and mapping; and we hear about the growing importance in our lives of numbers, facts and games.

CHAPTER 8

ENERGY EFFICIENCY, MY OLD CAR AND THE JEVONS PARADOX

That's always been the promise; that's always been the thought, that growth in the economy is what raises people up. But there comes a certain level where growth really isn't improving the quality of your life. We're not asking the important question: How much is enough? Because with all of this profusion of stuff, there's certainly no correlation with the improvement in whether we're happy.

David Suzuki, Canadian environmentalist and author[41]

Shedding some light

Here's a confession ... It's a bit of a surprise to me that the publisher actually decided to leave this chapter in. Not that it's a bad chapter by any stretch of the imagination. Judge for yourself, but it carries my mother's recommendation, and why would she lie? It's just that, on the surface of it, a chapter about energy efficiency is a really efficient way to get people to stop reading, turn out the light and go to sleep.

The very word efficiency speaks of dullness — nothing exciting is ever efficient — try imagining efficient sex or efficient cuisine and I'm sure you'll grasp what I'm getting at. But it's important to explore the concept, because it's one of those terms we hear all the time, and it's one of the main goals we're supposed to strive for as we charge into the future.

Let me cut to the chase and be brutally honest: the biggest problem I see with society's push to become more energy efficient is that it's a bit like people and exercise machines. Just because you fill the garage with bikes, treadmills and the like, doesn't mean you're going to get fit. In other words, the technology is only of benefit once you've changed your mindset and your habits. Owning it, but not using it, is no good at all. In fact, it's counterproductive, because at the end of the day you're still just as unfit, but with less room in your garage and less cash in your wallet.

It's hard to imagine anyone arguing against energy efficiency. It's self-evidently a good thing. It's a goal even normally divergent groups can agree on: from an environmentalist's point of view, energy efficiency means less pollution and less waste; and from a manufacturer's perspective, it offers the chance of reducing costs and thereby maximising profit. So energy efficiency can make for a greener future and also a stronger economy. Win-win, as they say.

Then there's sustainability. Again, who would argue against that concept; surely if our world was run on the pursuit of sustainability we'd all be better off — no question about it.

But here's the odd thing: while we talk a lot about the pursuit of energy efficiency and the need for sustainability — the desire to conserve resources — the reality is something entirely different, because growth in public awareness about energy and resource depletion has perfectly coincided with the explosion of a lifestyle that actively promotes rather than discourages consumption.

Sustainability is a dangerous concept, according to international design expert Tony Fry, the head of the Design Futures Program at Australia's Griffith University, and he calls for the abandonment of the term, though not necessarily its original intent. 'We're at a watershed,' he says. 'The future of humanity as we understand it is really about a choice which says, "Do we change direction or do we try to maintain what we already have?" Now the question in terms of sustainability and sustainable development, to a large extent reduces to the proposition of sustaining what we already have, sustaining, in a sense, the unsustainable.'

Dr Fry argues that our focus on sustainability has impeded progress and diverted energy away from a nuts-and-bolts reassessment of how we can reshape modern life to match the economic and resource capacities of the world. 'In the end, we are the problem,' he declares. 'Unsustainability isn't a problem of the environment. It is us, it is our way of treating the resources that we utilise, it's our way of living or not living together. It's the way in which we treat all the things that we depend upon pretty carelessly.'

So it's not just that we don't 'walk the talk' when it comes to genuine sustainability and moderation, we're not even off the couch!

Here are some extremely disheartening figures to illustrate my point. The US Government's Energy Information Administration estimates fossil fuel use during the twenty-six years to 2006 grew annually by around two per cent. And energy usage in the G20 group of nations in 2010 grew by more than five per cent.[42] And the G20 countries, don't forget, are meant to be among the smartest, as well as the wealthiest, in the world.

Now, we don't like to admit it, but we all secretly know that human beings are pretty stupid, as evidenced by the fact that we invented reality television and the means to blow the entire planet to smithereens hundreds of times over. But it's not as if we're the dumbest creatures on Earth. We're not brush turkeys, are we? And the average person has more smarts than a cow. So why haven't our efforts to create a more efficient and less wasteful planet actually matched our ambitions? It's entirely possible, of course, that it's simply a matter of not trying hard enough. I can't help thinking we're a bit like those people who drink diet cola and talk all the time about calories, but then sit down to lunch and eat three times their own body weight in chips and hamburgers.

But what about that issue of language I mentioned? Sustainability, as we've already seen, isn't really a helpful term. It can whitewash over some pretty significant problems. And what about efficiency? Well, there is a school of thought that says that it, too, is more of a hindrance than a help. To understand why, we have to journey back in time to meet a nineteenth-century Liverpudlian gentleman by the name of William Stanley Jevons.

Jevons made his name as a professor of economics at University College, London, in the 1870s. He specialised in political economics and logic and he's credited with being one of the pioneers of modern economic thinking. At the age of nineteen, Jevons had left a reasonably comfortable life in the UK for the frenetic madness of the colonies, taking up a job at the Macquarie Street Mint in Sydney.

Colonial Australia wasn't all sheep stations and bushrangers. It was sheep stations, bushrangers and gold! The place was booming and so during his time Down Under, Jevons had a chance to observe the raw dynamics of an economy undergoing massive change. And it obviously had an effect on him because, upon returning to England, he began publicly questioning contemporary economic thought. Then in 1865 he published an influential book on the future of the British resource industry called *The Coal Question*. In it, Jevons foresaw a rapid depletion of the UK's coal reserves brought about not by a lack of initial resources, but by increasing efficiencies in the way in which coal was being used. He suggested that efficiencies in the extraction and use of coal simply fed greater demand, as people found new ways to use the excess. And that in turn, he argued, led to greater extraction. He wrote: 'It is wholly a confusion of ideas to suppose that the economical use of fuel is equivalent to a diminished consumption. The very contrary is the truth.'

So, as a general principle then, his argument centres around the idea that efficiency actually increases, rather than decreases consumption. And that's what's become known as the 'Jevons Paradox'. It's also sometimes referred to as the 'efficiency dilemma' and it's one of the major reasons why striving to be energy efficient in the modern world so often ends up as an exercise in pedalling faster, rather than moving ahead.

Dr Miles Park from the Faculty of the Built Environment at the University of New South Wales explains it like this: 'When you buy these new "eco-efficient" products, it can change your behaviour. This is referred to as a "rebound" effect, whereby there's the psychological thinking that "Well, this product is saving me energy." So therefore you may be inclined to leave the lights on longer, or perhaps you've bought a new eco-efficient car so you'll drive further and more frequently.'

Walk inside the modern house and it's easy to see what Dr Park means. Newly constructed dwellings are now built with energy-efficient lighting but whereas a room used to have, on average, just one 'inefficient' incandescent light bulb, today the fashion is to have as many energy-efficient globes as the ceiling space will allow — or the bearers in the roof will hold. * I visited a beach house in the fashionable Sydney suburb of Avalon not so long ago that had more than forty downlights in the open-plan entertainment area alone! At night time the ceiling looked like a planetarium. You could have mapped your path to another galaxy just by sitting at the breakfast bar and looking up.

And lighting is just the beginning of it: we build more freeways and overpasses in order to make our traffic flow more

---

* Someone once described it to me as the Washing Machine Syndrome because he said: 'In post-war Europe the introduction of the washing machine did not lead to more spare time, but to more washing.' Not a bad analogy, but after all that fighting everything probably needed a damn good wash anyway.

efficiently, only to end up with an increase in vehicle usage and eventually even greater levels of congestion. Then there's the internet. The web was meant to herald the age of the paperless office, but in reality the online environment has vastly increased the flow of correspondence between people, resulting, in turn, in an increase in energy costs from the electricity required to run the world's computers and servers. And to make matters worse, an awful lot of the digital correspondence that's sent between offices often ends up being backed up on paper anyhow.

But there's also another problem with computers: the faster they've become, and the greater their capacity, the more applications we've found for them, which means more usage, which, in turn, means more energy consumption. It's now estimated that information communication technology (ICT) infrastructure accounts for around twenty per cent of the energy consumed in the standard modern office.

'It's certainly the case that our information and communications technology devices are chewing up more and more energy and there's a huge effort in the community, in the computer and electronics community, to reduce that amount of energy, to look for lower and more efficient devices,' says Dr David Skellern, a former head of the technology research organisation National ICT Australia Ltd (NICTA). 'But inevitably, as we have more and more systems connected, we are going to see an increase in the amount of energy that's used.'

In 2007, a study by the tech research company Gartner found that ICT accounted for around two per cent of total greenhouse gas emissions. That doesn't sound like much, but put into perspective, that's around about the same percentage as emissions from the aviation industry. And Lachlan Andrew at the Centre for Advanced Internet Architectures at Melbourne's Swinburne University says all the relevant indicators are pointing upward.

'The most recent figure I've heard is about fifteen per cent annual growth in the energy consumption of the internet.

Another figure that I've heard is around six per cent or so in total due to e-commerce type activities, which includes things like buying a book online. Now, you don't have to physically travel to a bookshop, but that book is in fact being shipped to you. If you consider all the packaging costs and suchlike, the energy cost of buying a book online is often more than driving to the bookshop and buying the book yourself.' *

The solution seems obvious enough: consume less. But encouraging less consumption is always going to be easier said than done in affluent countries like Australia and the United States. It shouldn't be, but political considerations do get in the way.

To show you what I mean, I need you to shut your eyes.

Shut them tight. I mean really tight.

OK, you might have to peek a bit in order to read what I've got to say, but only a little bit. Now, imagine a politician running for election on a campaign platform based on cutting back. Not slicing away at the size of the national deficit or the public service, but forcing voters to seriously cut back on the gadgets and good stuff that we as a society of consumers just love to have. Imagine a campaign message that said to voters that they needed to spend less time on their computers and other digital toys. Or that for the sake of the planet and future generations, they should rip out almost all of the mood lighting in their home, and be content to have just one bathroom in the new house they're building. Or better still, imagine advising people that perhaps they could get by with just one giant flat-screen plasma television in their home, not one per room.

It's just not going to happen, because it's a message that none of us want to hear. The future is meant to be about more not less; and besides, aren't we already doing our bit for energy efficiency by turning off the lounge-room light once a year in support of Global Earth Hour?

---

* An e-book, of course, is going to be cheaper, but there are still energy costs involved in its production and delivery.

In summary, weaning people off at least some of their gadgets is never going to be easy in a world that's saturated with advertising and where, as I pointed out earlier, the term *consumer* has now begun to replace the word *citizen*. Part of the answer is always going to have to be about thinking smarter and trying to reduce energy usage without inadvertently stimulating greater demand.

So what sorts of initiatives could work? Well, I thought about it for a long while and couldn't come up with any myself, so once again I turned to David Skellern for help.

'There are sophisticated ways in which you can save energy,' Skellern assures me, and the example he gives involves motor vehicles. Manufacturers, he says, are experimenting with systems that connect the engine management of a car to the outdoor environment. 'If we knew, for example, when a light was going to turn on or off, a traffic light, and we let the computer in the car determine that we're actually going to be in a braking mode, then it could change the whole energy system in the car to save energy,' explains Skellern. 'And the savings are not trivial. General Motors has recently estimated that you might save fifteen to twenty per cent, or something of that order of magnitude, by being able to alter the energy usage in the car during a braking circumstance.'

And Lachlan Andrew and his colleagues at Swinburne University have also been researching ways in which the efficiency of personal computers can be improved, without getting people's backs up. 'Computers can run much faster at a peak speed than they often need to in quiet times,' says Andrew. 'And so one of the things we're looking at is optimally controlling the speed at which computers run, so that they're only running as fast as they need to at a given time. And this can save a lot of energy in the quiet times, but still give reasonable performance in the peak times when it's really needed.'

It's a noble cause, but Dr Andrew is well aware that it's also a difficult one to realise, given human nature. 'It's a very fine line to tread,' he agrees. 'It's important the user experience not be significantly harmed by the techniques we're introducing. It's important that the user experience be as if computers were running at full speed all the time. But at the same time, if people aren't aware of the resources that are being consumed, then we run the risk of encountering Jevons Paradox, which says that if we make something more efficient, then it becomes cheaper to provide, and so the total amount of energy that is used in the system might actually increase as a result of energy-saving measures. Many people are concerned that is happening with IT already. If we make computers more efficient, then it's going to dramatically increase the amount of computing that's done, which will potentially increase the total amount of energy consumed.'

And around we go again.

The Volvo revelation

It was around 2005 that I first noticed that not only was technology experiencing exponential growth, but that exponential growth was itself on an exponential upward curve. A startling revelation to be sure, but it came in simple brown-paper packaging: there was no epiphany, just a sudden realisation one day while out driving that all the old cars had disappeared. This probably won't make sense to anyone living in Cuba, or Lagos, or Somalia, but it's certainly true in my neck of the woods.

I was driving a faded orange-red Volvo 240 GL, the kind that nerdy academics used to own in the late seventies/early eighties, very box-like, very secure and very old: twenty-six years old at that stage. Don't get me wrong, it was a good, safe car. So good, in fact, that it was threatening to keep chugging along forever. And being slightly mean with my money, I couldn't see a valid financial reason for discarding a vehicle that still worked, even though it had a carbon footprint bigger than the shadow cast during a full solar eclipse.

So I'm in a large bitumen car park on a hot summer's day with the car violently idling and the windows down (the air-conditioner had long since given up the ghost). And I was waiting for a very small Mercedes to vacate its parking space — the last one available. As I sat there, sweltering, I began to notice the number of new cars around me. I'd better qualify that statement. By *new*, I mean anything up to five years old; newish, perhaps. Anyway, what I quickly noticed was that all the cars around me were new. Mine was the only vehicle in the entire car park with what is often euphemistically referred to as 'character'.

Now, I don't necessarily want to wave a flag for the 'frugality' movement — I like new things as much as anybody else — but it does strike me as not a particularly healthy situation for society, or the planet, when cars are now considered old even before their warranty expires. I'm overstating things, of course, but the serious point I'm trying to make is that we're not just living in a consumption-focused world, we're living in one long cycle of replacement — the era of the uber upgrade.

If you'd asked me a few years ago to sum up the essence of the average person's life in a single sentence, my guess would probably have been something like this: Life, for most people, is about having things, getting more things and then trying to find room to store all of those things.

But today, I think I'd say something more along these lines: Life is about having things, getting more things, regularly replacing those things, replacing them again, and then building an extension on the back of the house for all of the things you've now accumulated, but still haven't got room for. Then it's about selling that house and upgrading to an even larger residence, which you'll then need to completely refurbish.

As frightening as this may sound, the total number of objects we have in our homes has more than doubled in twenty years, according to Miles Park. The future is looking very cluttered indeed. And not only that, we now have more energy-consuming products within our houses than ever before. 'The cumulative impact of all those products burning power is increasing. In fact, it's doubled household energy consumption in the last thirty years,' he says.

But, as I mentioned, modern life is not just about accumulating, it's about upgrading. And while it's easy to poke fun at the serial refurbishers, it would be remiss of me not to point out that one of the other main reasons why people are constantly upgrading, particularly in the area of electronics and digital devices, is because they often have little choice in the matter.

Nothing lasts forever is sage advice, but why is it that the smarter we get technologically, the less able we are to build products that actually last longer than the time it takes to get them out of the box? When I bought a new desktop computer for my home office recently, the man in the shop estimated its lifespan at somewhere between two and four years. And he was in the business of selling the damn things.

Of course, the fact that today's products stop functioning after such a short period of time has nothing to do with workmanship or knowledge, it's because they're meant to do a Kurt Cobain — to die young — it's expected of them. In fact, they're actually engineered to be quickly superseded. It's rarely referred to outside of design and manufacturing circles, but the principle that underpins our material world is an American business concept known as 'planned obsolescence', which apparently had its roots in the Great Depression, when industrial designers in the United States first hit upon the idea of lifting sales in a stagnant market by deliberately creating products that needed to be replaced. And Miles Park says planned obsolescence in the technological sector is a huge driver of the current turnover of digital products — all those devices we're consuming and discarding with increased regularity.

Aside from technological obsolescence, another pertinent variant, according to Dr Park, is what's called 'eco-obsolescence'. 'Eco-obsolescence is based on the assumption that it's better to replace old, inefficient products with more, or newer, eco-efficient products,' he says. 'So we have enforced obsolescence happening, not because products are breaking down, or that we just want new ones, but in an actual encouragement to upgrade and buy new stuff which is supposed to be more energy efficient.' Like the energy-efficient lightbulb.

And the end result of all these forms of obsolescence is an ever growing stockpile of unloved gadgets and products. E-waste is one of the fastest growing sectors of municipal waste, and it's only going to get worse: 'It's growing three times faster than any other type of municipal waste, and that is reflected in approximately 17 million televisions and computer-related products being discarded each year,' calculates Miles Park, using Australian figures for his example. 'Most of that's ending up in landfill. This is compounded by 14 million to 16 million unused mobile phones, which languish in people's desks and drawers across the country. Worldwide the volume of e-waste is expected to grow from three to five per cent a year.'

For Dr Park, the logical and obvious solution to the problem is for governments to frame 'policies and measures' to try to limit planned obsolescence and therefore its negative consequences. The only problem with that idea, though, is that many of the world's economies — both advanced and developing — are now increasingly reliant on consumption to underpin or bolster their stability. This was particularly evident during the Global Financial Crisis, when governments and central banks initially tried to push themselves out of financial difficulty by exhorting people to buy more, to shop, to consume in greater quantities in order to stimulate cash-flow. And that approach is still being followed in many countries today. Governments are less inclined to take the difficult path of root-and-branch restructuring, in favour of trying to grow their way out of difficulty by encouraging people to spend more on consumer products.

The Canadian environmentalist David Suzuki speaks of a 'frenzy of disposability', which, in turn, has led to an economic addiction. 'I think most of the speed up to now has to do with the drive for greater economic growth. We've come to feel that growth is the very definition of progress,' he argues. 'So if you talk to a businessman or someone in government, "How well did you do last year?" within seconds they'll be talking about whether GDP grew, or about their share of market or profits or jobs. Growth has become the definition of whether or not they did well. Growth has become a driving part of the destruction of the life-support systems of the planet. It just can't continue.'[43]

But it is continuing, of course, and when you factor in the socio-economic changes that are now underway in parts of the developing world, the prospects for the future look truly disturbing. China is expected to be the second largest consumer market in the world by 2015. Not so long ago a land of bicycles and foot power, by 2011 there were already more cars on China's roads than in the United States.

Such dramatic growth has become a point of environmental concern for many Western leaders who publicly, and often loudly, worry about the new industrialisation underway in Asia. But that has to be coupled with the fact that Western politicians and companies also see countries like China as a cheap source of products, and a market for commodities and high-end goods.

'Schizophrenic' is the way Hong Kong-based business consultant Chandran Nair describes the West's attitude. Nair is the founder of a think-tank called the Global Institute for Tomorrow and he's also the author of *Consumptionomics: Asia's Role in Reshaping Capitalism and Saving the Planet,* which he told me was inspired by the way he saw global politics playing out during the financial crisis of 2008–2009. 'We had leading economies who were mainly Western, leading politicians, urging Asians to stop saving and start consuming. I don't think you need to be a rocket scientist or a climate denier to know that if Asians consume like the West, well the game is over, to put it crudely,' said Nair.

So, be responsible and reduce your emissions, is the message from the West on the one hand. While on the other, it's buy more of our fossil fuel exports, build more factories and develop bigger consumer markets in order to keep the world economy pushing ahead.

Nair speaks and writes with conviction about his hope that, sooner rather than later, Asian nations will realise the folly of consumption-driven economics and begin to follow a different economic path to the one they, and we, are currently traversing. It's a positive and constructive message. But given the incredible growth of the middle class in China and India, isn't it already too late? I ask. Hasn't the train already left the station?

'I don't think any person, be it Asian or European or Western, is necessarily programmed genetically to just consume endlessly,' he replies. 'If you look at the consuming classes in Asia they are still the minority. If you take the population of Asia to be anywhere between 3.5 and 4 billion people currently, I would argue that the true consuming classes are probably only about a half a billion people. So the opportunity lies in reshaping the way we create prosperity. I remain hopeful that the crunch point between moving along this trajectory and the consequences that we're seeing, particularly in terms of the marginalisation of large sectors of the population, degradation of resources and declining quality of life, will get the politicians in this part of the world to think much more clearly.'

It's certainly a big hope and I for one am not convinced that any country at this stage has the answer to the consumption versus economic decline dilemma that we currently face. Or, for that matter, that any of the world's major leaders are actually looking for one. I find it hard to share Nair's guarded optimism, which also means that, despite my original intentions to the contrary, I'm going to have to end this chapter on a pessimistic note.

But if I can't conclude in an upbeat fashion, the very least I can do is leave you with something else to think about. And that something takes the form of an entirely new term. Well, I don't really know whether it's new, but I'm going to plant a flag on it anyway. I call it the Christ, It's Four In The Morning And I'm Panicking Because I've Got To Have This Assignment Finished Before The Sun Comes Up Rule, or, for the sake of brevity and convenience, the Morning Panic Principle. It goes like this: The greater the size and complexity of the task, the greater the chance that no one will get around to doing anything about it until the eleventh hour.

In other words, some tasks are so daunting that, despite our better judgement, we ignore them until the very last moment, until the time when there is absolutely no other choice but to act.

When I was at university, many late nights and early mornings were spent desperately finishing assignments. For students of my generation it was standard operating practice to leave things until the eleventh hour, and I'd be shocked if much has changed. In fact, that tendency to procrastinate and postpone, and then to try to solve problems in a mad, desperate rush right at the very end, appears to be an historic human trait: the Morning Panic Principle was clearly at play in Europe in the 1930s when, despite years of warnings, the great democratic powers did almost nothing to combat Nazism until Poland, Czechoslovakia and Austria had all been swallowed up, and the German High Command were making presumptive dinner reservations at the Savoy Grill; and in more recent times, it guided the international community's decision to do diddlysquat about banning the use of chlorofluorocarbons (CFCs) until somebody realised we already had a whopping great hole in the ozone layer and all the polar bears were threatened with sunburn!

So, why should we expect it to be any different with energy in the future? As was pointed out at the beginning of this chapter, the more efficient we get with energy usage, the more of it we consume, and the evidence already suggests that the only thing that might make a significant difference to our consumption habits is a shot of that eleventh-hour panic. Just ask New Mexico-based architect, Edward Mazria.

'In 1973, we had the first energy crisis; we had an energy embargo, essentially the price of oil went way up, and consequently that dragged all the other energy sources way up, and so there was a surge of research and development into alternative energy sources and design techniques,' says Mazria, the founder of the not-for-profit organisation Architecture 2030, a group dedicated to the concept of the energy-efficient city. 'In the US we had a huge number of buildings that were built to very, very efficient standards, and that continued from 1973 all the way through to 1983. In fact, during that period, we added about 40 billion square feet of US building stock, and we didn't increase our emissions or our energy consumption in the building sector at all,' he says.

So, it can be done. We can genuinely reduce our energy consumption on a large scale if we are truly desperate to do so. That's the good news. But, history tells us that things pretty quickly go back to business as usual once the time of crisis appears to have eased. That's the bad news. According to Mazria, as soon as the oil crisis passed, energy consumption in the American building sector immediately began to rise again.

And I'm sure you don't need me to tell you that it's still rising today.

CHAPTER 9

NEW COMMERCE, VIRTUAL CURRENCY AND THE ICELANDIC ECONOMIST

This is a fantastic time to be entering the business world, because business is going to change more in the next ten years than it has in the last fifty.

Bill Gates, co-founder of Microsoft

The virtue of gruel and a good day's work

Time, I think, to personally go out on a limb and make a big call — a bold statement.

Money is on the way out. It's history!

Looking ahead, I see lots of things that exist today and which I'm confident are still going to be around in the decades to come — cars, nation states, aeroplanes, reality TV, possibly Kim Kardashian — but not money. At least not in the way most of us currently know it; which is not to suggest that we're all going to be wearing orange and living in an ashram somewhere, exchanging homemade tofu cakes for services. But things are changing in the world of currency and it's going to affect us all.

When Google unveiled Wallet, an application developed for the smart phones that use its Android-based operating system, the company got loads of attention. It was heralded as the death of both cash and plastic. Wallet is an application that allows you to pay for things simply by swiping your phone across an electronic payment point, rather like scanning barcodes at a supermarket checkout. The phone just needs to be in close proximity to the scanner to make a transaction, so you no longer need to insert a credit card or dig around in your bag for cash.

Simply put, it makes your mobile phone into a payment device. It's been painted by the media as a breakthrough. And it is of sorts, but it's also just the latest development in a long line of changes to the way in which we think about both currency and finance; changes that are going to have a direct bearing on our future.

Now, if you've got a few quid to spare, and you're not averse to the odd bet, here's a sure-fire tip. Within a few decades or so, coins and banknotes will pretty much have gone the way of manners and civil debate: interesting relics of the past that no longer seem to have a place in the modern world. And that's really what I meant by the disappearance of money. All, or almost all, financial transactions — personal as well as business-related — will likely be done digitally. At least in the wealthy developed world, that is. And just as coins gave way in large part to paper, and paper has given way to credit and debit cards, so too our digital devices will become the instruments we use for our everyday buying and selling. And eventually the only place you'll be able to find a coin will be in a collector's album or at a casino (playing two-up by tossing a pair of mobile phones into the air is never going to catch on).

But we shouldn't get too teary-eyed about it all, because many of us have actually been making digital transactions online for more than a decade, don't forget. And besides, the whole notion of coinage is a pretty recent invention, anyhow.

Talk to any numismatist and, yes, he or she will tell you that coins have been in circulation for aeons. And that's true, but that's not to say that in bygone days the major part of the world's population actually owned many of them, or even had access to them, in the case of serfs and slaves.

It was only in the 1800s that the Scottish historian and essayist Thomas Carlyle made popular the phrase: 'A fair day's wages for a fair day's work'. And you don't have to go too far back to find a time when most people, particularly those living in the countryside, had no wages at all, instead they eked out a miserable and pathetic existence through payment in kind. Life for the lucky ones went something like this: you rose early, sweated all day in the sun while dutifully tending to his lordship's crops or livestock, and then on Sunday — your only day of rest — you were rewarded for the good and loyal service you'd performed during the past six days with just enough victuals to make several decent bowls of muck for you, your wife, your ten children and the extended family. And then you repeated that process every week until you were lucky enough to die. Whence came the phrase: 'Goodbye gruel world!'

Sure, it was character-building stuff, but without a wallet stuffed with coins, at least the back pocket of your pants didn't stick out like a goitre.

So, as I say, coins and paper money are on the way out. And it probably won't be as disruptive as it possibly seems.

'Most of our transactions are already digitised, let's not forget that. If you pay for something with a credit card, that's digital money, that's not real money moving around, that's zeroes and ones,' says Richard Watson, editor of the quarterly report on global trends called *What's Next* and author of the book *Future Files*. 'The idea really is, when you leave the house there's probably three things you have on you: you have some keys, your mobile phone and your wallet. Now there's no reason why a bunch of coins and potentially some notes couldn't be digitalised and put inside your phone. So if I need to pay for a bus ticket, or lunch, I just wave my phone at something in the same way that EFTPOS works at the moment. I think what the phone will do is it will suck in all of these basic transactional services.'

And why wouldn't the phone become your wallet in future? It's already your camera, your access point to the internet and email, your listening device for music, your book, your mini TV and your carpenter's spirit level (as long as you've download the right app). In fact, the least important thing about the modern phone seems to be its ability to actually make a phone call — the audio quality on most of them is rubbish.

'Goodbye wallet, the phone will take over from here,' was the tag-line in an online promotional video run by Google in late 2011 to promote its new phone-centric payment system. But Google isn't the only one working on the idea. Handset makers like Research in Motion, which makes the BlackBerry, and Nokia are also onboard, as is Apple. While in Japan and South Korea — two countries that seem to be ahead of the curve on most matters digital — making payments by phone is already a bit old hat. Commuters in both places have been swiping their phones to pay for bus and train tickets for several years now.

Without getting too technical, what makes the system work is a form of wireless technology called Near Field Communication (NFC), which allows for a financial transaction to occur without the need for direct contact, hence payments can be made by swiping an NFC-enabled device rather than by inserting a card or punching a PIN into a keypad.

Now, you could just as easily put an NFC device in a credit card or a keyring or a child's toy, for that matter. But it's not hard to see why the phone pairing makes sense for those pushing this new technology. And who are they? Well, the banks and financial institutions like Visa and MasterCard, along with technology companies and the big retailers. For a start, there's the point Richard Watson made, that almost everyone already carries a mobile phone in their pocket. Secondly, there's the fact that smart phones are two-way communication devices, so retailers can, at the same time, use them to promote products and specials to their customers. Quite a few major retailers now have smart-phone apps that alert shoppers to bargains or help them to price goods or find items while they're in store. So paying with your phone would just be another graduation on that. Thirdly, there's the fact that an increasing number of people are already accustomed to mobile banking, using their phones to do online transactions, so it's familiar territory for some smart-phone users.

There's also huge potential savings to be made for retailers and banks in eliminating the staffing and infrastructure costs involved with the handling and processing of physical money: and, just as importantly, huge amounts of additional data to be gathered about people's shopping and spending preferences. Remember, digital data is much easier to collate than physical data, so by making absolutely everything digital, every single financial transaction can be recorded and analysed. And that means the big retailers will be better able to spot spending trends among their customer base, thereby helping them to anticipate what items are likely to be big sellers. At least that's the theory. They've already been tracking spending to a limited extent in recent years with customer loyalty cards, the ones that get swiped when you're paying for groceries and which then give you a small discount on your petrol, for example. Those cards are dressed up as customer rewards, but they're actually about data gathering. The retailers use them to match every purchase you make against a digital profile of you as a shopper. Then they gather the profiles of millions of such shoppers and look for emerging shopping trends and patterns.

So there's much in the new system for the corporations. But what about us? What pros and cons would there be for we ordinary plebs in a future without small change?

Well, convenience, of course, is a positive. You wouldn't need a wallet or a change purse any longer and your phone could potentially replace all your credit and debit cards. And you'd never again find yourself in a situation where you were caught a few cents short at the cash register.

On the other hand, doing away with physical currency represents one more step in the ongoing process of making it harder for people to keep track of their hard-earned cash. And that's a significant downside. Perhaps I'm old fashioned, but paying at a cash register with a mobile phone just won't feel like real spending. And that's also a point not lost on Richard Watson either: 'If you have physical cash in your hand, you spend it in a very different way from digital cash. You are a little bit more carefree when you're using the digital equivalent. I used to get a lot of statements in the mail, on paper, and I would look at them. I'm talking about Visa bills and bank statements and airline miles. I would look at them very, very carefully. The minute that they [the bills] are digitalised — and they're not really digitalised for my convenience, they're digitalised for the corporations' convenience, saving them money — I don't check them. I mean, anything that is digitalised is so ephemeral.'

As with everything involving the digital world, there are also huge privacy and security implications to wade through. The financial sector has been at the vanguard of digitisation. And at the very, very front of the push has been the banking sector, which, for more than a decade, has been quietly covering the huge costs of cyber crime, while encouraging people to do more and more of their financial dealings online. Why? Because the money the banks have lost to online criminals has been more than offset by the enormous savings they've made through dramatic reductions in staffing numbers, office space and all of the other overheads associated with doing business in the physical world.

The trend towards the movement of financial services online is only set to continue. In the last few years numerous insurance providers, including very large players like AAMI in Australia, have closed all their physical outlets and relocated their operations almost entirely online (call centres excluded). And it's not hard to imagine the banks soon following that example — they're already halfway there.

Now, I spoke of 'encouraging' people to do more of their financial dealings online, but, of course, it's been much stronger than that. Financial institutions have actually gone out of their way to make it as difficult as possible for people to avoid doing anything other than online commerce. Penalty fees for face-to-face interactions are commonplace and while it's true that many people increasingly find online banking and shopping easy and convenient, the choice to do otherwise is slowly but surely being removed. And the rhetoric cloaking all of this, surprise, surprise, is that it's all about *you*. About giving *you*, the customer, a better, faster service.

It's a sleight of hand that isn't confined to the financial sector. Airlines now force you to use ticketing machines to process your own boarding pass and to check in your own luggage, while supermarkets now increasingly expect you to scan your own grocery items.

I don't know about you, but having to do my own check-in every time I fly, or take on the role of a checkout attendant whenever I go to Woolworths isn't actually a benefit to my life. I don't get paid for it, I don't even get a discount for the fact that I'm suddenly doing work that others were once employed to do, and more importantly, when everybody's forced to do the same thing, there isn't even any real saving in terms of time. So for me there is no upside.

But, like it or not, it is the way of the future.

Alternative means, alternative money

I started this chapter with a bold prediction, now let me give you the bookend to that: a statement of the bleedin' obvious. Here goes ...

E-commerce is booming.

Please note that it's so obvious I didn't even attempt to dress it up with an exclamation mark.

E-commerce is going gangbusters, we all know that: eBay, iTunes, buying food and clothing online; it's a major economic growth area. And I'm telling you nothing new in saying that we'll all be doing more and more of it as time goes on. But there are aspects of the e-commerce explosion that have largely passed unnoticed. And it's those I want to concentrate on now. I'm going to start with a look at alternative currencies.

Here's the definition from Wikipedia: 'Alternative currency is a term that refers to any currency used as an alternative to the dominant national or multinational currency systems (usually referred to as national or fiat money). Alternative currencies can be created by an individual, corporation, or organisation, they can be created by national, state, or local governments, or they can arise naturally as people begin to use a certain commodity as a currency.'

Alternative currencies have long existed — barter is perhaps the most well-known alternative currency system, but it's pretty small-scale stuff, associated with highly localised environments, say a commune or a collective. Even the name 'alternative' suggests it's not for the mainstream. But as I'll show in this part of the chapter, the growth in alternative currencies is no longer small beer. In fact it's huge and ever growing.

Many of us are already using very basic alternative currencies without realising it. The 'customer loyalty cards' I mentioned earlier are a form of alternative currency, and so too are Frequent Flyer points. In both cases you get credit (get paid) for giving a retailer or airline your patronage. And then at a certain point in time, you get to cash in those points for air travel or petrol, as the case may be.

But the real growth in alternative currencies has been online. Hundreds of millions of people across the planet spend huge amounts of time in what are called 'virtual worlds'. Second Life is one of the most famous — a sort of online game that mimics the real world and where you use your own personal animated figure (an avatar) to represent you. It's extremely popular and there are lots of rival virtual worlds out there. Then there are the huge interactive games like World of Warcraft, which allow thousands of people to play online at once. Not my cup of tea, but once again, they are very, very popular. What's pertinent though, is that within these online environments, genuine economic activity has begun to flourish.

With Second Life, for example, participants are required to use the game's own currency, called 'Linden dollars', in order to buy things. And you purchase that currency using traditional money, Australian dollars, UK pounds, etc. So Linden Labs, the developer of the game, makes its profit by selling people Linden dollars, which those people then use when they're playing. Those Linden dollars are a form of online alternative currency.

And, that's just one game, albeit a very large one. Now if you can imagine the same sort of economic activity occurring in multiple virtual worlds all at once, you can start to understand the size of the economic activity that's possible using such alternative currencies. It makes bartering look as irrelevant as … well, bartering!

Edward Castronova is a professor of Telecommunications at Indiana University in the United States and he says economic activity is now 'nearly universal' in virtual worlds. 'Most people who make one, immediately and without thinking about it, put in a market, and put in money,' he says. 'So everywhere there's a virtual world, there's an economy that's put in place. So it is, in a sense, universal. In almost all virtual reality systems today, the economies are growing as fast as virtual reality is, and virtual reality is really taking off.'

For the record, Dr Castronova also includes social media sites like Facebook in his definition of what constitutes a virtual world. He calls Facebook a 'light virtual reality system'. And certainly Facebook has been active in the last few years in promoting its own version of an alternative currency. Called Facebook Credits, they're designed for people to use when playing games on the social media site or purchasing products.

BBC Worldwide has been using Facebook as a video rental platform for several years now, with Facebook Credits as the designated currency of payment.

And there's considerable profit to be made through such a relationship. The company Zynga, which makes the popular Facebook game FarmVille, was estimated to have creamed a US$630 million profit during the 2010 financial year.

So again, at the risk of repeating myself, we're talking about seriously big money. In fact, and this is bound to set your Fukuyama reflex spasming, according to Dr Castronova, Norrath, a fictional planet in the online game called EverQuest, now has a GDP per capita roughly between that of Bulgaria and Russia.

'I mean, it sounds insane,' concedes Castronova, 'but remember we're talking about Gross Domestic Product — production per person. The value of that currency is going to reflect the wealth of the people who are playing the game. Stuff being made in that virtual economy is being made on the time of pretty well off, high-wage Americans, in the case of Norrath. And the people buying are also high-wage people. That's how the value of production per person can actually be pretty high. It is play money, but in this case play money actually has a value and it's not trivial.'

The author and technology commentator Douglas Rushkoff argues that to understand the current boom in alternative currencies, you have to first understand why we ended up with traditional national currency — the dollar, the pound, etc. Rushkoff points out that in the first millennium BCE there were actually many different currencies in use in the countries of Europe, including the use of grain, but he says all that changed in the late Middle Ages, when the feudal system started to break down: 'The feudal lords, who were really the proto kings and the aristocracy, were wealthy, but their wealth relative to people's wealth was going down, and they really needed to institute some laws to prevent the further decline of the aristocracy.'

And thus, argues Rushkoff, the primacy of centralised national currency — coin of the realm — was established: 'What they did was they made all of these other kinds of money illegal and forced people to use coin of the realm, which was loaned into existence by a central bank. So this way, people who had money, could get wealthy — or wealthier — simply by lending their capital and making everybody use it as a coin, as the only really valid currency for exchanging anything they wanted to exchange. And this has really come down to us today as central bank-issued currency.'

So the explosion in online alternative currencies — or digital currencies as they're also known — is really, in a sense, a return to the past. To a situation where there was greater currency plurality.

But what exactly are people buying in virtual online environments?

A shopping basket full of code

A great deal of the commerce surrounding online currencies is actually about the trade of virtual/digital goods. In fact, the lion's share, by far. And the thing to remember about virtual goods is that they don't really exist — they have no actual physical value.

'A digital good is really just a piece of code, which has been turned into something that's graphically seen as being a good of some sort. It doesn't have any intrinsic value but it has a perceived value by the user,' says Mandy Salomon, a senior researcher with the Smart Services Cooperative Research Centre, which works out of Swinburne University in Melbourne.

So, if you're playing World of Warcraft, for example, you can buy swords and shields and whatnot for your avatar (your digital representation) to use in battle, or say you're on Second Life, you can pay Linden dollars to buy a house for your avatar or furniture. It's not a real sword or a real house, but they exist in the game — you can see them and use them.

Now the important thing to remember is that digital goods aren't just normal goods that you happened to buy online. They're not the physical products you purchase through an online shopping or auction site like eBay, for instance. As Salomon says, they're just pieces of 'code'. So the obvious question then is: who would want to pay money for something that isn't real?

Well, a lot of people, it turns out.

'The digital or virtual goods industry is becoming a huge phenomenon, with enormous projections as to how it's going to continue to grow. It's very hard to talk about figures in any finite way,' says Salomon, 'because everybody seems to have different ways of measuring them, but in Second Life, US$1 billion has now been traded in that world. PayPal in 2009 processed US$500 million worth of virtual goods payments. US$500 million just on PayPal. So for a burgeoning new industry, US$500 million is a significant indicator of revenue exchange. And that's just when people pay for goods on PayPal; there are many other ways that they can pay for goods. So we're talking about a multi-billion-dollar industry that's growing very, very quickly.'

But here's where it starts to get murky. The 'sweet spot' for those looking to make money from virtual trade, says Mandy Salomon, is the kids' market. That, she says, is where businesses see the biggest potential growth: 'With micro-transactions, which are tiny payments, you don't have to commit as a user to getting a subscription. You can just have very small, incremental charges, which a child can handle through various payment services such as a phone card.'

And, says Salomon, growth in the age group between three and sixteen is phenomenal: 'Habbo Hotel, which is probably the grand old daddy of kids' virtual worlds, has 16 million users per day, and about 157 million sign-ups globally. Games that are based on entertainment products, like *Star Wars*, are coming into social networks; games that are related to, say,

Disney products, branded entertainment products, are coming into the gaming environment, and kids are very receptive to this. They have a very natural inclination to want to acquire and share things among their social network.'

Now, tar and feather me and call me a fool, but as I was researching this area I just automatically assumed that with so much money involved in the growing virtual goods trade, the regulators would be all over it, particularly taxation departments. But it seems many governments are yet to catch on. Although the Australian Government, I note, has ruled that real-world income generated from the sale of virtual or digital goods is to be treated as any other form of income. What that means in terms of actual compliance, I have no idea and it's difficult to establish.

But, a situation with hundreds of millions of dollars in annual trade, most probably billions, and very little government interest or regulation sounds to me like the perfect incubator for criminal activity; for money laundering at the very least. And that's also the way it seems to criminologist Ian Warren, from Victoria's Deakin University.

Dr Warren says 'harmonisation' is the biggest problem in coordinating global cyber-crime regulation. That is, harmonisation in terms of inter-agency cooperation between law enforcement agencies, as well as harmonisation between relevant national laws.

Then there are the service agreements that site administrators insist people sign before they're allowed to set up an account with a particular game or platform; agreements that, at least on paper, bind players to certain rules and regulations. But let's face it, service agreements are like instruction booklets — no one actually reads them. You just tick the box and away you go. So, the question still remains, if you buy digital goods, or invest in virtual property, how much protection does your investment have, and what sort of sanctions exist for those who transgress?

'Well the difficulty,' says Ian Warren, 'is that the program administrators don't necessarily have the resources or the desire to police every sort of behaviour, and so this generally works on a victim complaint basis. Where a complaint is lodged with the site administrator, there'll be a minimal investigation into what's happened, and in Second Life, for example, you have penalties like a twenty-four-hour ban for the perpetrator. They're normally pretty trivial, but it's usually related to denial of access or inability to enter the site for a limited period of time. I don't know of any cases where any of these sites have actually implemented financial penalties. There have been examples where there's been confiscation of property, so people who have built up virtual capital, and have been found to have built that up through a fraudulent method, have had their property confiscated by the site administrators. But that's a fairly rare occurrence; generally it's going to be a banning order for one to seven days.'

One to seven days in the naughty corner doesn't sound like much of a punishment or deterrent, does it? After all, human beings are human beings, and some of us just can't keep our hands off other people's stuff. So surely there must be a push developing for greater external regulation of online virtual commerce. But there isn't, and Ian Warren believes that's because the culture of regulatory freedom is so entrenched in the online world that making any change would be no easy task.

'I think there's going to be an incredible resistance to real-world law applying to any virtual environment, mainly because the rules of the game and the internal mechanisms and informal mechanisms that communities develop over time actually become quite strong, and become a driving force. The main people who seem to be affected by some of these trade practices violations are new users who don't know how to use the system all that well, or haven't developed the expertise to be able to get out of bad situations and become, I suppose, streetwise to economic problems, economic fraud and that sort of thing.'

But that's not to say that some governments aren't keen to bring a little old-fashioned law and order to proceedings. In 2009, enforcement authorities in Finland proudly announced that they were investigating more than 400 cases of theft involving digital goods. And in that same year in China, the government in Beijing introduced new regulations to restrict the use of virtual money after large numbers of people began using a form of online game currency called QQ coins to buy real-world products and services. Edward Castronova says the Chinese example should give us pause for thought. Because, he says, along with the benefits, there are legitimate potential dangers in the development of virtual trade and alternative currencies.

'Let's say a virtual currency like QQ coins got out of control and everybody's using the virtual currency to do their day-to-day transactions. I don't think we are anywhere near that now, but let's say it's something that could happen. In that case, the people managing QQ coins would become very influential in the real-world economy. And who are they? People who developed a game. They're not elected officials, they're not appointed by any government, they're not trained necessarily in anything. And so that would be a case where the people who run a virtual environment have significant influence over what happens out here in the real world.'

And in the longer run, Dr Castronova also foresees much larger potential social problems from people losing a perspective on what's real and what's not: 'You can imagine future generations of people who, as they grow up, spend some time in virtual worlds, and some time in the real world — back and forth. And they develop this idea of what an economy should be, and how things should work, partly by being in the real world and partly by being in the virtual world, where the way people have set up the rules can be totally different. And it might affect their expectations,' he cautions.

And that, for the authorities in a place like Beijing, might perhaps be the scariest notion of all.

Life in the economic snow dome

Despite the many obvious differences between a virtual economic world and its real-world equivalent, there are also important similarities. The basic economic thought processes of those involved in the trade or purchase of virtual goods, it appears, mirror those in the physical world. In other words, whether you're in Second Life or real life, people still know and appreciate a bargain when they see one; and it seems those operating in a virtual economy pretty quickly establish for themselves what the fair market price is for commodities, be they goods or services. Which got me wondering whether anyone was studying virtual-world economies for lessons that could be useful in dealing with real-world problems? Well, it turns out there are quite a few such people — it's a growing area of academic interest.

In the Icelandic capital of Reykjavik, Dr Eyjolfur Gudmundsson leads a team of four economists employed by the company that runs the sci-fi-themed game EVE Online.

When you visit the game's website it isn't initially obvious why they need a group of numbers boffins on staff. EVE Online is set in a galaxy at the 'far end of the universe', 20,000 years into the future and when you join the game you become a spaceship pilot. So it all reads like simple fantasy. But dig a little deeper and you soon see that economics is at the core of it all. The game has its own currency, of course, Interstellar Kredits (ISKs) and people are encouraged to engage in trade and to form 'corporations'. There's even initial commencement advice on how players can 'make money', with specific encouragements to 'trade to make a living' by conducting 'mining operations' or marketing 'your fighting skills as a mercenary'. Or even to 'camp the spacelanes for profit as a pirate'.

Now the inhouse economics team has three functions, according to Gudmundsson. The first is to provide players of the game — around 330,000 apparently — with economic updates and advice: his team produces a regular newsletter that monitors market prices within the game and even calculates inflation on a monthly basis. Their second role is to then feed that data back to the game's development team. And the third function, says Gudmundsson, is to provide forecasts: 'If the developers want to change a certain aspect of the game, they come to us and ask, "What do you think will happen within the economy?" So we have 330,000 subscribers and we play in the same environment. Which means basically that we have a universe of 330,000 people, participating in a player-driven economy and when it gets to this size, it has basically all the same characteristics as any other small-scale economy in our modern world.'

It sounds weird, I know, but it's all very serious indeed. Remember, Dr Gudmundsson has three other colleagues, and before taking charge of the team, he was one of the nation's senior economists. Gudmundsson reckons that in the not too distant future, studying games will become a legitimate part of real-world economic forecasting.

But what exactly is it, I wonder, that makes EVE Online such a useful microcosm for economic experimentation? 'Basically we have a contained world where we know all the rules and regulations, we know how they are implemented and we have logs of anything that happens within the world,' Dr Gudmundsson tells me. 'The big problem that economists often have is that they don't have relevant up-to-date data. That problem does not exist in my world. In fact, we have too much data. Even though it's a virtual world, we are dealing with real people. It is another universe, it is another world out there, but it is real people that are playing the game, that are participating in the environment, and by so doing, they are using the experience that they have from real life to make decisions within the game.'

But Eyjolfur Gudmundsson does concede there are some notable economic differences between the real world and his virtual world. For instance, in a virtual world like EVE Online, the notion of unemployment simply doesn't exist; which is a far cry from the reality outside the doctor's own office window in Reykjavik. The global financial crisis of 2008–09 brought the Icelandic economy to its knees and saw many people forced onto the dole queue as a result.

Still, despite the harsh economic realities of life in modern-day Iceland, Eyjolfur Gudmundsson says he's confident that prosperous times lie ahead — at least for those economic tea-leaf readers who've managed to go digital.

'We are just starting to scratch the surface of virtual-world economies in general. We have already worked with a couple of academic institutions on research related to virtual-world economies, and we're hoping to extend that further in the future. And as these virtual worlds are getting bigger and they're getting more popular, I am predicting that the field of studying virtual economies, using our conventional economic knowledge, will actually grow as a discipline within economics,' he says.

So, if you're an economist with a passion for games, you're going to be alright. The rest of us, though, might need to make other arrangements.

Now, I'm going to stay with games in the next chapter, because Icelandic economists aren't the only ones who believe that play is likely to have an increasingly important role in our future lives — with implications that go far beyond entertainment.

CHAPTER 10

GETTING SERIOUS ABOUT FUN AND GAMES

We don't stop playing because we grow old; we grow old because we stop playing.

George Bernard Shaw, British essayist and playwright

Didn't we have a lovely time the day we went to Brighton?

Let me begin this chapter by introducing you to Suzanne Conboy-Hill. She's a bit of a player. Not, I hasten to add, in a derogative corporate raider or stone-faced Texas Hold 'em Poker sort of way, I mean in a nice game-playing kind of sense — where no one gets hurt or loses the money set aside for the children's education on a bad hand and an unconvincing bluff.

Dr Conboy-Hill works in two worlds, a virtual one and the real one. She's a clinical psychologist and a Visiting Research Fellow with the University of Brighton in the UK, and she's also one of a growing number of people fascinated by the potential that fun and games have for serious endeavour, because, as we glimpsed with EVE Online, in the twenty-first century, play is finding a new purpose.

Our attitude towards games has long been a contradictory one: games are great when it comes to children, they can stimulate the imagination and be used for education, but conventional wisdom dictates that adults don't play games — football, the horses, poker, backgammon and nude Twister notwithstanding. Games are strictly for the young, be they kids or youth. There's even that famous quote from the Bible that gets dragged up every now and then to remind us that being a responsible big person is a very serious matter indeed: 'When I was a child, I spoke as a child, I understood as a child, I thought as a child: but when I became a man, I put away childish things.'[44] It's a powerful idea that comes with the authority of the Holy text. But I would just point out — without trying to provoke the wrath of fundamentalist Christians — that intelligent modern people, even pious intelligent modern people, don't take everything in the Bible as gospel.

Exhibit A: 'Woman shall not wear that which pertaineth unto a man, neither shall a man put on a woman's garment: for all that do so are abomination unto the LORD thy God.'

And then there's this very useful tip I found about matters culinary ...

Exhibit B: 'Every beast that parteth the hoof, and cleaveth the cleft into two claws, and cheweth the cud among the beasts, that ye shall eat. Nevertheless these ye shall not eat of them that chew the cud, or of them that divide the cloven hoof; as the camel, and the hare, and the coney: for they chew the cud, but divide not the hoof; therefore they are unclean unto you.'[45]

I'm actually not in the habit of eating much hare, and I'm not even sure what a 'coney' is, but I think you get my point — and it has nothing to do with cross-dressers and camels.

Games, as far as adults are concerned, have long been portrayed as trivial and unworthy. And where we do see value in them, it's purely as entertainment. But what if that's changing?

You could mount an argument, of course, that one of the main attractions of social media platforms like Twitter and Facebook is that they allow for the incorporation of an element of playfulness into our staid work-a-day lives, which is why many of us are on them throughout the day. Even the very names employed by social media tend to give the game away, pardon the pun; 'poking', 'tweeting', 'Facebooking', finding new 'friends', it all sounds much more like mucking about than work, which is no doubt why many companies actually ban their employees from Twitter and Facebook during office hours. But what I'm interested in exploring in this chapter is the appropriation of games technology by individuals and organisations interested in using play to pursue a higher purpose.

There's definitely a buzz in technology, marketing and business circles around the employment of game dynamics as a motivational and organisational tool. But how much of it is real and how much of it is nonsense? Well, the answer is that it's both: there's music and there's madness in the mix. There are those achieving interesting things in the areas of health and education, and there are also those at the very extreme who'd like to fashion the whole world into a sort of giant play pen.

Now, I'm sorely tempted to go with the madness first, but in the interests of rewarding good effort, let's start with the thoroughly sane. Which brings me back to Brighton and Suzanne Conboy-Hill. You see, Dr Conboy-Hill was involved in a pioneering project with both Imperial College London and the Royal Sussex County Hospital, to create a virtual hospital environment using Second Life. Yes, I know, there are lots of game pedants who dispute the fact that Second Life is actually a game, but in this case, I think that's splitting hairs.

Anyway, the aim of their experiment was to see whether an online hospital environment could be used to give patients with intellectual impairment a better understanding of medical procedures and thereby make it easier for them to give 'informed medical consent'. So, twenty people with quite severe learning difficulties were chosen to take part in the test and each in turn was given their own personal avatar.

What was gratifying, says Dr Conboy-Hill, was that all of the subjects very quickly engaged with their avatars and took ownership of them. The first within a couple of minutes. 'We'd set it up so that they got a visual experience that they would recognise, which was the seafront and Brighton Pier, and we established that they knew what that was by asking them, "Where do you think you are?" and "What can you see?" and they would say, "The sea and that pier", "Which pier?" "Oh, it's Brighton Pier." And then we would say, "This person in front of you is pretending to be you." But within a few minutes they would say things like, "I'm running down the seafront", or "I'm going on the pier."'

According to Conboy-Hill, that initial period of play was crucial. 'We didn't want it to feel like an exam. We didn't want it to feel like a test. It's that thing about being able to engage people by giving them something that is enjoyable and fun, and that way, they do something that you want them to do.' And once the virtual excursion to Brighton Pier was out of the way, the patients were then taken on their hospital tour, with avatar doctors and nurses talking them through the environment and explaining the medical procedures the patients required.

Now the Brighton Hospital experiment was exactly that, an experiment. But the results were so promising that further research is being planned and Dr Conboy-Hill believes her virtual-world technique could prove useful for other forms of therapy and medical inquiry. In fact, since starting the study she's already been involved in getting together a number of other bids around different ways of using 3D virtual environments: 'We're also looking at facial disfigurement and something called the "Proteus effect",' she tells me, 'where you behave more confidently if your avatar is attractive, and this transfers back into the real world, which is surprising. You wouldn't think it would. And so we're looking at that in terms of facial disfigurement, to try to see whether having that kind of positive experience makes people feel more confident in the real world.'

Noah Falstein has a label for what Dr Conboy-Hill and her colleagues have created. He calls it a 'serious game' or a 'game for good'. He's been in the game development industry since 1980 and he's the president of a California-based company called The Inspiracy, which specialises in game design and production consulting. Now I've heard those terms used before in different ways, so Falstein seems to me like the perfect person to shed some light on exactly what they mean.

'Serious games are a new enough thing, and a nebulous enough thing, that people are still arguing about definitions,' he says. 'But the one that I find most accurate is "a game or something that uses game techniques and technology for a purpose beyond entertainment". It may well be entertaining. Many of the serious games are fun as well, but its main purpose is not the entertainment, but rather something else; often teaching or some sort of instruction, sometimes research or persuasion.'

One such game that Noah Falstein was actively involved in constructing was called ReMission and it was designed to help teenagers with cancer better understand the importance of keeping to a chemotherapy treatment regimen. 'The idea was that a lot of teens with cancer go off chemotherapy because the pills make them feel sick,' says Falstein. 'So the game essentially showed them what was going on in their body and let them play out scenarios of what's going on with fighting cancer cells and infections.'

Both ReMission and Suzanne Conboy-Hill's Brighton experiment were targeted at very specific groups and so their appeal was intentionally limited. But Noah Falstein talks about other serious games that have what he terms 'crossover value', appealing to both a target group and a broader section of the community at the same time. The two examples he gives are Microsoft's Flight Simulator, which has been popular for years as both a pilot training aid and a game, and Full Spectrum Warrior, which, according to Falstein, was developed in the US as a training tool for the military, but was later released to the public, with only minor changes.

And, says Noah Falstein, crossover value can also work in the other direction. Here he quotes the example of Civilisation, a game, or series of games, initially designed purely for the entertainment market, but which some schools in the United States have recently been using to teach students about history and the evolution of cities.

That crossover effect is of particular interest to Brisbane researcher Daniel Johnson. Johnson is a senior lecturer at the Queensland University of Technology (QUT) in the Bachelor of Games and Entertainment Program, and he focuses on studying the benefits of using games to improve wellbeing. In that respect, Johnson talks about using games as a sort of 'scaffold' for developing a patient's mental strength and building their resilience. And the sorts of games he's talking about are all off the shelf, not purpose built. Says Johnson: 'In some cases you're seeing video games being used in hospitals to help distract from pain and to help people deal with difficult situations. One of the other obvious adaptations are things like Wii games or other physically controlled games — those games that can be used literally for physical rehabilitation.'

And that's exactly what's happening down the road from QUT at Brisbane's Princess Alexandra Hospital, where therapists in the brain injury unit have been using motion-based consoles alongside traditional therapies. One of those involved in that initiative is occupational therapist Erin Griffin. 'Our focus is primarily on the combination of cognitive, physical and perceptual skills required to interact with the Wii. We are also really keen for patients to benefit from the social aspects of playing a video game, particularly a competitive video game in a social context. They often cause a lot of competition and rivalry, which is fantastic for keeping patients motivated, and encouraging patients to continue to attend therapy sessions,' she says. 'It gives the therapists a great opportunity to monitor patients' social interactions and to use the video game as a tool for facilitating improvements.'

And because those who pass through the brain injury unit tend to be younger than other rehab patients, Griffin says, the hospital has found the use of games particularly beneficial: 'Video games are contextually very appropriate for this patient group, and are a lot more motivating than traditional therapy means.'

But younger patients aren't the only ones responding to games therapy. In another part of Brisbane, Robyn McMullin is employed by an aged-care facility as what's called a lifestyle team leader. Her role is to keep residents motivated. And in order to do that, she's also been experimenting with a Nintendo Wii. Now, you couldn't accuse McMullin of taking the easy option, because one of the very first patients she used a games console with, a man named Dennis, had significant disabilities: he was paralysed down one side of his body, was an amputee, and had no power of speech. 'He came here pretty much completely incapacitated, so we got him up into a wheelchair but he was very depressed, couldn't really feel like he could do anything,' recalls McMullin. 'Then we got the Wii and tried him out on different games, and he had the best time. His face lit up, and his whole self changed. He thinks he's the Greg Norman of Wii golf. If anyone comes in and wants to play the Wii with him, he is more than happy to show them how to do it. So his attitude has changed a lot, and he looks forward to doing that one thing that he feels he's capable of doing.'

You can look at these examples in two ways: either as interesting, small-scale initiatives or as the beginning of something new and powerful. Daniel Johnson is convinced we're on the cusp of a type of therapy that will, in the future, be commonplace. 'We're about to make some major advances in terms of realising how to apply video games to improve individual wellbeing, as well as the larger wellbeing of our global community,' says Johnson. 'And I think the sorts of developments we're going to see in the near future will include more and more people realising how they can adapt video game technology to improve the work they're doing; or adapt video games to get solutions to problems that otherwise couldn't be solved.'

A university for the avatar age

Now, I promise I'll get to the madness shortly, but there's still a bit more of the good stuff to get through first, particularly regarding education.

In Europe, researchers from nineteen institutions, including a variety of continental universities, are working to create what they're calling a Euroversity — a full-scale education facility with a virtual campus, that is, a campus that exists only in the online world. The idea is to take that same immersive quality that Suzanne Conboy-Hill found so useful in her Brighton experiment and to apply it to education. But instead of creating a hospital environment in a virtual world, you create an entire university, complete with virtual lecture theatres and an online resource library.

So that's the end goal. Stage one of the project, which commenced with European Union funding in December 2011, is to build a framework for the university's construction and to begin pulling together the knowledge already accumulating across the globe about how to best use virtual worlds for educative purposes.

Another confession: I really like this project, because as out there as it sounds, it's actually based on a proven model for education, one that transformed the Australian outback in the mid to late twentieth century: the School of the Air. From the 1950s, teachers worked with two-way radios to bring children from all over the bush together in a virtual-classroom environment. And it seems to me that building a lecture theatre in a virtual-world environment like Second Life isn't that much different. If anything, it just builds on what the School of the Air started, adding a visual/interactive component to the mix. It's distance education for the twenty-first century.

One of the brains behind the scheme is Luisa Panichi from the University of Hull. Between December 2009 and late 2011, Panichi and other researchers ran a test of the concept focusing specifically on language education. That test was called the Avalon Project and it was supported with funding from the European Commission's Lifelong Learning Program. [46]

'The students and teacher-trainers we brought in under the Avalon Project, went through different phases,' says Panichi. 'We had what we called our Welcome Area, where students would come on the first day of their lessons, and this would usually be a wide space, so people would be free to move around and practise their walking and their movements, and then usually after the Welcome Area, we would then move on to a more specific learning space. Sometimes that would be a replication of a lecture theatre, if we were having a more traditional teacher-centred lesson. But other learning scenarios we created were smaller, cosier environments. Sometimes you could walk into a room or a learning hut, and sometimes we had students sit around a campfire for good discussions.'

But the point is that everything was virtual, including the campfire, and students from various countries interacted with each other, and their teachers, only through their avatars. 'We found it was more creative than video-conferencing,' says Panichi, 'because it was a dynamic environment, and there was movement, and you could manipulate the environment by creating objects, by changing your appearance and by interacting with other people and the environment itself. Video-conferencing often tends to be extremely static; even in terms of looking at the screen, video-conferencing tends to engage you all the time, whereas with virtual worlds you can actually stand back from the computer and rest your eyes. So you're not forced to engage, to be looking at someone constantly through a video screen.'

Still, Panichi freely admits there were difficulties in adapting the virtual environment to the project's educative requirements.

And the biggest problem of all related to lingering perceptions about what is and what is not a proper 'space' for learning. 'First of all, virtual worlds create fear in some people because they're not quite sure what they're getting involved in,' she tells me. 'Also some of the students who were familiar with virtual worlds used for gaming, like World of Warcraft, couldn't quite see how a gaming environment, or a gaming-like environment, could actually be used for educational purposes.' And she adds: 'Unfortunately, there still seems to be a general misconception in the educational community at large that gaming and games are not related to learning. And that's one of the challenges we faced under the project.'

And that misconception is also prevalent in the international development sector. The World Bank's senior education specialist, Bob Hawkins, tells me he faced significant internal bank resistance when he came up with a plan to develop a game for getting young people in Africa to engage with development issues. But he eventually won the argument and the end result was a multi-player online game called Urgent Evoke.

'We very much wanted to have a game that captured the aspects of social networking and collaboration that are growing and continue to grow through Facebook and platforms such as MXit, which is a text-based social network in South Africa and now Kenya,' Hawkins says. 'So we wanted to try to reach students through means in which they are already spending a lot of time — and communicating and engaging with each other. We worked with gamers to develop it, and gaming consultants, but there were a number of challenges since it was so new and not something that is part of the World Bank's normal business. So it was very much an innovation in the way that the bank reached out to young people.'

Urgent Evoke ran for only ten weeks. It had a comic book feel to it and players were set a series of development challenges around issues like poverty, hunger and education. Once a week they were given a specific challenge and then asked to research the issue in their local community, making their findings available to other players using photos, blog posts and/ or videos. And at the end of each challenge or mission, points were awarded for the suggestions received. Pretty solid stuff. The sort of game only a teacher could invent, perhaps.

Hawkins is open about the fact that the project was an experiment and he had no clear idea exactly who it would attract and what type of activity the game might generate. But as it turned out, the results were not quite as expected. Although originally designed for young Africans, a decision was made early in the piece to allow anyone, anywhere in the world to get involved. And provision was also made for people to access the site via mobile phone, in recognition of internet connectivity problems in many parts of Africa. In the end though, only around 8000 young people took part, and only 400 of those were from Africa.

So, without being unnecessarily rude, based on the project's original goals, you'd have to say it was only a modest success. Encouragingly though, it caught the eye of teachers and education organisations and the game is now enjoying a second life as a classroom-based teaching aid.

Now the conviction that both Luisa Panichi and Bob Hawkins share about games having a growing place in education seems borne out by the results of a recent study into children and technology undertaken by the US-based research group Latitude. The organisation quizzed children twelve years and younger from the US, Australia and a variety of other countries about both their current technology usage and the ideas they had for the sorts of technology they'd like to use in the future. The overwhelming majority of children surveyed — eighty-three per cent — said they desired interactive technologies such as 'responsive virtual environments', in other words, game-like environments. And thirty per cent of participants suggested ideas for future technologies that had a gaming dimension.[47]

'Kids are naturally imaginative,' says Latitude's CEO and founder, Steve Mushkin, 'so we expected to see some good material from them, and we did. And we thought that kids could give us a bit of a window into where things might be going. What we're calling the "near present", which is what is right around the bend.'

I've seen research looking at teenagers and how they use technology, what they want from technology, but I haven't seen it in terms of children, particularly around the age group surveyed. Steve Mushkin says one reason for the lack of previous research is that very young children are often looked upon simply as passive recipients of technology, rather than as creative users, or even potential developers of technology.

'Since these were young kids, we contacted them through their parents, had their parents give us some basic information about what their online behaviour was, and what kind of devices they were using, and so on. And then we asked the kids to do something very simple for us, which was to answer the question: "What would you want the computer to do, or the internet to do, that it doesn't do right now?"'

Among the key findings, according to Mushkin, was a desire to blend the physical with the digital; and secondly, a strong response to anthropomorphic applications. That is, applications that have a human quality about them.

'We saw from some of the results that one of the things that many kids do is personalise the computers, the internet, and they do that in a variety of ways. Obviously in terms of the literal physical sense, but also they very much want to be able to speak to, and become "friends" with any computing device that they're dealing with,' says Mushkin. 'They want to be the creators of the next generation of computing, and be able to be the creators of the next generation of games.'

Now, having the desire to create is one thing, but desire without a skills base can simply lead to frustration. In his 2011 book *Program or Be Programmed*, Douglas Rushkoff argued for a back-to-basics approach when it came to computers and education. Society will do itself a great disservice in the future, he tells me in an interview just after the book's release, if we don't once again start teaching the young about the actual nuts and bolts of computing.

'I'm advocating that we raise people with some knowledge of programming,' he says. 'In the same way we think of it as important for kids to know basic math and long division, I think kids should understand the very basics of programming. So that when they operate a computer they don't think of the computer in terms of what it has come packaged with, but they think of the computer as a blank slate. It's just like introducing kids to reading and writing. You know, you show them books, but you also give them blank pieces of paper where they can write their own words. I feel like those few schools that do teach computers, teach kids not really computers, they teach them Microsoft Office, which is great for creating the office worker of the 1990s, but not for creating the people who are going to build the twenty-first century.'

Shakespeare only got it half right — apparently

So games can be used as an effective learning tool and can be built or adapted to help people overcome adversity, but what are the limits? Well, according to Noah Falstein the potential is 'staggering', not just for serious games, but for the possibilities a games-based approach can offer us as individuals and as a society: 'As somebody who's been making games for nearly thirty years, one of the things I'm most excited about is the diversity that we've been seeing just in the last few years. Serious games are one great example of that but I would say mobile games are yet another. It all points to a world where game play — or perhaps interactivity is an even better way of putting it — will become an absolutely essential part of our lives.' And he adds, 'You can't get by without computers and mobile devices and so games are kind of creeping into almost every facet of life.'

Now, that creeping process he describes has already been given a name. It's called 'gamification', a word so devoid of poetry it makes 'crowdsourcing' seem lyrical.

To 'gamify' is essentially the process of turning things that aren't games into games, or introducing a gaming element to an activity. Let me give you an easy to comprehend example: air travel is not a game (it's not even fun these days, but that's another story) however, the customer reward system that many airlines employ, frequent flyer miles, is arguably a game, in that you earn points by travelling and then you cash in those points at various levels for free or discounted air travel or in some cases, even prizes. That's an example of gamifying. And using such game dynamics to get people to buy products is as old as the practice of marketing, but what's new is the idea of trying to insert game dynamics into all aspects of our lives. And that's what gamification is. Gamification is essentially the belief in turning everything into a game.

The first-ever international conference on the subject was only held in San Francisco in January 2011, but within a very short space of time it's begun popping up all over the place as a future trend.

Alright, we've just reached the point where you need to pause, put the book down momentarily, go to the craft box in your storeroom, find some masking tape and wind a couple of lengths firmly around your Fukuyama. Otherwise, it's likely to start fitting.

Shakespeare once wrote: 'All the world's a stage.' But I have a feeling that if Seth Priebatsch, the co-founder of a Boston games company called SCVNGR could somehow transport himself back to Elizabethan England, he'd have the Bard sit down and add the words: '... and a game too!'

Priebatsch is so young he looks like he still belongs in high school, but he's actually a very successful businessman who's already made a small fortune out of the media industry. His company — it's pronounced 'scavenger' — has partnered on various initiatives with both Harvard and the Massachusetts Institute of Technology. He's fond of telling people that he dropped out of Princeton. He seems to mention it in every interview and presentation he gives. And he's given more than a few of them in recent years on the subject of gamification. Priebatsch speaks of a 'game layer on top of the world'; of using gaming dynamics to blur the line between 'digital interactivity and real-world interaction'.

Without mincing words, Seth Priebatsch is a gamification evangelist and as such he confidently and bravely predicts that what he calls the 'decade of social' is now transitioning into the 'decade of games'. Here's how he describes that transformation: 'People have been social networking since we all lived in caves. We just weren't very good at it. Now we've gotten very, very efficient at it. What's happening now is that that framework has been built, that sort of social layer has been created and the next shift that's occurring, the next evolution in the way that we interact with technology is what we think of as the "game layer", where instead of digitising our social connections and trafficking in who we know, and making the web very personal, the game layer actually traffics in individual human motivation. It takes the game mechanics that have been so powerful at motivating billions and billions of hours of action and game play online, and moves those game mechanics into the real world to motivate what we do and where we go.'

English translation: For the past decade or so, social networking has been king. But in this next decade, playing games will become even more important. People won't just want to socialise with others using social media, they'll want those interactions to be more like a game. And, as a result, eventually many of the things that people do in their everyday lives will involve elements of a game.

So, Nirvana for Seth Priebatsch isn't just having everybody in the world playing a game, it's about turning as many activities as possible into some form of rewards-based play. Still, he's not arguing that gaming dynamics could and should be used to solve every single problem we as human beings face. No, that's the line being pushed by Jesse Schell, an assistant professor of Entertainment Technology at Carnegie Mellon University in the United States. Like Seth Priebatsch, Schell doesn't just believe in the idea of gamification, he's out there preaching it far and wide.

'When I talk about the "Gamepocalypse",' he tells me, '[I'm talking about] the moment when every second of your life is involved in a game in some way, where everything that you do during the day from brushing your teeth to eating meals, to choosing how you're going to get to work, ends up being something that somehow gets you points in one of many games that are woven through your life.'

Jesse Schell is also a frequent conference speaker and he's one of those responsible for popularising the notion of gamification. His idea of a coming 'Gamepocalypse' is cute, playful and an attention grabber. But does he really believe that one day, in the not too distant future, gaming dynamics will be a component of every activity we undertake?

'I believe that there's a lot of reasons to think we're heading towards something that is very much like that,' he replies. 'Look at the encroaching number of loyalty systems that are closing in on our lives bit by bit: at the grocery store, you get points for that. When you play normal video games, you get all kinds of point systems that aren't just in the game but are outside the game. There are points when you go to buy your coffee and certainly airline points and so I think we're seeing more and more of these things creep in and getting more and more efficient. A big one people are talking about is Foursquare, you know, the ability to check in at different geographical locations and get points for that; so it certainly is something I think a lot of people are experimenting with.'

Sure, the examples he mentions are real, but they're all pretty low-level, you'd have to say — hardly evidence of a significant trend. But that hasn't stopped the buzz.

Already in this chapter we've had a quote from Shakespeare, now here's something from Isaac Newton: 'For every action, there is an equal and opposite reaction.' And in the case of gamification, much of that reaction is actually coming from within the tent — among the idea's biggest critics are people within the gaming and technology industry itself.

'Why "Gamification" is as stupid as it sounds', read the headline of an article in *The Drum* written by one of the ABC's senior online technology innovators, Sam Doust; while soon after the San Francisco gamification conference the very popular Sydney-based blogger and technology consultant Stilgherrian let fly with a post entitled 'Gamification: Hot, new, unethical?' Stilgherrian wrote: 'If the "rewards" and "status" we seek are about how many times we visit a coffee shop, then as a species we're doomed. The problem with gamification isn't just that it gets users and customers addicted to increase business profits, it also gets the businesses themselves addicted to gamification.'[48]

And that's a view shared by Margaret Robertson, one of the UK's senior and most respected game developers. Robertson acknowledges that games have untapped social potential, but she rejects the popular Priebatsch/Schell vision as too shallow, as a 'snake oil solution' being peddled to gullible companies, government agencies and charities seduced by the possibilities that games have to offer.

In late 2010, she wrote a blog post about gamification entitled 'Can't Play, Won't Play' and in it she stated her desire that gamification should 'Take a long walk off a short pier'. At the core of Robertson's argument is the idea that many of those who talk about applying game dynamics aren't really interested in the complexities of what makes for a successful game. Instead their focus, she argues, is on a simple and potentially exploitative use of trivial prizes: 'It's a problem with suggesting that they're turning these things into games, when all they're really doing is adding systems that allow you to earn points or badges or little signals of reward.

'There's a huge amount of very, very complex and subtle theory out there about how you define a game,' Robertson adds, 'and a useful starting point is to think about, at the very least, games being things that you can win or lose. It's quite an interesting little litmus test if you look at some of the things that people are speaking of as having been gamified and ask whether or not you can in any meaningful way lose them, it's often a quick way to spot something that is claiming to be gamified when it's only been pointified. We know that points and badges are brilliant and work incredibly well, there's a reason why we've been using them for centuries. But I think in the same way that it distracts us from really understanding what's good about adding points to things, it does also distract us from understanding the complexity of building games around things.'

She may be right, but that doesn't mean gamification won't continue to capture attention and converts, particularly in the media and technology spheres. However, Sam Doust is crossing his fingers and living in hope — and also counting on the power of natural selection. Says Doust: 'One of the most exciting early promises of the digital revolution is that good ideas will win over the bad ones. And in this viral, incredibly fast incubation chamber of ideas and information, we can separate the good from the bad much more quickly than ever before. If that's true, gamification will wither and die.'[49]

CHAPTER 11

MAPPERS, TRACKERS, SELF-LOCATORS AND TALKING TYRES

If you have something that you don't want anyone to know, maybe you shouldn't be doing it in the first place.

Eric Schmidt, Executive Chairman and former CEO of Google[50]

Location, location!

I was young once. It's hard to convince myself of that fact sometimes when I look in the mirror, but it's true. And I remember in the early 1990s sitting in front of the television watching live coverage on CNN of American military commander General 'Stormin'' Norman Schwarzkopf introducing some grainy black-and-white footage of a laser-guided missile strike on a building in Iraq. A 'surgical strike' it was called. The idea being that new aiming technologies allowed for almost pinpoint precision when it came to 'taking out' targets.

It was pretty impressive stuff and it was meant to be so. We later found out that Schwarzkopf's claims were largely hyperbole, that while the precision of aerial bombing had improved markedly over the decade-and-a-half since the end of the Vietnam War, in 1991 it was still pretty much a hit-and-miss affair. And worse than that, even if you managed to blow up the correct building, there was no guarantee that the human target you were really after was actually still inside.

Fast forward to the mid 2000s and I'm now sitting in front of a computer screen watching satellite footage of an Israeli air strike. It has that same blurry, slightly surreal quality about it, but this time it's the real deal: an Israeli jet fighter fires a missile at a designated target and within seconds of the command to fire, a leading member of Hamas and several of his colleagues are no more. Blown into tiny fragments.

What doomed the man from Hamas wasn't superior on-the-ground Israeli intelligence, or the skill of the pilot involved in the operation, although they may well have been factors. What ultimately sealed his fate was the mobile phone he was carrying in his pocket. That phone, even though it was probably turned off, was actually the electronic equivalent of a bull's eye, because in order to communicate with a phone tower, mobiles have an ID inside them that identifies their position at any given moment. So for the Israeli military, once they knew they had the correct telephone number, all they had to do was zero in and bombs away. He might as well have painted a great big X on his roof and lots of arrows pointing to it.

And that, of course, is why Osama Bin Laden severed all online and digital connection with the outside world the moment he became the West's public enemy number one. He certainly wasn't using that old video cassette machine in his Pakistani compound because of a nostalgic love for VHS, or a lack of cash.

So the message is: if you carry a phone around in your pocket, or any form of mobile device in your briefcase or bag, you're potentially already on somebody's radar, whether you realise it or not; which is not to say that you're likely to have an Israeli missile punch through the roof of your home any time soon, but just to be on the safe side, I'd try not to do anything that's likely to get Tel Aviv's nose out of joint.

Increasingly our world is one in which location matters, and I'm not just talking about real estate. As we saw in Chapter Six, everything we do in the digital world leaves a trail and the same technology that's now making it easier for us to map our way around the world is also making it easier for other people to map *our* movements.

Naturally I'll try not to go over ground we've already covered. Yes, this chapter is about tracking, but it's also about exhibitionism, voyeurism, narcissism and probably a few other isms I can't quite put my finger on. My argument here is that we're turning into a society of mappers and trackers, even though it's not always obvious to us. And that has both good and bad elements to it, as we'll see. At the very least, it's certainly something we need to be aware of.

Essential to that change has been a shift in our relationship with maps. Paper maps were once our main way of understanding location. Go out and ask people on the street how often they use a map these days and you're likely to encounter a blank stare or a shrug of the shoulders. We don't tend to think about maps anymore. When absolutely necessary we give them to somebody else to read, like instruction manuals. Even the old street directory has fallen out of favour in the world of GPS navigation. But we're actually using maps like never before. We may not necessarily recognise them as maps, but we see them on a regular basis.

'People now are used to having maps pop up on the screen when they do internet searches. People are used to having maps on their iPhones. It's just brought the whole arena of mapping much closer to people. Particularly at a local scale, where mapping is about navigating through cities, through strange places,' says Michael Goodchild from the University of California, Santa Barbara, a prominent name in the cartographic world.

And people are not only using maps more, as Professor Goodchild points out, they're also becoming more involved in the creation of maps — once again, without always necessarily comprehending the fact. Dr Mark Harrower received a traditional training in cartography, but he now works for a private US-based company called Axis Maps. He's on the lecture circuit and he also provides advice to the corporate sector. Harrower says the change that's going on in his industry isn't just about technology, it's also crucially about involvement: 'One of the really exciting things is people have become data-collectors in a way that they never were before. Data used to always be collected by surveyors, or by paid professionals. Now data is collected and shared by just about anyone, including people who have cellphones with cameras and GPS units. They can do things like record whether a bridge has been washed out, take a photo of it, upload it, locate it with their GPS and then share that in real time with the rest of the world.'

Government agencies used to sit at the top of the cartographic totem poll, but the king of maps today is Google — it's the biggest maker of maps in the world. It has Google Earth, Google Maps and Street View and increasingly its maps are used as the basis for the creation of other people's cartographic efforts. So its influence extends far beyond the obvious. There is, of course, nothing wrong or unusual about a private company getting involved in the map business. You could argue, as Google's chief technology advocate Michael Jones does, that it's doing a public good for the world. That it's providing a service that governments in many countries have abandoned. Jones says only around a quarter of all countries have what he considers 'world class' maps and that's something he says his company has a commitment to change. But the company's dominance and at times questionable approach has sometimes caused problems. Earlier in the book, as you'll recall, I mentioned the controversy surrounding Street View, where field staff were discovered to have inappropriately and illegally gathered private information from people's wi-fi-enabled home computers, but there have also been several other occasions where Google has managed to find itself at the centre of an international fracas.

In November 2010, the Secretary-General of the Organisation of American States, Jose Miguel Insulza, was called on to settle a flare-up between Costa Rica and Nicaragua. Costa Rica accused its neighbour of invading sovereign territory after Nicaraguan troops went walkies over their joint border, occupied a contentious area of land near a river, and then raised the Nicaraguan national flag. * 'Costa Rica is seeing its dignity smeared,' the Costa Rican President, Laura Chinchilla, was quoted as saying. In response, the Nicaraguan military immediately blamed the armed incursion on Google, which was then forced to admit that it had made an error in demarcating the border between the two countries. 'This morning, after a discussion with the data supplier for this particular border, we determined that there was indeed an error in the compilation of the source data,' a company spokesperson conceded.[51]

And there was a similar, if not quite as fiery, incident between India and China when all the names in the disputed Indian-governed state of Arunachal Pradesh suddenly turned from Hindi to Mandarin on one of Google's maps.

'I think [these incidents] raise some very important issues,' says Michael Goodchild. 'There's a lot of sensitivity in mapping. Maps are very powerful devices. They've always been recognised as such in foreign policy, and agencies that have traditionally made maps have been very sensitive to this. They've been very careful not to offend national sensibilities when maps are made of other parts of the world. Those sorts of sensitivities don't have the same tradition in companies like Google, that therefore, almost inevitably, find themselves getting into hot water by making mistakes of a diplomatic nature. Within the context of diplomacy, there's nothing new about this, but of course there is within the context of the internet.'

---

* I do feel duty-bound to point out that if it had come to fisticuffs, the smart money would have been on Nicaragua, because while Costa Rica has some defence troops, it has no actual military. President Jose Figueres Ferrer abolished the nation's permanent standing army back in 1948. And it doesn't have much of a police force either — for a country of 4.5 million. In 2011, there were only around 11,000 police officers in the entire country.

But Google's main interest in cartography isn't really about border lines and marking out unexplored regions of the world, its primary focus is on using the location mapping capacity of modern technology to support and enhance its gigantic search engine empire. In fact, Michael Jones thinks so little of the traditional map, that, wherever possible, he even avoids using the very word itself; instead, he talks about maps as 'place browsers'. A piece of jargon that only makes sense if you think about marrying the functions of a traditional map (a document that helps you locate your position) with a web browser (a search engine for finding information). But not just information for its own sake, information, Jones argues, that's specific to a user's immediate needs.

That change — that merging of maps and search engines — is already well underway and only going to get more sophisticated into the future. Mark Harrower has a good example of what I mean: 'For me, a real a-ha moment, was the time when I was using Google Maps on my iPhone, and I typed in "Thai", and it knew that I wanted Thai food and it also knew that I didn't want any Thai restaurant, I wanted to know about Thai restaurants that were geographically close to where I was,' recounts Harrower. 'So the fact that it knows my location, and the fact that it is able to combine the power of the traditional search engine with the power of GIS [Geographic Information Systems] means that you can now do what are being called "location-based services". And location-based services are the most exciting thing that's happened to cartography in a very long time, because when we want to know what's here, we mean here, where we are, typically. So if you have a device that's smart enough to know where you are, you can really ask pretty complex questions in a very simple and quick way, the way I did with the Thai restaurant.'

To my way of thinking, tracking and mapping are two sides of the same coin. Despite justifiable concerns about the way in which companies like Google treat our data, there are obvious tangible benefits in technology that allow ordinary people to tie information to location mapping in the manner just described, and there are other very useful aspects to our ever growing taste for mapping and tracking — many in fact: GPS-enabled devices have assisted in rescue operations and have made things like sailing and bush-walking far safer; tracking bracelets can help keep violent offenders under surveillance and stop them from attempting to get close to their victims; and even being able to target and eliminate insane terrorists has its pluses. But it is also true that modern communications technology is making it harder and harder to move about the world quietly — unnoticed.

British comedian Stephen Fry, who has an enormous international following on Twitter, admits to sometimes being lax when tweeting. 'I was in St Petersburg not long ago and I'm very proud and happy to say that I do have a particularly intense and kindly following in Russia. For some reason the Russians like me very much,' says Fry. 'I was very excited at seeing the cathedral in St Petersburg outside the window of my hotel. And I took a photograph of it — not saying it was outside my hotel, but from the height of it, if you knew St Petersburg, it was pretty obvious I was at that hotel.'

So Fry took his photograph, posted it and then tweeted a link to the post. And that's when he got a surprise: 'I had a shower afterwards and went downstairs, came out into the street and there was a huge crowd of fifteen-year-old Russian girls screaming and waving and carrying things for me, you know, gifts for me and wanting photographs. And it was rather a severe lesson in being a little bit more discreet about those sorts of things.'[52]

The Sydney-based technology analyst Peter Marks tells a similar anecdote about Adam Savage, one of the co-presenters of the hit American television show *Mythbusters*. Savage took a picture of his car, which was parked outside the front of his house, and then posted it online, but because the photo was taken with a GPS-enabled phone, which geotags the pictures it takes, Savage inadvertently revealed the exact location of his house. In other words, latitudinal and longitudinal coordinates were recorded when the photo was snapped and they were then automatically embedded into the photograph's digital code.

'You've got to be careful, because it's easy, even though the software does the right thing and operating systems like Android from Google, and IOS from Apple, specifically ask you, and warn you, that you are enabling location-based services, it's very easy to turn them on, and then they're just on from then on,' cautions Marks. 'So there's a false sense of security that comes from just using these gadgets, pulling them out of the pocket and putting them away again and forgetting.'

Sound advice, but then we shouldn't forget that the benefits derived from location-based services only happen because people are willing to use GPS-enabled phones and cameras to let themselves be tracked. That's the trade-off. Google Maps, for instance, needs to know where you are in order to tell you which Thai restaurant is closest.

Now, while some of us still cling to the fast perishing shreds of our privacy, there are many other people who just don't care. No, that's not right. It's not that they can't be bothered to protect themselves from being tracked, it's that they find the very act of tracking, and being tracked, both advantageous and fun, as difficult as that may be for some of us to understand.

Australian legal academic Peter Black is one of those who might fondly be described as a Foursquare tragic. Foursquare is a social enabler, it's perhaps the most well known and popular social tracking platform of recent times, and it works like this: when you join the service you install an application onto your smart phone, and the idea is that whenever you arrive somewhere, say a coffee shop or a book store, you register where you are and then in return you get information telling you about other Foursquare users in the same location or vicinity. It's then up to you to make contact, should you wish to.

From my experience, many people who use Foursquare also like to link it to their Twitter and Facebook accounts so that even their friends and followers who aren't on Foursquare get regular notification of their movements. Peter Black is one such person. On any given day it's easy to find him — he's constantly telegraphing his whereabouts. So, as you can imagine, it wasn't all that difficult to organise a face-to-face meeting.

'I guess it's so other people can see where I am, and if they're in the same area, they can potentially meet up with me,' he says over coffee. We'd been following each other on Twitter for some time, but we'd never met in person. So our coffee-shop sojourn gave me the perfect chance to get an insight into why someone who's smart, well educated and apparently well adjusted, would want to spend their days digitally tagging and publishing their every move. 'It's actually a record for myself as to where I've been as I move around Brisbane, where I live, other cities in Australia, and around the world. I suppose I'm a little bit cautious, in the sense that I don't ever give out my apartment number or my office number, but that's about the extent of it. So where I live and where I work and where I'm having coffee, or where I'm seeing a movie, that's all publicly available for anyone who wants to stalk me, to stalk me,' he says with a slightly disconcerting smile.

Now, everything but your apartment and office number doesn't sound like much of a safeguard to me, but then I have to confess that I'm a bit of a nervous type, and I'm also a natural-born pessimist, as I think I've already mentioned, so I'm always looking for the bad side in things.

Sipping his coffee, but sensing my reservations about the whole practice, Black smiles again and makes a small concession: 'I probably can't argue that it's a little bit strange,' he says, 'but I suppose I see that the benefits outweigh whatever the potential detriment may be. It works because other people will see when I've checked in and if they're in that same area, they will then either send me a tweet or a text message or a phone call and say, "Hey, I see you're in the same area, would you like to catch up for a coffee, or come around for a drink?" And you'd be surprised how regularly that actually happens, that someone is in your neighbourhood, or you're in their neighbourhood. I haven't seen a downside at all yet. I've only seen positive things about geotagging my location.'

So, the primary benefit you get by using a location-centric service like Foursquare is social, but there are also a variety of gimmicks and motivational devices to be had. Explains Peter Marks: 'There are advantages to giving up your location, and products like Foursquare leverage this. You can find out what's nearby, so if you've got a few minutes to spend, is there a nearby coffee shop? Of course, other people from the crowd have provided information and they may make recommendations about local restaurants or cafes. Sometimes there are other benefits. Shops will have what's effectively an electronic version of a loyalty card. You know how you get a little stamp every time you go to a coffee shop, and you'll get a free coffee after number ten or something. Well they're starting to do that [digitally], and in the US they have a very popular voucher system where you get a discount, or you get something for free, if you're a regular visitor. In Foursquare, you eventually become "the mayor", the person who's there the most, and you get a little crown.'

Marketers and advertisers call the sorts of benefits Foursquare offers 'geosocial' services. Which sounds a lot more appealing than geotagging or geolocating, doesn't it? And a lot less creepy. Now, I know for a fact that Peter Black has more than a few 'mayoralties'. How do I know that? Well, because he's forever tweeting about it, of course.

OK, let's now figuratively put Peter Black into the basket marked Happy and Contented and move on to Sydney-based

Neerav Bhatt for another perspective on the geolocation trend. Bhatt is a professional blogger and freelance journalist and, like Peter Black, he's a big user of social media. But he's much more cautious and undecided about the whole phenomenon: 'Usually I say where I've been. You know, that I've just been somewhere five minutes after I've left,' he explains, detailing the precautions he takes. 'It helps you know where you are. Which can be handy if, like me, you get lost easily. Then again, it helps the companies that provide those services tell where you are — at this stage in aggregate more than personally, but who knows how they'll get in the future. I don't know if you've ever watched *Minority Report*, but I just heard the other day of a marketer who said, "We're really close to that *Minority Report* future where a person walks past a billboard, the billboard knows who they are, where they are, and shows them something that's specifically targeted to them." I find that kind of world a big worry.'

And it doesn't help to ease one's concerns when you recall some of the things Google's Eric Schmidt has said over the past few years. Like the quote I used to open this chapter: 'If you have something that you don't want anyone to know, maybe you shouldn't be doing it in the first place.'

Or this little gem: 'The Google policy on a lot of things is to get right up to the creepy line and not cross it.' Or even the wonderfully reassuring statement: 'We know where you are. We know where you've been. We can more or less know what you're thinking about.'

Not crossing the 'creepy line'? Of course not! How could you think such a thing?

But let's not be too hard on Schmidt. I mean, there's a whole lot of creepy going on if research by the East Carolina University in the United States is anything to go by. They questioned 804 undergraduate students about their attitudes towards social tracking and found that five per cent of male respondents admitted to using a GPS-enabled device to track their partner, while three per cent claimed to have, at some stage, hidden a camera in their partner's room to monitor her activities.

But don't get the impression it was all one way, because the women surveyed weren't without sin either, with more than a third admitting to secretly checking their partner's email, and almost sixty per cent admitting to monitoring their boyfriend's Facebook account.[53]

With friends like that who needs to go stalking on Foursquare?

But I digress. Let's go back to Sydney and to Neerav Bhatt and a question about whether his twenty-something friends share his niggling concerns about GPS-enabled devices. 'Some of them do,' he responds. 'In the inner-city technology/ marketing crowd, there are a lot of people who just use all of them, and play with all the technologies to learn how they work. And I've used most of them myself. But a few people are a bit unsure about how wise it is to always tell people where you are. For example, there was one person I'd talked with on Twitter for quite a while. I didn't exactly know where he worked and I wanted to say, "Hi, let's meet for a coffee and a chat." I found that he updated his Google Latitude coordinates quite often, so I was in the city one day, I checked, and it said that he was at these particular coordinates on this particular street, and so I tweeted him to say "Are you here? Can we chat?" And he was a bit surprised because he didn't realise anyone could tell to that granular level exactly where he was.'

And echoing Peter Marks's words, Neerav adds: 'It doesn't have to be a conscious choice on your part; these days so many devices geotag location into updates or even photos. I was at a press event and one of my friends took a picture of me using that particular technology so I could use it in a review. I uploaded it to Flickr, and I saw he must have left the GPS on because Flickr showed exactly which building and in which street that photo was taken.'

The Devil is in the detail — and now Beelzebub knows where you live!

Please Rob Me is both an invitation and a caution. It also happens to be the name of a Dutch website set up by the youthfully named Boy van Amstel.

As we've seen, both Neerav Bhatt and Peter Black are selective of the information they communicate — to different degrees and in different ways — but there are a lot of other people who aren't. At least that's Boy van Amstel's experience. The Amsterdam-based multi-media programmer set up the Please Rob Me website with a colleague after he and his friend became alarmed at just how much information people were publicly communicating online, not just about where they were, but more importantly, where they were not.

'First we noticed people mentioning they were going to their jobs, which you would expect, and what their favourite lunch locations were. But at some point, we also started noticing people sharing their own home locations, or those of their friends and relatives. And we thought, "Well, maybe this isn't information people really want to share", or they're not aware who can actually read it,' says van Amstel. 'So we made this very provocative way of letting them know, and that's what Please Rob Me has become.'

On the website, van Amstel began posting examples of some of the really stupid correspondence he came across where people had left themselves and their security wide open. The examples came from simply trawling social media platforms like Twitter and Foursquare.

'It's a pretty wide range of information people are sharing,' he tells me. 'The most dangerous? It depends on what you think is dangerous, but showing your own home location is probably not very wise. You'd probably not stand up in a full Metro station and scream your home address. But also there's people mentioning that they're going to a faraway holiday location, that kind of stuff.'

Like Neerav Bhatt, Boy van Amstel's concerns aren't born out of a dislike of social media technology, or even a failure to understand it. In fact, when I spoke to van Amstel he was at pains to stress the fact that he wasn't 'anti-sharing', only anti-*over*sharing: 'As a product developer I really like the concept of location sharing. It has a lot of potential and there's a lot you can do with location information. But what it seems all about right now is sharing your own location without getting anything substantial in return for it. You're just sharing your location, you're getting a badge or whatever. I'd like the idea a lot more if you're sharing your location to get something from it. For instance, you're at the supermarket and they're letting you know what the latest offers are, that kind of stuff. But I think a lot of messages on Twitter and stuff, it's probably a lot of narcissism that's going on. People just letting everybody know where they are just because they can and because they think other people think it's interesting.'

Now, one person's narcissism is another person's personal genomics.

That wasn't very clear was it?

Let me try that again ... one person's narcissism is another person's medical biometrics ...

Alright, let's forget that. Instead, let me tell you about Gary Wolf. He's the co-founder of Quantified Self, which is a blog and also a sort of coordinating body for people involved in the practice of 'self-tracking'. Not to be confused with self-locating, the sort of thing indulged in by the likes of Peter Black. Established in 2007, Quantified Self is now at the heart of a growing movement of people using all manner of tools to self-analyse and to 'quantify' aspects of their life; to gather the genomics and biometrics I was talking about — medical data.

I wouldn't ordinarily want to pass judgement on the way people live their lives, but I have to say that the self-trackers seem to me to be at the slightly weird, verging on fanatical, side of the mapping and tracking equation. They even talk in a strange way. Wolf's blog speaks of adding a 'computational dimension to ordinary existence'.

A lot of self-tracking focuses on health-related issues, and while Wolf says he recognises the danger of self-diagnosis and obsession — which was obviously the substance of my first questions to him — he believes that medical self-tracking is a positive thing and will one day be commonplace. 'We've seen an explosion of people using numbers for insight into their own situation, their own state of mind, their physical state, physical condition,' Wolf says passionately. 'I think it came more or less out of fitness, where there's a real benefit for tracking. But it has spread to many, many other dimensions of people's lives. I think the people in health are sort of excited about it because managing health is such a complex thing, and we know that data's really valuable in clinical trials and things like that. People are starting to try to find out whether you can use some of the same methods and techniques on individuals and on yourself.'

So how detailed is the level of medical self-tracking that's currently taking place? And who exactly is likely to want to self-track?

Wolf admits it's probably still a minority pursuit. 'These are people who don't necessarily match the mainstream profile,' he concedes, telling me nothing I couldn't have guessed for myself. 'All of us are highly interested in self-tracking as a phenomenon, and so these are people who tend to go much further than ordinary people go. But there's a lot to be learned from sharing experiments and seeing what comes of them, and we've seen some incredible gains,' he says.

But exactly what sorts of things are people tracking about themselves?

'We've seen people who have tracked their sleep, for instance, in really ingenious ways. You know typically the normal way you get information about your sleep is to go into a sleep lab and sleep there, wired up to a bunch of devices, and that's a very poor substitute for finding out about your sleep in its natural environment. Well, we've seen people hook up really amazing instruments to find out what happens when they're not conscious of what's happening. We've seen people who track everything they've done. We've had a guy who showed us a project where he tracked virtually all of the things he thought about for more than ten years. We've seen people do very interesting experiments with nutrition and their diet. A very wide range of things, and some of them just really make your jaw drop.'

And leaving aside whether it's actually healthy for people to be analysing themselves to that extent, Gary Wolf says a big part of the reason why the self-tracking movement is growing is because modern technology is making it much easier to feed people's desire to quantify their own lives: 'It's not necessarily the easiest thing to do. A lot of the people who get very, very into it are people who are willing to suffer some of the inconveniences, because they're very interested in learning about it for its own sake. But I do think some of those lessons are going to apply very, very widely. Nike made a little device that you can put in your shoe, and it tracks how you run. More than 2 million people have used that Nike Plus System, as they call it, to track their running. And, you know, little devices they call "accelerometers", which measure changes in velocity, they measure movement, manufacturers can get them for under one dollar a piece and put them into a little device that looks like a credit card and you put it in your wallet and it keeps track of your movements. These tools were simply not available five years ago, much less twenty years ago.'

The walls have ears — and so too do the footpaths, street lights and stairways

Now the sheer availability and relatively cheap cost of censors and other quantifying devices have also led to an explosion of smart technology in our homes, workplaces and cities. I have a friend who works in an office that has motion sensor lights, they come on when they sense movement in a room and go off when the room is empty. A sensible way to save electricity you might think, although she tells me it's not so good if you're a particularly thoughtful person who ends up working back late; on those occasions spending a little too long in quiet contemplation can suddenly find you sitting in complete darkness.

Increasingly, engineers and urban planners are envisioning a world in which sensors of one variety or another are built into the very fabric of our urban spaces — not just turning things on and off, but measuring the overall health and vital signs of our built environment, our buildings and cities. And also, it has to be said, getting the measure of us.

Adam Greenfield sees the city of the twenty-first century as a place that monitors and reads its inhabitants; that tracks and quantifies them. Now we all know about the growth in the deployment of closed-circuit cameras. These days big cities like London have more street cameras than trees. And there are some other obvious examples to mention: censors that turn on our taps or the hand-dryers in public lavatories, or register when you've crossed a toll station on a bridge, for instance. But Greenfield talks about something far more subtle and pervasive. He talks about the age of 'ubiquitous computing'.

A former executive at Nokia, he's now the managing director of a New York-based design practice called Urbanscale that specialises in urban design and technology. Ubiquitous computing isn't a term he's invented, it's a phrase that's popular in technology and computing circles and, like most monikers relating to the tech field, it's suitably vague and elastic; it's actually as much a goal as it is a label. It refers to a period when computers, censors and monitors are located in so many objects and places that they are literally everywhere — ubiquitous. And it's not as futuristic as it seems. Just think about your car and your washing machine and your television, they all have little mini computers of one form or another inside them. In late 2011, technicians at Nokia's research lab in Tampere, Finland turned a large slab of ice into an interactive touchscreen display in order to demonstrate the fact that any surface can now be made into a computer interface. And they called their ice creation Ubice, short for ubiquitous ice.

I specifically wanted to speak to Greenfield about his interpretation of the modern city because, unlike so many of those who talk about ubiquitous computing, he has a balanced view of its potential.

That mass of computers, sensors and monitors slowly infiltrating our city structures, are generating all sorts of data about our movements, our habits, our likes and our dislikes, he says. And he cautions that both as individuals and as communities, it's time to start understanding that the urban structures around us are no longer passive, and recognise that the scale of that development is going to be massive. 'When you walk over a stretch of sidewalk that has embedded censor grids in it, and your presence is tabulated, and possibly even your identity is accounted for, you have no way of knowing that that's even happening. So we've multiplied by orders of magnitude the numbers of people who are exposed to these technical systems, and yet they're surreptitious, they're minuscule. You don't even know you're engaging them.'

But the reason for greater public awareness, he maintains, isn't about trying to restrict technology's spread, because censors are neither good nor bad — they're neutral — it's about ensuring appropriate oversight of how they're being used and for what purposes. 'It's very, very hard to be appropriately critical and to make good decisions about things either as individuals or as societies when you don't understand their implications and when you don't understand their method of operation and how different systems connect to one another, and how they create their effects,' Greenfield says. 'My argument would be that we need to become much more savvy as individuals, to welcome this particular system into our life, or not. How do we go about designing these systems in such a way that they're respectful of our prerogatives, our prerogatives of privacy, our prerogatives of autonomy, respectful of us as human beings?'

And a significant part of that reassessment, according to Adam Greenfield, involves not just rethinking, but renegotiating the way we interact with our urban environment: 'We need to start thinking of ourselves as potential generators of usable, actionable data in most spheres of our life, certainly in the public sphere. As we move through public space, I think we have to be conscious of the fact that there is at least the potential from here on forward that the environment is alive, that the environment recognises our presence, it senses our presence, it might even, as I said, sense our identity, and that's potent, and it's dangerous and it's valuable at the same time.'

What I find refreshing about Greenfield's argument is that it's made by someone within the industry, someone you might expect in normal circumstances to be blindly talking up the benefits of ubiquitous computing, not cautioning us about its development. Whether or not the environment he describes will come to pass is hard to say. It seems to me that a significant limiting factor in the future could be the cost of production. Censors and computers are incredibly cheap to produce right now, and that encourages their widespread usage, but if we keep over-consuming and energy and material costs eventually start to skyrocket, then the situation could change quickly and significantly.

There's also, of course, the possibility of a public backlash, but given the way in which people have acquiesced to the widespread deployment of security cameras in public spaces, that seems highly unlikely.

So, if things continue as they are and the age of ubiquitous computing becomes a reality, what then? Well the next stage after that, according to hopeful technologists, is to make all of those devices not just readable, but also able to communicate with each other. And that concept also has a label. It's called the 'Internet of Things'.

I say concept, but NICTA's Dr David Skellern says it's more than just a futuristic vision, it's already a work in progress. 'We're increasingly seeing that objects, everyday things we buy, are now smart. You know your mobile phone's extremely smart, a lot of appliances that you buy, white goods and so on, have computers in them; certain clever lighting systems have computers in them — many, many things around your house. Lots of cars, of course, even the low-end cars now have ten to twenty computers in them. And all of these computers are able to provide lots of information and, moreover, we're moving into the situation where some of these things can actually be controlled.' At the 2011 Frankfurt Motor Show, Volkswagen unveiled a concept car called Sharan, which could reverse park itself using a series of sensors coordinated by an onboard computer. And crucially, the signal telling the car to start its engine and perform the manoeuvre came from somebody using a smart phone.

So the world Skellern sees ahead of us is one where almost every physical item, from lampposts to tyres to toothbrushes, not only have some form of low-cost electronic tagging device built into them, but connectivity with the web.

And what would be the benefit of that? Well the example I've often heard quoted goes like this: your car tyre, which is equipped with a sensor, sends a message to the local mechanic's computer when its tread wears down to a certain level. The communication it transmits tells the computer that it needs to be replaced, and then that computer, in turn, sends its own communication to the local tyre supplier ordering a replacement. It also automatically books your car in for a refit and then sends your smart phone a text to tell you the time and location of your appointment — all without you (the vehicle's owner), or any other human for that matter, needing to be directly involved.

It's not hard to see the seductive nature of such a world, but would the benefits outweigh the costs? For David Skellern the answer is an unambiguous yes. But there are the doubters. Brian Cute, the vice-president of discovery services for the internet infrastructure company Afilias, isn't convinced it will all work out the way Dr Skellern and others envision. While Cute confirms there is a great deal of interest in the concept from both industry and government, he says the sort of object identification system that would be needed to make it all a reality is still a long way off.

'Having been in the communications and internet industry for about twelve years now, whenever I hear the phrase "the next big thing", I always take that with a grain of salt. There's no doubt that we're moving and evolving towards object identification, that we're seeing implementations of track and trace in particular industries, but we're still very much in the early stages of adoption,' he says. 'The European Union has definitely taken a lead position in trying to understand what the implications of the Internet of Things are going to be for consumers, for businesses, for the market. They have been very active in developing forward-looking policy frameworks because when the Internet of Things does become a reality, you will have active sensors in many environments in data collection where you didn't before. Issues such as privacy, issues such as security, even network architecture issues, are going to become very important, and governments have a unique interest in making sure that those issues are addressed.'

And privacy was indeed a central issue discussed at a 2009 conference on the Internet of Things organised by the European Union. Still, Brian Cute believes the EU and other bodies need to be careful not to overreact, not to become too guarded against change. The Internet of Things is going to evolve in stages, he says.

'We're not going to wake up tomorrow and be surrounded by sensors. You'll see it in the supermarket. There'll be tagged shelves and tagged products. And I think once we get to that next stage, then the consumer being comfortable with that sort of interaction, the notion of having RFID [radio frequency identification chip] in your fridge at home doesn't become such a cold, distant, threatening type of scenario. So I think as a matter of stages, consumer attitudes will evolve,' says Cute.

OK, time for yet another personal confession. It's entirely possible that I'm paranoid, but the idea of the objects in my house talking to each other (behind my back) doesn't personally thrill me at all. Imagine if my fridge, my oven and my cutting board suddenly got together and started ordering things from the supermarket that I actually don't care to eat. What if they did it to spite me?

And I'm not sure I want to have a two-way relationship with my toothbrush either. I might be swimming against the tide, I know, but wanting to communicate with inanimate objects seems ... well, a little odd. And that's not meant to reflect in any way on Dr Andy Hudson-Smith from the Centre for Advanced Spatial Analysis at University College, London, who I know for a fact likes to talk to buildings. Let me qualify that: he likes to converse with them, not in a slightly strange Prince Charles chatting with trees kind of way, but through a system of electronic tagging that he's devised, and which he hopes will allow people to better understand the history and uniqueness of their immediate urban environment.

In fact, he's been busy darting across London putting little digital tags on buildings and other pieces of architecture in order to record 'place, space and time'. What's more, he's been having fun while doing it. And between you and me, I don't mind a bit of madness as long as it's enjoyable. 'I really like the science that we've been able to make buildings talk, so these little tags talk to our website which is Tales of Things and there's an iPhone app, an Android app, and if you point your phone up at these little tags, the architecture will talk back,' he tells me.

And what those tags then give you, according to Hudson-Smith, is a history of that particular building. But — and here's the really inventive bit — because the tags are read/write, as soon as you read one, it thinks you own the object you've just scanned, so you can then add your own message for other people to read later. 'It's sort of like a mix between Facebook, Foursquare, the *Antiques Road Show* and eBay. An interesting little mix,' Hudson-Smith says dryly.

Over time each tagged structure develops its own historic story that's accessible to passersby: 'How it works is that you point the phone at the app and you can either type in text or you can record movie clips, and that will always live with that place and that tag, and the only way it can ever be played back is if you're in the actual location.'

But Dr Hudson-Smith and his colleagues haven't only confined their activities to London, or to history for that matter. 'We've just turned on 4200 transport links in Norway,' he tells me, 'and they've got little QR codes, and the nice thing about that is that you can read the QR code, it will tell you how long you've got to wait for your next bus, and it allows you to write back your thoughts. And it's fascinating to see bus stops tweeting, because every time there's a tag there, the architecture — the place — can actually tweet back.'

But is there, I wonder, a benefit other than just the fun of it all, bus stop information aside? 'Yes, I definitely think there is,' Hudson-Smith replies, a little indignantly. 'We walk to places now, and we don't think of their past, whereas from now on, every bit of architecture, every place, every space, can record memories and record thoughts. So, whereas it's very new now, in fifty years' time there'll be an amazing history that we can just play back. It would be really nice just to walk around either St Paul's or your local church, or your local library, and see who used it twenty years ago, to see them actually talking about the place.'

And, no doubt, to also find out who was the Foursquare 'mayor' of St Paul's way back when.

PART THREE

IS IT JUST ME, OR IS EVERYTHING GETTING A LITTLE ODD?

In which we study the role of science fiction as a predictive tool; learn about two real-life sci-fi inspired projects — one of which is mad and the other even madder; and then, finally, explore the quasi-religious nature of our relationship with technology.

CHAPTER 12

THERE'S A KLINGON ON MY DESK

There are known knowns; there are things we know we know.
We also know there are known unknowns; that is to say,
we know there are some things we do not know. But there
are also unknown unknowns — the ones we don't know
we don't know.

Donald Rumsfeld, former US Secretary of Defense

A warrant to think big

Dr Kevin Grazier is sitting in an open-plan office in the
Jet Propulsion Laboratory at the US National Aeronautical
Space Agency. He's a planetary scientist and he's been
working on the Cassini mission to Saturn. He's on the phone.
He's talking to someone on the other side of the world. And
that someone happens to be me. We've been chatting for
twenty minutes or so about the role science fiction plays in
influencing and inspiring future scientific endeavour — *real*
science, that is.

I've already gauged that he's clearly a big fan of sci-fi, a
really, really big fan. But I can't help wondering how many of
his colleagues are as well. I mean, are all boffins interested in
the genre or is that just a fiction in itself?

'If I stood up right now,' he replies, 'I'm at work, I'm at
NASA. If I stood up and looked around the room, you would
be astounded how many sci-fi posters and action figures are

in direct line of sight,' he says. 'Personally, right now, I am looking at a model of a Klingon Bird of Prey.'*

Science and science fiction have a long symbiotic relationship. In this chapter I want to tease out some of the characteristics of that association and the value sci-fi has in helping us to imagine the future; and also, in some instances, to shape it. After that, I want to highlight two of the many real-life science projects that have clear sci-fi DNA; initiatives that are currently being planned, plotted and worked on by scientists in various parts of the world. One of them is barking mad and probably has very little chance of coming to fruition any time soon; and the other is also an insane idea, but one that's so crazy it clearly has every chance of being realised in the not too distant future, particularly if you take my Morning Panic Principle as a guide.

So, having hopefully created a little anticipation, let me push on.

Sci-fi is future focused. Yes, there is a popular and growing stream that draws some of its inspiration and content from the past: think of Matt Smith's *Doctor Who* whizzing back to Blitz-era London to aid a befuddled Winston Churchill, or even the capes and monk-like garments worn by various characters in the *Star Wars* series; there's also what's called Steampunk, which has a heavy emphasis on Victorian-era machinery and industrial design. But what I think separates sci-fi from technological fantasy — like the 1999 film *Wild Wild West*, starring Will Smith and Kenneth Branagh — is that science fiction is about the potential of what lies ahead, what might be.

Science fiction is a way of thinking and communicating about Donald Rumsfeld's 'known unknowns' and even 'unknown unknowns' in a way that doesn't get you laughed out of class. It's fiction, right? It's made up. It's entertainment.

---

* Don't feel bad if you didn't get the reference, I had to look it up myself. The Klingons were the baddies in *Star Trek*. The ones who looked like they had lobsters stuck to their foreheads. *Bird of Prey* was the name of the specific type of spacecraft they flew.

What's the harm? And if it proves prescient — well, all the better. So those who play at sci-fi have the freedom to imagine ideas and concepts, and to inspire others to create and develop future ways of doing things. Says Kevin Grazier: 'The engineers who designed the flip-open cellphone have come clean and admitted their motivator was the *Star Trek* communicator. And how many scientists and engineers, irrespective of discipline, went into their field because of an interest in space or science fiction? I guarantee it's a lot.' *

Including the good doctor himself, of course.

I don't mean to suggest that sci-fi is just a safe way of speculating about the future, because I think it's much more than that: it gives creative people a warrant to think big. Within the genre, anything is possible. And according to writer Robert J Sawyer, who's also an occasional advisor to NASA, what makes it liberating is the fact that things don't need to be automatically verifiable: 'We're not beholden to skittish funding bodies and so are free to speculate about the full range of impacts that new technologies might have — not just the upsides but the downsides, too. And we always look at human impact rather than couching research in vague, non-threatening terms.' [54]

Now NASA isn't the only organisation that regularly uses science fiction writers to help with its forward thinking, or as a sounding board for ideas. The giant US technology company Intel uses them as a tool for consumer trend spotting. In 2010, the company trialled an initiative called the Morrow Project. Essentially they got four well-known writers, including Douglas Rushkoff, and commissioned each of them to produce a new piece of sci-fi. The brief was to fashion a story incorporating Intel's products, in order to help give the company 'a way of

---

* In a 2011 patent dispute, Samsung reportedly tried to argue that Apple had no right to a patent over the general appearance of the iPad because, said Samsung's lawyers, Apple's tablet computer was clearly similar to a device used by characters in the film *2001: A Space Odyssey*.

envisioning how people could use our technologies', says Intel's Brian David Johnson.

And it seems, even in the darkest corners of the US military industrial complex, sci-fi is also highly prized. The American journalist and writer Michael Belfiore is one of the few outsiders ever given exclusive access to scientists at DARPA, the secretive research and development arm of the US Department of Defense. He subsequently produced a book about the organisation called *The Department of Mad Scientists*. Belfiore described for me their unique way of assessing project ideas: 'It has to meet the definition of what they call "DARPA hard",' he says. 'In other words, something so outrageous that no one is going to attempt it except for them. And in fact, if a project doesn't have a fairly high chance of failure — not success, but failure — then chances are they won't take it on.

'There's one program manager I talked to and he was quite upfront with me about the fact that he developed some of his ideas for programs from reading science fiction. In fact, he would convene little mini conventions of science fiction writers, fly them out to Washington and sit down with them and have brainstorming sessions so that then they could come up with new ideas that they could farm out to their laboratories and workshops around the country.'

So some science fiction writers, it seems, have found a second job as science consultants. And there's even an organisation, a US-based think-tank, dedicated to furthering that role. It's called SIGMA and it was set up by Dr Arlan Andrews, a sci-fi creator who was once a member of the science office at the White House, the OSTP.

SIGMA's website describes its mission in this way: 'SIGMA is a non-profit organization dedicated to improving the understanding of the future and the long-term consequences of government actions. As the future is the common ground for science fiction writers, so SIGMA is willing to share its knowledge of this unknown territory for the good of the nation.'[55] And on the same website Dr Andrews personally declares: 'I formed SIGMA because I had heard more original and appropriate futurism on panels at any given science fiction convention than in all the forecasting meetings I ever attended while in DC.'

Annalee Newitz, who runs a very popular and influential sci-fi blog out of San Francisco called i09, points out that references to science fiction regularly pop up in everything from the names of genes to the names of computer programs. 'A great example is the Google Android phone,' she says. 'When Android was being developed, a little sort of red Cylon eye would move across the screen when you booted up your phone.'

The Cylons were androids in the *Battlestar Galactica* series, which, coincidentally, Kevin Grazier worked on as a scientific advisor. And even the name itself, Android, is a sci-fi reference, of course. Newitz, I discovered, has a very different take on the value of science fiction and its role. Sure, it's entertainment, she says, and a means of refining product design too, but she also sees it as a 'cultural test bed'. She maintains that the narrative aspect of sci-fi is an important tool for enabling society to adapt to technological advances. And one of the ways that we begin that process of transforming, she says, is by telling stories about what we'd like to see happen in the future: 'Science fiction becomes a thought experiment for as many people as can share those stories.'

And the stories that are told aren't always pleasant ones, Newitz is quick to remind me. 'There are movies and books and comic books that deal with the horrible outcome of any number of different kinds of technologies,' she explains, 'and right now, of course, biotechnology has become a very terrifying factor and you see dozens of zombie stories, which are basically about runaway disease, caused by some pharmaceutical industry shenanigans or caused by experiments in the lab. And so I think that we express both our anxieties, but also our hopes, in this fictional test bed.'

It's a compelling argument and 12,000 kilometres away across the Pacific in Sydney, Mike Jones has been thinking along similar lines. Jones runs courses in Screen Studies at the Australian Film, Television and Radio School (AFTRS). Over the decades the popularity of sci-fi has waxed and waned, but based on the number of Hollywood releases in recent years, the genre is currently on a high. Jones has no doubt that science fiction is resurgent because he says it offers something that other forms of storytelling don't.

'Science fiction gives us a chance to test out our morality, test out our ethics, and test out the way we relate and make sense of the science in our world. And when we live in a world that is science saturated, in our daily lives, in the way we communicate and use devices, in the way we think about how we engage with the world, whether it be medicines or genetically modified foods or the environment or communications technology, when we live in a society like that, it is crucial that we are testing the ideas that those things represent. And when we fail to test them, I fear we run foul of them. It's a community service. Science fiction is a community service.'

Androids are humans too

A community service and also an aid to civil libertarians, at least in the United States, that is. The pace of technological change is now so great that, believe it or not, the American Civil Liberties Union (ACLU) has turned to science fiction to help it keep pace with developments.

'It's an implicit part of how we think about things,' says Jay Stanley, a senior policy analyst for the ACLU's Speech, Privacy, and Technology Project. And he says he's been repeatedly surprised during his ten years with the ACLU at just how quickly technology has moved from science fiction to fact: 'We've seen technologies emerge — such as body scanners, biometrics and radio frequency or RFID chips — and we've seen them go from being sexy media issues that really are very future-looking and theoretical, to very real civil liberties issues, to technologies that are being used by the authorities.'

And he argues that from the classic science fiction of the 1950s right through to modern times with films like *Gattaca* and *Minority Report*, sci-fi has often been about the story of an individual struggling against the larger social order. Although I think you could argue it goes back even further than that. Certainly that struggle was at the heart of Fritz Lang's silent film *Metropolis* in the late 1920s.

Jay Stanley first put forward his thoughts on the importance of using sci-fi for issue identification in a 2002 paper for the ACLU called 'Technology, Liberties and The Future'. He admits the initial reception the document got was mixed, but he says the idea of looking to sci-fi for hints about what's to come is now accepted practice. Still, he concedes, even with a forward-looking approach, it's difficult to keep up. 'Technology is moving at the speed of light, but the law, or jurisprudence and the ability of our culture and society to digest these new technologies moves very slowly.'

He points out that it took the United States Supreme Court more than forty years to extend the right of privacy to cover phone calls. 'So when you're talking about email and internet chat and Facebook and video, texting and all the rest, our courts are just very, very slow to extend our constitutional protections the way they need to be extended,' he says. 'So we're always looking down the road to figure out what's going to happen next, and science fiction is a help in doing that.'

In summary then, science fiction can be used by scientists and others to inspire future innovation, to project our fears and aspirations, and to track change. But can it also be an impediment? I mentioned earlier that sci-fi and science have a symbiotic relationship, but, of course, symbiosis isn't always mutually beneficial in the long term. So, can the societal fears that science fiction helps reflect actually get so frightening that they turn people away from certain fields of scientific endeavour?

'I think one of the areas that has been most troubled by science fiction is in genetic engineering,' says Annalee Newitz. 'Just the phrase "genetic engineering" causes people to become quite frightened because they get this image of *Brave New World* in their mind, where there's a manufactured society of people who are basically clones and don't have much control over themselves or their society. Of course, now we have all kinds of synthetic biology and genetic engineering, which are intended to improve crop yields, they're intended to improve health, but when you say that someone is working on designing a new life form, people immediately think "Frankenstein". They think, "Oh, somebody is going to create a monster; it's going to run amok, it's going to be like the movie *Species* where beautiful women with weird horns in their back are going to start randomly humping people." And you know, it's not a good picture, and I think it does really stand in the way of a lot of scientists explaining to the general public what they're doing, and getting grants to do perfectly legitimate work.'

The world's slowest lift

Now, as promised, let me walk you through two sci-fi-inspired projects currently being explored by the international scientific community. The successful development of the first is possible, but improbable, and it involves a new way to launch spacecraft.

I mention it for several reasons: because I think it's a fascinating idea; because I think it's good for us to realise just how out there and speculative genuine science can be (we often only hear about the white bread stuff, the work-a-day material that it suits the PR people at research institutes to tell us about); and because it's a good example of the fact that even highly improbable ideas can spawn genuinely useful spin-offs.

So, imagine this, if you will: It's the near future and you're about to head into the heavens. You're going to a space station orbiting just above Earth. It's time to get ready. You blow your nose and do a lucky last pee, because that's what your mother always told you to do before long journeys, you put on your space suit and lock down the helmet. You load some trashy magazines into your digital reader, grab a couple of tubes of astronaut food, and a handful of those pills that taste like Black Forest cake, and you're off.

It's just a short drive in a minibus from Mission Control to the launch pad. Then it's into an elevator and … Oh, that's it.

There's no rocket, it's just the elevator.

Ground floor — Earth.

Going up!

First floor — space. Mind your step!

As a concept, the space elevator is definitely out there: it's mad, it's so ambitious it seems implausible and impossible and yet a great many scientists around the world have it on their drawing boards. I kid you not. There's even a day marked out for the first journey into space using the elevator: 27th October 2031.

That date isn't one that everybody's working towards. It belongs to US businessman Michael Laine, who describes his LiftPort group as a sort of coordinating body for elevator activities. I'll come back to Michael Laine shortly, but let me first give you a better understanding of the idea itself and its origins.

In 1979, sci-fi supremo Arthur C Clarke gave a speech to the 30th Annual Astronautical Congress in Munich entitled 'The Space Elevator: "Thought Experiment", or Key to the Universe?'

'What I want to talk about today,' Clarke told his audience, 'is a space transportation system so outrageous that many of you may consider it not even science fiction, but pure fantasy. Perhaps it is; only the future will tell. Yet even if it is regarded as no more than a "thought experiment", it is one of the most fascinating and stimulating ideas in the history of astronautics.'

Most people now date the original space elevator concept back to a nineteenth-century Russian scientist named

Konstantin Tsiolkovsky, but it was Clarke's embrace of the idea that proved a turning point. He popularised it among science types by using it as a device in one of his novels, *The Fountains of Paradise*. The main premise is simple enough: You launch a satellite into geosynchronous orbit, so it's essentially keeping pace with the Earth as it turns. And then you lower a long cable or ribbon-like 'tether' from the satellite and let it drop all the way down until it touches the ground. After that, a self-powered elevator is attached to the cable and slowly begins tracking its way up the tether and into space.

Describing how it will work is the easy bit, actually making it a reality is another matter.

Dr Charley Lineweaver from the Research School of Earth Sciences at the Australian National University, and also a senior fellow with the university's Planetary Science Institute, estimates that across the globe there are currently about a dozen or so 'serious groups' working on the idea, with another '100 or so scientists, or semi-scientists, or retired engineers who think this is an important challenge'.

A cursory internet search found teams hard at work in Japan, the United States and Europe. And some of the weighty organisations who've also come on board in different ways include NASA, the Massachusetts Institute of Technology and Microsoft.

Now, as I've already pointed out, while it's mad, it is a serious project. And in one sense, as a concept, it's no more ridiculous than the reusable flying Space Shuttle was when it was first proposed in the 1960s. But more than that, there is actually a sensible rationale underpinning it.

The conventional way of launching objects into space — whether satellites or spacecraft — is to strap them to a rocket. In fact, rockets are still the only way of getting things into genuine orbit. But rockets, as Charley Lineweaver points out, are dangerous and costly: 'If you take a spaceship and all of the power and energy that goes into making one launch, you can see why the concept of the space elevator would be so convenient and easy. It would just be a string sitting there and you'd switch on an engine that climbs up, and keeps on climbing, like a highway to heaven.'

In theory, then, you could do away with all the drama associated with rocket launch and replace it with a system that gently carries a space vehicle into orbit. And once up there, you'd simply open the elevator door and push it out.

David Horn was one of the organisers of a space elevator conference held in 2010 in Seattle. The conference was sponsored by Microsoft, for whom Horn works as a program manager. 'I've seen estimates of US$10 billion to build the first one,' he tells me, 'which is really in the same ballpark as the Apollo program. The benefit is that launch costs will come down dramatically as well as safety [risks]. If you're going on a slow, gentle elevator ride you can build bigger things and not have so much engineering in them and expense. You can bring material back. It's just going to change economies. New businesses will open up.'

Michael Laine from the LiftPort group also pushes the spin-offs argument. 'There are going to be breakthroughs in communications, computing, robotics, nanotech and material sciences, energy systems and space applications,' he enthuses, before adding: 'I think it's going to be pretty lucrative also. So it's a situation where we can make buckets of money and do the world some good. So it's pretty compelling for me.'

However, to date, it's been more of a money drain than a fountain. Laine's consortium ran into financial difficulties late last decade, but between 2003 and 2007, LiftPort conducted a series of tests, including fourteen high-altitude balloon experiments with the agreement of the US Air Force, Navy and the Federal Aviation Administration. Michael Laine claims that the most successful of these saw a tether extend a mile into the air for a duration of six hours. Another test lasted for sixty days, but Laine admits the tether in that case didn't reach a very high altitude.

Now at six hours or sixty days you and I might be tempted to give up, but what's really pushed the enthusiasts along in recent times has been the advances made in nanotechnology. One of the project's principal stumbling blocks has always been the ability to make a tether that's light enough to traverse the tens of thousands of kilometres required to reach orbit, yet tough enough to resist the elements, principally wind and rain. That seemed an almost impossible task, until scientists developed the carbon nanotube. Light and strong, its invention reignited the space elevator's fuse. And it's towards perfecting a tether made from carbon nanotubes that the Japan Space Elevator Association is now directing its efforts.

The other major problem yet to be overcome involves powering the elevator. Even if you could develop a long enough tether, one that was stable and capable of withstanding adverse weather conditions, how do you get the elevator from the ground to the satellite station in a cost-effective way? Obviously rockets are out of the question, because the whole idea of the space elevator is to reduce the costs associated with rocket launch, so you don't want your elevator strapped to a large fuel tank or a massive engine. And while a long tether or ribbon makes sense, a really, really, really long extension cord certainly doesn't. So what's the alternative?

Well in 2009, at an event called the Space Elevator Games, various groups from across the United States competed to demonstrate new methods of powering a small craft along a ribbon, with two of the major prizes sponsored by NASA. One of the winners was a company called LaserMotive, run by a man named Tom Nugent. Nugent's company has been pioneering a process called 'laser power-beaming', a system he says involves the transfer of energy without wires: 'Just as sunlight when it shines on solar cells will generate electricity out of the solar cells, we use specialised solar cells and we shine laser light on to those, and the lasers act as a very bright light source that we can direct in a very narrow remote location.

'One of the areas that we are interested in developing is called "laser launch", where you use laser beams to actually launch rockets. This allows you to leave all the complicated, expensive machinery on the ground, and transfer your energy up to the rocket. Similarly for the space elevator idea, where you would have a vehicle that has to climb a cable, rather than carry your fuel, or say a combustion engine on board, you can leave most of the complicated elements on the ground and simply transfer the energy to your vehicle.'

So it's not hard to see why NASA is so interested. Nugent says the company now has 'proof of concept', having successfully moved an object over one kilometre under laser beam power. And once again there's talk of spin-offs. The most obvious, according to Nugent, being the use of power-beaming technology with the US military's unmanned aerial vehicles. 'The space development is something that has much longer ranges and higher power levels, and rather than trying to go immediately to those longer ranges and higher power levels, we're trying to go after commercial products that start at the shorter scales and lower power levels and build up from there. Because by doing so, we gain revenue to keep us going as a business along the way. We gain operational experience as we expand the envelope of how this is going to perform, and we start to build familiarity and deal with the regulatory issues that will come about as we try to transmit power through the air.'

All sounds promising, but here's the twist: despite having won a prize at the Space Elevator Games, Nugent is not a believer in the final concept, at least not fully. Something in the tone of his voice made me suspect that he had his doubts. And when I prompt him, out they come.

'I hate to be a spoilsport,' he says, 'but I actually spent a couple of years doing technical research on the space elevator, and ultimately I came to the conclusion that it's not something that's going to be built on Earth in my lifetime, for a variety of both technical and economic reasons.'

One of those reasons being that Nugent's not convinced the recent work on carbon nanotubes has lived up to its promise. But that's not to say that he's completely down on the idea: 'It [a space elevator] can be built on the Moon, or on Mars,' he tells me. 'I know there are groups who are looking at using it, for example, on the Moon, as we start expanding lunar operations.'

Now I have to confess the Moon and Mars reference stopped me in my tracks. It came from out of the blue. But Nugent said it without a snigger, so I took the idea back to Michael Laine to get his reaction. Remember, Laine's LiftPort group is already counting down to an Earth-based launch: 27th October 2031. However, as I soon found out, LiftPort is one of the very groups Tom Nugent is talking about.

'What we're going to do as a precursor demonstration is develop a lunar elevator, a Moon-based elevator,' Laine informs me, in a matter-of-fact tone. 'See, the Earth elevator cannot be built with current technology. We don't have a string strong enough. But because of the much simpler environment of the moon, its lower gravity — we don't have an atmosphere, we don't have lightning, we don't have a whole raft of issues there — we've got current technology that can build a lunar elevator in between five and seven years. So while LiftPort is still looking towards the future of an all-encompassing Earth elevator, our immediate horizon is we're tackling this lunar elevator.'

OK, but what, I ask, is the point of a lunar elevator? I mean, how would it benefit us here on Earth?

'The lunar elevator allows for what we call soft landing,' Michael Laine replies. 'If you remember back to the Apollo days, the reason that the Saturn V rocket was so darn big, was it had to carry an awful lot of fuel for that last 100 miles, so that Neil Armstrong and Buzz Aldrin didn't crash into the moon. They had to fire their rockets and slowly descend. The goal of the lunar elevator is not to get off the moon — that's actually surprisingly easy, you could do it practically with a slingshot — it is to soft land on the moon.'

So a Moon-based elevator would make it safer and easier for a spacecraft to touch down on the surface of the moon; and it would be cheaper too, given that less fuel would be required. And the overall point of it all would be to establish a research facility on the moon. As Michael Laine says excitedly: 'You could build colonies, you could build settlements up there.' And he adds, 'That's really not going to be possible without the space elevator. I mean, it's a complete game changer.'

Possible? Sure, but highly improbable, particularly given the fact that the richest country in the world, the United States, seems to be turning its back on space, having recently canned its Constellation mission, which was centred around getting US astronauts back to the Moon by 2020. And that cancellation came in spite of the fact that NASA had already spent over US$9 billion on the project. In 2010, the Obama administration also cancelled work on the Challenger project, which was tasked with building a replacement for the Space Shuttle after its phasing out in 2011. On those considerations alone, you'd have to imagine there's not much real US Government interest or money to be garnered from building a lunar elevator.

I could be wrong, of course, so just to be on the safe side I ask Charley Lineweaver for his thoughts. He seems like such a sensible chap. 'You know, it's hard to trace the evolution of an idea from science fiction into serious research, and in some ways this concept of a space elevator is still science fiction, it's not there yet,' he cautiously replies.

It may never be there, of course. But as I said earlier, I like the space elevator concept even though I think its chances of success are probably highly dubious. Sometimes it's necessary to think big and crazy, and, like DARPA, to intentionally take on seemingly impossible challenges because of the difficulties they present, rather than in spite of them. And at the end of the day, if all that's achieved is a spin-off like laser beam power, well that's not necessarily a bad thing by any stretch of the imagination.

As you can no doubt tell, I have a bit of a soft spot for creative insanity. But then there's madness and complete madness ...

Fixing the world by mucking about with it

Outrageous sci-fi inspired concept number two is every bit as ambitious as the first, but far more serious in its implications. If scientists ever do create a space elevator and for some reason something goes wrong — like, I don't know, mad terrorists decide to fly two fuel-laden commercial jets into the tether, for instance — then the worst that can happen is that a lot of money will get wasted, and a decent number of people and their houses will get squashed by the thousands of metres of carbon nanotube cabling that plummets back to Earth. But with concept number two, if everything goes belly-up, there's the potential for environmental catastrophe.

I asked the respected British sci-fi writer Charlie Stross what he thought the future trends for science fiction would be over coming decades, and he replied: 'We're going to be dealing with the consequences of climate change.' And that's where this next scientific concept fits in.*

When San Francisco-based businessman, Dan Whaley, looks out at the ocean, he doesn't necessarily see what you and I see. Forget the seagulls and the sand dunes, forget the shimmering water and the gentle waves, when Whaley looks out over the ocean he sees a bloody good place to dump huge amounts of powdered iron oxide. And all for the good of the planet, I might add.

---

* Out of interest, he also listed biotechnology (the genetic modification of organisms) and the consequences of ubiquitous computing.

'We need to do more than we're doing,' he declares. 'I think countries are obviously trying to work together, but both national politics and international politics make that a complicated goal. So we think it's important to also start exploring ways that humans might do more than emissions reduction; might actively pull CO_2 out of the atmosphere.'

I realise, of course, that it's not at all obvious why pouring large amounts of iron oxide powder into the sea has anything to do with CO_2 levels and the climate. What's important to know first off is that the process is called Ocean Iron Fertilization, and it's just one of several ideas that fall under the rubric of 'geoengineering', sometimes also known as 'terraforming', 'terra' as in earth.

Essentially, geoengineering is the deliberate manipulation of the environment on a massive scale, in order to try to redress climate change. And, like the space elevator, it's a real-world concept drawn straight from the pages of sci-fi.

In the film *Star Trek II: The Wrath of Khan* — so I'm reliably informed — two doctors working for the Federation Department of Scientific Research were assigned to an experiment called The Genesis Project, and their work resulted in the construction of a device that allowed them to alter the atmosphere of barren planets in order to make them habitable. Don't ask me what happened next because I haven't seen the film. The point is, The Genesis Project was all about geoengineering/terraforming.

And *Star Trek* wasn't the first piece of sci-fi to make use of the idea of deliberate human-induced atmospheric modification. According to Wikipedia, the term 'terraforming' was coined by a fellow named Jack Williamson who wrote a story called 'Collision Orbit' back in the early 1940s.[56] And somewhere between then and now, the concept began morphing from science fiction into scientific experimentation.

In mid 2010, more than 175 scientists from fifteen countries gathered in California for a five-day conference on the issue, and among those in attendance was Dan Whaley. As I mentioned, the focus of Whaley's company Climos is Ocean Iron Fertilisation. So how exactly does it work? Well, the iron oxide powder basically acts as a fertiliser for the phytoplankton living in the sea; it gives them a massive growth boost by helping to increase the amount of photosynthesis that occurs. Then as the phytoplankton start to grow on the surface of the water they begin absorbing carbon dioxide from the atmosphere. 'It's really a direct analogue to planting trees on land,' says Whaley. And the idea is that the more phytoplankton you can produce, the more carbon they'll consume.

'There's actually been thirteen iron-fertilisation projects done out in the open ocean over the last fifteen years, at scales of several kilometres to tens of kilometres across,' he says. 'And those projects have shown definitively that adding iron in the ocean produces a response. You get phytoplankton to grow.' If you're having trouble trying to picture that, just think of those massive algae blooms that break out every now and then on the surface of lakes and rivers and then multiply them manyfold.

Of course, a natural response to such a suggestion is to worry about the environmental risk. After all, history is littered with the debris of good scientific ideas that went horribly wrong and actually ended up causing more harm than good. The disastrous introduction of the cane toad into Australia is the most obvious example. Instead of eating cane beetles, the toads immediately began whipping out Indigenous fauna. And the controversial practice known as fracking is another. It involves blasting water at high pressure into rock to release the natural gas trapped inside. Natural gas is highly sought in many countries because it's meant to be a more environmentally friendly alternative to coal. But a study by the British Geological Survey in 2011 found there was a 'high probability' that drilling for the gas in the UK had actually caused two small earth tremors.

Dan Whaley is convinced his approach is not only safe, but also natural — in an artificially induced kind of way. And that's true enough, except for the fact that the sort of scale that would be required to make any real difference to the CO2 levels in our atmosphere would clearly have an impact on ocean ecology.

And that impact could be considerable, says one of the world's leading marine scientists, Professor Tony Haymet, from the San Diego-based Scripps Institution of Oceanography. 'The life in the ocean is about ninety per cent micro-organisms, bacteria and viruses. We know very little about that, and so people who want to go and seed the ocean with iron and so on, don't really understand how that's going to affect the way in which energy and matter is transported around the oceans,' says Haymet. 'I think it would be a foolhardy idea to try this before we have a lot more information about the ocean. The ocean, after all, not only dissolves a third of the CO_2 but it also produces fifty per cent of the oxygen that we breathe.'

Although as Dan Whaley points out, more than a dozen ocean fertilisation experiments have already been conducted, so the idea has gone well past the theoretical stage.

But fertilising the oceans with iron isn't the only form of geoengineering currently being explored by some of the world's leading scientists. Eli Kintisch, a staff writer for *Science* magazine and the author of the book *Hack the Planet*, breaks the geoengineering concept into three streams.

Firstly, methods he calls 'carbon sucking' like mass tree planting and Ocean Iron Fertilization, which involve trying to reduce the amount of CO_2 in the air to allow the planet to cool. Secondly, methods that attempt to block the sun in some way, including seeding clouds with reflective particles and even covering vast areas of desert with reflective plastic sheeting, effectively mimicking the reflector shields people use in their cars to keep sun off the dashboard and steering wheel. And the final stream is what Kintisch calls the 'Pinatubo option', where minute particles are introduced into Earth's upper atmosphere, the stratosphere, replicating the cooling effect of a volcanic eruption. Explains Kintisch: 'In 1991, when Mount Pinatubo erupted in the Philippines, about 10 billion tons of sulphur spewed up into the stratosphere. As a result, over the next year, the planet's temperature went down roughly about a half a degree centigrade. And so there's talk of using this Pinatubo option in the future as an emergency procedure to cool the planet.'

Well, unless you've got a better plan

Eli Kintisch dates the embrace of geoengineering by serious boffins to a 2006 paper by the Nobel Prize-winning Dutch atmospheric scientist Paul Crutzen, who won his award for his work on the hole in the ozone layer. Crutzen favours Kintisch's 'Pinatubo option', arguing that one day it might be necessary to try to cool the planet by spraying large amounts of sulphur into the Earth's upper atmosphere, so it acts as a giant reflective shield — the ultimate sunblock.

But it would be a mistake to read Crutzen's endorsement of the idea as enthusiasm for its implementation. He's actually one of a growing number of scientists and academics who believe it's necessary to start investigating the feasibility of geoengineering, not because they like it, but just in case it's ever needed. Says Eli Kintisch: 'I think that there is an almost visceral repugnance when scientists or members of the public think about this hubristic act of trying to control the planet's temperature. After all, we've failed in so many ways to manage the planet sustainably. But it's increasingly hard to find a climate scientist who doesn't feel that, at the very least, we need to think about it and work in a serious way to understand what its risks and possible benefits will be.'

Even the Green Party of Canada is arguing along those lines. In a blog post titled 'Fair is Foul, and Foul is Fair', the party's Benjamin Donato wrote: 'Geoengineering will be used. Countries should accept this and integrate it into a global framework on climate change. It would be an understatement to call geoengineering contentious. Despite its disastrous potential, it offers much to humanity.'[57]

A necessary evil? That's certainly the way it's viewed at the Royal Society, Britain's prestigious national academy of science. In September 2009, the Royal Society published a report called 'Geoengineering the climate: science, governance and uncertainty'. One of those involved in its drafting was John Shepherd, a professor of Earth Sciences at the University of Southampton.

'It is an unpalatable truth that unless we can succeed in greatly reducing CO_2 emissions,' Shepherd said at the time, 'we are headed for a very uncomfortable and challenging climate future. And geoengineering will be the only option left to limit further temperature increases.'[58]

Those sentiments were later endorsed by three leading experts in the field, professors Andy Ridgwell, Chris Freeman and Richard Lampitt. In an article for the Royal Society's website they declared: 'It is essential to reduce emissions as quickly as possible in order to create the most room for manoeuvre. It cannot be overemphasised that geoengineering must never be relied upon to stop global warming. For that, emissions cuts remain key. However it would be foolhardy not to formulate our "Plan B".'[59] The article ended with the line: '... should policy makers fail to grasp the urgency of the problem and emergency action be required in decades to come.'

The Royal Society's concerns about government unpreparedness in the event of a catastrophe are also shared by staff at the Institute for Sciences, Innovation and Society at Oxford University's Said Business School. Steve Rayner is the James Martin Professor of Science and Civilisation at the School and he and his team believe there's a strong possibility that someone, either a company, a nation state, or a group of nations, will one day make a unilateral decision to give geoengineering a go. 'The boundaries between experimentation and implementation are quite fuzzy,' he tells me. 'It's all very well to say, "in the experimental stages we don't need to worry". The problem is, when does a sub-scale field experiment, putting sulphate in the atmosphere, actually become the implementation of putting sulphate aerosols in the atmosphere for cooling?'

The institute's approach then has been to start setting some international parameters for 'Plan B'. And to that end they've drawn up five 'high-level principles' as a regulatory starting point. The principles were presented to that mass meeting of scientists in California I mentioned earlier. And they've also been delivered to the British parliament.

The first of the 'Oxford principles' as they've become known, is that geoengineering should be regulated as a public good. Says Steve Rayner: 'We're arguing that that's the model whereby governments will be ultimately responsible for specifying what kind of geoengineering technology will be developed; governments will be responsible for implementing it, and the contribution of the private sector will be in the framework of governments providing for the public good in stabilising the climate system.'

The second of Rayner's principles argues that there needs to be public participation in decision making about geoengineering. Something that could be well near impossible to achieve, one would think, given that so many countries operate political systems that are far from democratic.

The third principle is about disclosure, both in respect of research and results. The fourth advocates some form of independent assessment of impact. And the fifth principle is about cooperation: 'Any decisions with respect to actually implementing the technologies on any global scale,' says Professor Rayner, 'should only be taken once robust government structures are in place. And that doesn't mean to say that we necessarily have to have new treaties for everything, or new international agreements. Wherever possible we feel we should be using existing institutions, existing regulatory agencies.'

And that, the institute believes, means a greater role for the UN, particularly with regard to conflict resolution.

The problem is, however, that the Oxford principles rely on governments around the world acting in unison and in a spirit of openness. Ironically, they were being formulated just as the 2009 UN Climate Change Conference in Copenhagen was floundering. And if the breakdown of the Copenhagen talks taught the world anything, it was that nations and their leaders aren't very good at working together towards a higher goal. And those who prove the most reluctant to cooperate aren't always the obvious bad guys. One hundred and ninety-three nations agreed to a moratorium on geoengineering research and development at a meeting of the United Nations Convention on Biodiversity in late 2010. But the moratorium has no bearing on countries that are not signatories. Chief among those still refusing to ratify the convention is the United States.

And as Eli Kintisch points out, tensions between nations and geographic regions are already starting to appear over climate change. 'There's already the sense of a kind of resentment among countries in the developing world that developed countries caused this problem, they're responsible for the vast majority of historical carbon emissions. I think now that the West is coming up with geoengineering techniques, I can see developing countries being extremely sceptical and maybe even hostile,' he says. 'By the same token, one can imagine a scenario where a small country with the means to do some of these methods, might choose to conduct sunblocking operations because they're experiencing the worst effects of climate change. So it could go both ways.'

In other words, when North Korea's Kim Jong-un starts importing large amounts of silver paint, plastic wrap and iron oxide, that's when we really have to start panicking.

'There is great disorder under Heaven,' Mao Zedong once wrote, 'the situation is excellent.'

Now, there are people in the world who thrive under stressful and adverse conditions — it brings out the best in them. And then there are people who just like to push things to the very edge to make situations as stressful as possible because they actually get a rush out of danger and chaos. That's OK, to my mind, if you're taking a personal decision about whether to parachute out of an aeroplane, or to bungee jump from a bridge in Zimbabwe (trusting that the jumping equipment has been properly cared for in the past); but we don't want the risk junkies making decisions for the rest of us about whether or not to flick the switch for the Pinatubo option.

One of the explanations now gaining ground for the global collapse of financial markets in 2008–2009 is that too many of the people employed by financial institutions in the 1990s and the first decade of this century were young male risk takers. In essence, they were gamblers and our trust in them almost brought the roof down. UK trader Alessio Rastani made world headlines in September 2011 when he gave BBC interviewer Maxine Croxall a glimpse into the way he and his colleagues think. Said Rastani: 'For most traders, we don't really care that much about how they're going to fix the economy, how they're going to fix the whole situation. Our job is to make money from it and personally, I've been dreaming of this moment for three years. Personally, I have a confession to make — I go to bed every night and I dream of another recession. I dream of another moment like this.'[60]

It seems to me that the idea of using geoengineering strategies to try to change the world is just the sort of insanely risky activity that's likely to attract the scientific equivalent of Alessio Rastani. You can hear the future BBC interview now: 'I don't really care whether it's bad for the entire world, I just wanted to see how much stuff we could pump into the clouds and whether we could put the whole of South America into the shade.' Or perhaps: 'I go to bed at night dreaming about whether we can fill the Mediterranean chock-full of phytoplankton!'

Another significant reason why geoengineering is such a dangerous idea is that it ignores the fact that the world's environment is a mass of interlinking bits, it's not a collection of self-contained systems; the trade winds that sweep across the oceans, for instance, influence the rainfall on land; while the level of ice and snow at our Poles influences sea levels along the equator. It's all connected. And the fear is that even if you could cool the temperature in one country — say, the United States — you might, as a result, cause increased heat in another — say, China — and wouldn't that be good for the planet?

But perhaps, what's most concerning of all, is not what a reliance on geoengineering might cause us to do, but what it might cause us not to do. I've already made clear my belief that we as humans like to leave really big problems to the very last minute before we attempt to solve them. The worry is that if we believe there is ultimately a technological fix to the problem of adverse climate change, we may be even less inclined to try to find a political and social solution while there's still time.

That said, when it comes to geoengineering, the frightening truth is that our hands may already be tied. As with the development of nuclear weapons in the 1940s, the genie, as we've seen, is already out of the bottle.

It's a scary scenario — and potentially cataclysmic for the world. But it sure would make for a terrific piece of sci-fi.

CHAPTER 13

CHURCH OF THE LATTER DAY GEEKS

(A CONCLUSION OF SORTS)

We are as Gods, and might as well get good at it.

Futurist and former 1960s counter-culture entity Stewart Brand

Technology as religion

You should always begin with a joke and end with a poignant thought, somebody once said to me about writing a good speech, and I'm thinking the same is probably true for turning out non-fiction. But I have to admit, when I sat down at my laptop to bash out this final chapter nothing came easily.

So eventually, in frustration, I made myself some sandwiches, grabbed a thermos of coffee (and my crocheted tartan throw-over) and headed down to the waterfront to gaze out into the distance, looking for inspiration; pondering what I could say that would pull some of the common threads of the previous twelve chapters together in a meaningful way.

As I sat there, I began a mental checklist of the book's major themes and before long I managed to narrow them down to just two. The first is the value of scepticism, the need to question what's dished up to us, and what's expected of us, in an increasingly digital world. It's difficult for many of us, as I hope I've shown, to sort out whether the future we're building, collectively and individually, is actually the one we want for ourselves. In part, that's the result of the incredible rate of change we're experiencing; and it's also made worse by living in a world saturated by spin.

Misplaced trust was the other key theme. Considering that we as humans are meant to be at the very top of the animal totem pole when it comes to smarts, we naively put our trust in a lot of really not-so-smart ideas: we increasingly talk of getting government out of our lives, while at the same time allowing largely unaccountable, profit-driven corporations incredible access to our once private thoughts, friendships and — particularly in relation to cloud-based storage — our financial and business-related records. Facebook alone holds more personal data on individuals than any Western democratic government has ever come near.

There's also the trust we place in location-based technologies. We increasingly use them to find the things we want, but we often blindly assume that no one is going to apply the same technology to track us and our movements, unless, of course, we want them to. And finally, by and large we trust the people with vested interests who repeatedly tell us that the new technologies they flood us with are all about servicing *our* needs, not theirs.

Too much trust and too little scepticism can be a dangerous combination.

So there I am sitting on a bench, eating corned beef sandwiches, making notes and staring out into the distance, when suddenly I see the light, I have a vision, an epiphany: Could our infatuation with modern technology actually be devotion? What if the blind trust we place in its usage is really a form of faith? And can our willingness to accept the incredible risks inherent in things like cloud computing and geoengineering only be fully understood when you think of them as signs of belief — belief in the inevitable power of technology to overcome all? In short, have we made a religion of technology?

It's a bit of a bizarre thought, I know, but no more so than thinking that covering the world's deserts with shiny plastic is going to save the planet; or that putting all of the US Government's digital files into a handful of giant data centres is actually going to enhance security, not diminish it.

OK, maybe it's equally as screwy, but I still think it's a line of thought worth pursuing. 'Much truth is said in jest,' as the old proverb would have it.

The High Priest

In mid 2011, Steve Jobs, the co-founder of Apple, logged off for the very last time and immediately became a technology saint, his three required miracles apparently being the iPod, iPhone and iPad. No church inquiry needed to be convened, nor a Devil's Advocate appointed, because he was canonised by popular vote.

But even before he ascended into the clouds — that's Heaven-type clouds, as opposed to giant data storage-type clouds — he was already well on the way to sainthood, having carefully constructed for himself a place at the High Altar of the Church of the Latter Day Geeks.

Jobs was certainly clever, with a great sense of style, but he wasn't exactly adventurous when it came to his attire. I always imagined him having a walk-in wardrobe the size of Corsica, filled with row after row of identical black polo-neck shirts: black shirt for Monday, Tuesday, Wednesday, every day of the week. Black shirts for playing with the dog, or for special occasions — product launches, weddings, black shirts for dining with the President, for getting an honorary knighthood from the Queen. Oh, that's right, that was Bill Gates. Anyway, just black shirts.

I wouldn't like to suggest that the giant of Apple was anything less than a good boss and a thoroughly decent human being, but as a journalist, and a lover of history, I feel duty-bound to point out the niggly little fact that not so long ago, the black shirt was chiefly the preserve of priests and fascists, and it still is to some extent. The black shirt has long spoken of authority and a certain spiritualism, qualities which pretty much summed up the Jobs persona.

Now technology as religion is an intriguing idea. And, rest assured, I am aware that it's possible to push these things a little too far, which seems to me the perfect reason for doing just that. So let's give it a whirl …

The computer scientist and early pioneer of virtual reality Jaron Lanier seems much too countercultural for organised religion, but he claims he sometimes feels surrounded by the techno born again. Says Lanier: 'There is a funny religious quality to it, particularly in the world of elite engineering where I tend to reside. It's sort of an odd world. Nerds sort of — we define ourselves as being a little odd and apart — and so a lot of us have come to believe that the internet is coming alive and turning into a giant global being of some kind, a sort of collective intelligence that actually becomes almost godlike, and there's a set of beliefs that recreate the beliefs of traditional religions around this perceived being. So for instance, there's an afterlife because the collective super-being of the internet will become so capacious that it'll scoop up the contents of all our brains and give us everlasting life in virtual reality, and so forth. And if you think I'm exaggerating, I'm not. A great many very serious and very powerful and rich people in Silicon Valley buy in to this set of ideas, so there is kind of a religious sensibility driving some of these designs.'

Whether or not Steve Jobs believed in that godlike collective intelligence, I'm not sure. But as I say, he did like to wear an awful lot of black and, as we'll see, he also seemed to borrow heavily from the evangelical handbook. Oh, and, of course, there was also a miracle: he rescued the company from economic oblivion.

Back in the late 1990s, when Jobs returned to Apple after a substantial absence, the company was on the slide. It had an historic record of innovation, certainly, but it had a distinctly small, rusted-on following and its profits were as slim as a communion wafer, while its market share was tiny in comparison to its rivals. His return was initially announced as a temporary measure and it was written off by some analysts as a nostalgic last-roll-of-the-dice for what, sadly, had once been a significant corporate entity. Fast forward a decade or so and by 2010, Apple had overtaken Microsoft as the world's biggest technology company, and an Apple product even headed my ten-year-old son's Christmas wish list that year, ahead of a toy machine gun capable of firing foam darts over twenty metres at a rate of three darts per second. Miraculous!

How Jobs succeeded in reinventing Apple was by refashioning his old firm as a sort of quasi-religion and, as I said right at the beginning of the book, not just some tiny cult, but a truly universal church.

Line up all the technology giants of the past thirty years or so and the former head of Apple stands out. What made him different was that he was a marketer as much as he was an innovator. He knew how to sell as well as create. And if Steven Levy, the author of *Hackers: Heroes of the Computer Revolution*, is to be believed, he was always that way even in the early days. 'Jobs did some programming. He programmed a computer game for Atari and got to know a lot of the technical aspects of it. But he never hacked for passion,' Levy says. 'He was not that kind of personality. He had the sense for marketing and what people would like for design and for more artistic endeavours.'

Design indeed, and a sense for making his products seem more than special, almost otherworldly. 'When you hold an iPhone, you have a Zen experience of divinity,' were the words that US advertising executive Rishad Tobaccowala used, if you'll recall.

If you have an Apple computer or iPhone you'll know there's long been an almost religious fervour that surrounds the company; they don't have customers so much as devotees and followers. And under Steve Jobs, even the iconography and theatrics of an Apple product launch always looked more like an evangelical gathering than a media conference: Jobs, priest-like in his trademark black shirt, alone on a darkened stage, summoning forth the spirit of that year's new product, which then miraculously appeared projected in the air above and just beyond him, like some sort of apparition; and then Jobs working the eager congregation of tech-heads and tech wannabes like a slick televangelist, sermonising to the tech writers and journalists in the audience, and filling them with the spirit of technological possibility and wonder. No surprise then that a very popular blog devoted to Apple products is called The Cult of Mac.

Suffice it to say that the devices produced by Apple weren't, and aren't, just used — they're revered.[*]

Even Apple's distribution system has long been structured to play on that feeling of being part of something special and spiritual. You may have noticed that whenever a new product is launched, people queue up on the footpath outside their local Apple Store like church-goers awaiting a Holy Sacrament. They'll line up literally for hours, regardless of the weather. And that's not to take away from the quality and sheer cleverness of the devices Apple creates, because they are clever and they are often beautiful (you know, in a plastic and metal kind of way).

But what makes Apple Apple isn't just the superiority of its goods, it's the knowledge that by buying one of their devices, you become part of an exclusive grouping, a brethren. And even with their increasing dominance of the market, that feeling of exclusivity still exists, although perhaps not in the way that it once did when the company was smaller and more niche.

Of course, Apple is not really a religion, or a cult, even though it might sometimes look and act like one. And Steve

---

[*] It helps if you don't think about all the poor young Chinese workers sweating away in appalling conditions in Dickensian factories, churning out iPads and smart phones.

Jobs, although gaunt and slightly tortured looking towards the end, was no Jesus. But what he and his company cleverly gauged was the emergence of a public attitude towards technology that over the past few decades has become increasingly devotional in its nature. Why, even the head of the Roman Catholic Church, the heir of St Peter, God's vicar on Earth, has felt it necessary to take to Twitter, though it has to be said, from looking at Pope Benedict's account, that he still hasn't quite grasped the idea that you're meant to follow others, not just expect everyone to follow you.

And if even the Pope is now tweeting, brothers and sisters, I think it's fair enough to declare that we have finally entered the second great age of techno-worship.

What's that?

The second?

Yes, that's right, because we've actually been here before. Well, not us, but our ancestors. The first great age of technology veneration began about two hundred years ago.

Déjà vu

You see, the Victorians — stern faces, mutton-chop sideburns and stove-pipe hats — also lived in an era of constant change driven by rapid advances in technology. In 1838, the second year of Queen Victoria's reign, the paddle-wheeler *Great Western* kicked off the modern age of intercontinental transport by crossing the Atlantic under the power of steam, not wind. Over subsequent decades, railways networked Europe, the United States and eventually the rest of the world. Skyscrapers were born, electric lighting was invented, along with the telephone, motion pictures, the machine gun, modern artillery, high-speed printing and the automobile, to name just a few of the many achievements that were realised during that period. It was a time of technological advancement at a phenomenal, often disruptive pace — not at all unlike today.

We remember the Victorians for being rather dour and for building and squabbling over empires, but arguably at the core of the Victorian spirit was an overarching faith in technology: an approach, a belief, a trust that all problems could be solved by clever design, by newer machines, by better science.

When I spoke with the author of *The Victorian Internet*, Tom Standage, about the similarities between our modern technology-focused society and that of the mid to late 1800s, he speculated that it was only the bloodshed and destruction of the Great War that ultimately brought about the end of humankind's initial period of techno-worship, the argument being that after the carnage of World War One, technology began to be seen more as a double-edged sword: it was still viewed as a means of advancement, but in the wake of the Western Front and the Dardanelles it was also treated as a point of fear, of distrust. People suddenly realised that it had the potential to make their lives more vulnerable. And if you think about it, that fear of technology mixed with wonderment was clearly there in the science fiction of a great part of the twentieth century: *Metropolis*, *Gattaca*, *Blade Runner*, *The Terminator*, *2001: A Space Odyssey*, and so on and so on.

So, if we have now entered the second age of technology worship as I've already boldly declared, when did it start?

Well, you could mount a plausible argument that a dormant utopian belief in all things tech was revived by the phenomenal growth of computer power in the very late stages of last century. Computers suddenly began to enhance existing technologies like never before: factories became fully automated; neurologists undertook delicate brain surgery via robotic arms and a 3D digital display; and aircraft could suddenly fly and land themselves without the need for a pilot.

Now, corresponding with that explosion in computing power and its application, we also saw the end of the Cold War. Nuclear weapons still pose a threat, of course, but with the demise of the Soviet Union and the arms race between the USSR and the US, suddenly the ever present risk that technology could at any moment see the entire planet blown into a wasteland began to disappear in most people's consciousness. And subsequently, technology lost some of the menace that first smeared it during the Great War.

Like the Victorians, many of us now believe in the idea that technology can be used to solve every problem, that the only limitations are adequate funding and the correct technical expertise. It's a belief that I think is particularly evident in the military. When US soldiers won the initial conflict in Iraq in 2003, but failed to prevent an insurgency, the Pentagon's answer wasn't just to deploy more troops, but to significantly boost funding for new technologies and their deployment: a state-of-the-art robotics-focused program called Future Combat Systems (FCS) was quickly rolled out, receiving more than US$230 billion in initial funding.

The Director of the 21st Century Defense Initiative at the Brookings Institution in Washington, PW Singer, told me in February 2009 that military robotics were taking on a new primacy within defence planning. 'I think the extent to which science fiction is becoming battlefield reality will surprise and maybe even scare people,' he said. 'We went into Iraq with just a handful of drones, unmanned air systems; we now have 7000 just in the US military inventory. On the ground, we went in with zero unmanned ground systems, unmanned ground robotics; we now have 12,000. The things that are coming are just amazing. I met with a US Air Force three-star general and he said, "Very soon, we're going to be getting to the point of talking about numbers of tens of thousands of robots."'

In fact, we've now reached the point where a desk-bound employee of the US Department of Defense, sitting in an office in Virginia, has the power and ability to launch successful missile strikes against insurgents in Afghanistan using an unmanned drone piloted by his or her PC, after first having watched their movements at close range and in remarkable definition via a series of satellites.

But it's not just in warfare that technology is taking on a new primacy, it's also now being pushed as the solution to all of our domestic problems as well — both real and perceived. A friend of mine, a somewhat frustrated senior public servant, recently relayed his despair at constantly being assailed by those within his organisation pushing an IT solution. The IT solution, he darkly mused, was 'the solution you had when you didn't actually know you had a problem in the first place'.

If you work in a government department, statutory authority or in any decent-sized organisation, you'll know that there's always somebody promoting an IT solution in one form or other: the notion that digitising, automating or computerising will *always* be better, because it will always be more efficient.

I'm sure you know what I mean. It's a mantra. It's a truth of the modern workplace, just as the inherent benefit of cramming employees into 'open plan' work environments is a truth — even though all the research I've ever seen suggests open plan is more stressful for staff and detrimental to their efficiency.* Anyway, the IT solution is a seductive concept, until you start to look around. The recent history of public transport in the Western world is littered with examples of automated bus and train ticketing systems that have cost far more in terms of repairs, fare evasion and public frustration, than any savings their proponents claimed would be realised by eliminating the need for costly human staff and wages. And does anyone really think that all those automated phone services — 'If this

---

* I tell a lie — in the late 1990s I knew a man who ran a large Canadian organisation with overseas branches, and when he decided to reconfigure the work environment and move to an open-plan model, he gave up his personal office and joined his staff out on the floor, so to speak. That certainly impressed people at first, until they realised that life was probably better when the boss wasn't sitting next to them all day listening to their telephone calls and conversations. Still, he's the only one I've ever come across who's led by example when it comes to open plan. So, in my book, he has to get points for that.

is correct, press one now. If this is not correct, press two' — make our lives better and more efficient? Or that getting rid of counter staff at airports and forcing passengers to do their own ticketing and luggage tagging via computer check-in kiosks is a good thing — particularly when there's no reduction in the cost of the ticket as a result?*

Trivial examples perhaps, but they do highlight the very strong association that's made in our society between technology and modernity. It's long been there, of course, but in our current gadget-infused world it's even harder to question. Technology *is* the future, and to query the universality of that idea, as my public servant friend admits he often does, merely ensures your own irrelevance as somebody who's simply 'stuck in the past' or 'resistant to change'. Dare I say it — a Luddite.

But I have to admit, to be fixated on technology, to be enthralled by its potential, is not the same as genuine full-on worship. And the people Jaron Lanier talks about, the people who 'believe that the internet is coming alive and turning into a giant global being of some kind, a sort of collective intelligence that actually becomes almost godlike', well, those people no longer see technology as just a tool, but as a thing of inherent transformative power.

I discussed the soft end of that belief in the chapters 'Horses for Courses' and 'Overstate, Oversell,' where we looked at a school of thought called techno-determinism, which encompasses the idea that computers have a sort of almost magical power in and of themselves: an ability to lift people out of poverty in the developing world simply by their very presence, for example; or to spark democratic revolutions a la the Arab Spring.

---

* At various McDonald's outlets in France they're now cutting back on counter staff by making customers order their own junk food via a touch screen and credit card. They'll be asking people to flip their own burgers soon. And in late 2011 one of the busiest Metro lines in Paris was fully automated — no drivers. The Metro's administrators reportedly believe that trains run by a central computer are safer than ones with a human in charge. Oh, and they're also anticipating their labour costs will be reduced over time.

As I say, they're at the soft end. At the other end of the scale are a bunch of people whose strength of belief in technology sees them wanting to push the very boundaries of what it means to be human.

A HAL of a future

The British computer scientist and gerontologist Aubrey de Grey is the nominal head of a movement known as 'transhumanism', which, according to Wikipedia, 'is an international intellectual and cultural movement that affirms the possibility and desirability of fundamentally transforming the human condition by developing and making widely available technologies to eliminate ageing and to greatly enhance human intellectual, physical, and psychological capacities.'

Put into plain speak, transhumanists are convinced that medical science will one day allow our species to control and counter the process of ageing — in fact, to indefinitely postpone death, barring of course the extremely prejudicial consequence of accidentally getting hit by a bus or falling down a set of stairs and breaking one's neck.

With a wild beard and a ponytail, the Cambridge-based de Grey looks like your classic eccentric, but his theories are taken seriously by a great many people and he lectures all over the world. Talk to anyone involved in research on ageing and you'll find they have an opinion on de Grey and his pronouncements. He might be eccentric, and possibly wrong, but that doesn't stop him from being influential.

In *Foreign Policy* in 2004, our friend Professor Francis Fukuyama even nominated transhumanism as the world's most dangerous idea. He called it 'a strange liberation movement' and he said that it wanted 'nothing less than to liberate the human race from its biological constraints'. It wasn't meant as a compliment, but I have a sneaking suspicion Aubrey de Grey would have taken it as one. There are others in the field who believe that the transhumanists simply misunderstand evolutionary biology: that being able to abolish disease (if that proves possible) is not the same as preventing ageing. Human beings, they argue, are actually hardwired to die after they've completed the task of passing on their genes. So human bodies are dispensable; it's the genes that matter in the end. And changing the behaviour of our genes is going to be a lot more difficult than tackling disease.

De Grey is also a member of an organisation whose very name speaks of the neo-divinity of technology. He's an advisor to the Singularity Institute, a somewhat mysterious body located in California and inspired by the works of the famous mathematician and sci-fi writer, Vernor Vinge. The organisation and its members represent the hard-core end of the techno-determinist spectrum, and their motto is actually a quote from Albert Einstein: 'The significant problems we face cannot be solved at the same level of thinking we were at when we created them.'

The Singularity Institute is dedicated to the research and promotion of the quasi-religious concept of the Singularity, which the institute's website defines in this way: 'The Singularity is the technological creation of smarter-than-human intelligence. There are several technologies that are often mentioned as heading in this direction. The most commonly mentioned is probably Artificial Intelligence, but there are others: direct brain-computer interfaces; biological augmentation of the brain; genetic engineering; ultra-high resolution scans of the brain followed by computer emulation. Some of these technologies seem likely to arrive much earlier than the others, but there are nonetheless several independent technologies all heading in the direction of the Singularity — several different technologies which, if they reached a threshold level of sophistication, would enable the creation of smarter-than-human intelligence.'[61]

I know it reads like gobbledygook, but it's all deadly serious. Briefly: 'artificial intelligence' simply means a really smart computer, one that can think like a human being; 'brain-computer interfaces' mean hooking people's grey matter up to computers and sharing information between the two; and 'resolution scans of the brain followed by computer emulation' — well, it doesn't matter, the point is that believers in the idea of the Singularity see a time when computers will one day become smarter in every way than the humans that build them. And the advantage of that, so the argument goes, is that at the 'point of Singularity', the point where the intelligence of a computer surpasses that of the smartest person on Earth, well, at that point computers will be able to start helping us answer questions that our human brains simply don't have the capacity to solve, or even to fully understand.

Questions such as: Where did the universe come from? Or one I wouldn't mind finding the answer to: Why do otherwise sensible people take Aubrey de Grey seriously?

I have to say, it's not apparent to me that believers in the Singularity have what could be termed a sense of humour. When critics of the concept began referring to it as the 'geek rapture', a blogger called 'Singularity Utopia' shot back: 'It is an insult to be deemed a geek due to my interest in the exponential growth of science and technology. I assure you I am not a geek. There's nothing religious or quasi-religious about the Singularity.'[62]

However — and without a sense of irony — the above writer also declared in the same blog post: 'Via science we will progress beyond the hypothetical omnipotence of God. Instead of an elusive fantasy regarding God's powers we will create actual real powers based on science not mysticism; we will supersede God's hypothetical supernatural powers. In the modality of Nietzsche the Singularity will declare God is dead.'

Potato, potahto, tomato, tomahto; it certainly sounds quasi-religious to me.

For some of us, the idea of a really super smart computer is a bit of a frightening thing. If you've ever watched *2001: A Space*

Odyssey, you'll know what I'm talking about. In that film HAL, the central computer on a futuristic spaceship, acquires so much knowledge from the crew that it eventually takes on a life and a will of its own, countermanding the orders given to it by Dave (the sole surviving astronaut) with a cold, deadpan, almost psychopathic voice: 'I'm sorry Dave, I'm afraid I can't do that. I think you know what the problem is just as well as I do.' And that's after HAL has already despatched all of the other astronauts onboard through a series of unfortunate 'accidents'.

Of course, if you asked the Singularity Institute, they would tell you that HAL was just a fiction, a Hollywood creation deliberately designed to scare people, to play upon their base fears. Which is true, of course. But on the other hand, if they are talking about the eventual creation of machines that are just like us only smarter, what's to stop some of those machines eventually developing the nasty side of human nature, not just the analytic and the good?

The quest to develop super-smart machines has been going on now for decades. The most well-known, and perhaps the best publicised, display of greater-than-human computer intelligence involved a chess match in 1997 in which the IBM computer Deep Blue won a match against the then world champion Garry Kasparov. The result made international headlines at the time and was a bit of a shock, although, perhaps tellingly, IBM refused repeated requests from Kasparov for a rematch. And they actually disassembled Deep Blue afterwards, so there was no chance of another bout at some later stage. Then in 2011 a supercomputer named Watson, also developed by IBM, competed in the US quiz show *Jeopardy*, and beat its human competitor. I'm not actually sure what happened to Watson, but given the fate of its predecessor, it's likely it was always destined to be a one-shot wonder.

There's also an interesting challenge held annually in the UK called the Loebner Prize, which pits people against computers to judge just how human-like machines are becoming. The prize follows the rules of the so-called Turing Test, named after the British mathematician Alan Turing, who in the 1950s predicted that by the year 2000, computer programs would have the ability to imitate intelligence to such a degree that it would be impossible to definitively say that they were 'less intelligent than humans'.

The Turing Test is a fascinating contest. Each year during the event, a team of judges are given the task of corresponding via email with a number of contestants, some of whom are human and some computers. And from that correspondence they (the judges) have to guess which contestants are which — the idea being that the Loebner Prize will be won the moment a computer is able to fool a quarter of the judges on the panel into thinking that it's actually a human being. The contest has been run since the early 1990s and while no machine has yet succeeded, a computer program in 2008 came within one judge's vote of winning.

But to the followers of the Singularity, such events are mere parlour games; the true 'point' of Singularity, they would argue, will be something much more profound. The Institute's website says: 'A future that contains smarter-than-human minds is genuinely different in a way that goes beyond the usual visions of a future filled with bigger and better gadgets. Vernor Vinge originally coined the term "Singularity" in observing that, just as our model of physics breaks down when it tries to model the singularity at the centre of a black hole, our model of the world breaks down when it tries to model a future that contains entities smarter than human.'

Now Vinge's theories might be at the heart of the organisation, but its figurehead, and chief spokesperson, is the American writer and futurist Ray Kurzweil. Kurzweil, the author of the best-selling book *The Age of Spiritual Machines*, not only talks about a time when the computers we make will one day surpass us in terms of intelligence, but also about the merging of computer technology with our physical bodies to create a generation of technologically enhanced human beings.

Here's how he describes it: 'The important thing to understand, and the core of my thesis, is that information technology, like computers, doubles in power in less than a year. It's exponential growth. We will match human intelligence and go beyond it by 2029. By 2045 this artificial intelligence we're creating — which is really part of our civilisation, it's not some invasion from Mars, we're already deeply integrated with it — it will make us a billion times smarter by 2045, according to my calculations.'[63]

As it transpires, Kurzweil is also a transhumanist, and like de Grey, he's the subject of numerous books, documentaries, newspaper features and interviews. And the mark of his influence is demonstrated by the list of heavy-hitting and wealthy founding partners he managed to attract in establishing his own Singularity University, among them, NASA, Nokia, Google, IDEO and LinkedIn.

The university is actually based at the NASA Ames Research Centre. It was described by the *Financial Times* at the time of its launch as 'a new school for futurists'. In one sense it's as much a finishing school as a university — it offers post-graduate courses aimed at trying to 'assemble, educate and inspire a cadre of leaders who strive to understand and facilitate the development of exponentially advancing technologies'.

When it first commenced business in 2009, I asked its executive director and trustee, Salim Ismail, whether it irked him that much of the initial coverage the university had attracted focused on the science fiction-like quality of its mission. His response, with what was possibly a slight tone of condescension, was to say that yes, it was a 'natural' viewpoint, but: 'Frankly, we are focused very much on the actual science, and we don't have to go very far out of what's actually happening today to get into the quite extraordinary and amazing developments. And so we're really just focused on that.'

He then went on to tell me: 'The singularity concept is a theoretical one, but we do, as a species, need to get a grip on how quickly these various domains are advancing, and try to understand them and be able to measure and forecast them as much as possible. And the institution is really aimed at using these technologies to solve some of the grand challenges that humanity is facing.'

Now, having started this chapter with Apple, let me return there. But not to Steve Jobs, instead to the words of his co-founder, Steve Wozniak, the man many believe is an underappreciated genius. When asked at a conference in 2011 whether or not he believed in the central idea of the Singularity, he responded: 'I think that awareness of machines is getting very, very close and we're getting closer to where machines will really understand you. Once we have machines doing our high-level thinking, there's so little need for ourselves and you can't ever undo it — you can never turn them off. I think we lost the battle to the machines long ago.'

And just to stir the pot a little, he added: 'We're going to become the pets — the dogs of the house.'[64]

Perhaps, but I'm not convinced. There may well come a time when computers are so smart they outshine us all. If it ever happens, hopefully that technology will be a benefit not a curse. But our gadgets and devices are really just tools, and as I said with geoengineering, the greatest danger is perhaps not what we do with them, but what we don't do because of our reliance on them. To me, waiting for the day when technology alone will solve our problems and lead us to some future promised land, feels a little too much like the Millerites waiting for the return of their saviour.

And as we know, all that came of that was disappointment!

AFTERTHOUGHT

One final thought to keep your mind ticking over. And I promise this is the last.

As strange as this may sound, sometimes the future isn't really about the future at all. Sometimes it's actually about the past.

I know, that's a pretty big call to make at this very late stage of the book and I probably should have mentioned it a lot sooner. You know, in the Preface perhaps. But it just seems to me like an important observation to share with you before pulling up stumps.

Douglas Hurd, the former British Foreign Secretary, and a writer of fiction to boot, once remarked: 'History provides no automatic system of navigation for our leaders. Knowledge of history does not change politicians into statesmen. But ignorance of history is foolishness. The most dangerous form of ignorance is that smidgeon of shallow knowledge which lacks any understanding of the characters or context of past decisions.'*

So history can be a guide to future decision making, but more than that, I think the past is actually a place we return to over and over again.

Many of us think of time as one long, forward-moving highway, when in fact the road to the future is full of detours

---

* Baron Hurd of Westwell is an interesting chap. Derided in the early 1990s for his patrician demeanour, he's actually the author of a string of political thrillers. And in 1998, he was the chairman of the judging panel for the Booker Prize for fiction. Not surprisingly, he has a first class degree in History from Cambridge.

and exit-lanes that, if you choose to take them (or if you're forced to), are just as likely to sweep back in the opposite direction before eventually rejoining the main thoroughfare. Things fall in and out of fashion, of course. Even Confucius is back in favour in China. After more than half a century of representing all that was wrong with the past — a reactionary historic relic — now the leadership in Beijing has declared the thinly bearded sage a modern symbol of traditional Chinese values, and a civic role model for the future.* Even many of our most modern creations, the world wide web and social media, for example, have their antecedents in what came before. Writing in 1999 about the burgeoning internet and the value he saw in its interactivity, the late Douglas Adams — he of *The Hitchhiker's Guide to the Galaxy* fame — argued: 'During this century we have for the first time been dominated by *non-*interactive forms of entertainment: cinema, radio, recorded music and television. Before they came along *all* entertainment was interactive: theatre, music, sport — the performers and audience were there together ... I expect that history will show "normal" mainstream twentieth century media to be the aberration in all this.'[65]

Another Brit, TV personality and comedian Stephen Fry, argues that in some ways we've set up a false dichotomy between our notions of modernity and of the past. A very popular identity on Twitter, Fry nonetheless has a deep-rooted affection for history, and he finds it puzzling that so many people have difficulty accommodating the two.

'For me it's all part of a continuum,' he says. 'Life, and the way life is lived, has always astonished and provoked my curiosity and whether that has been in the past or whether it is the forefront of the future, doesn't make any difference.'

---

* They even erected a large bronze statue of him in Tiananmen Square in early 2011, though its presence turned out to be temporary. Still, not a bad effort for an historical figure who, as I say, was reviled by the Communist authorities only a few short years ago.

In fact, Fry suggests it's impossible to truly understand digital technology without a grasp of history. 'I think those who object to modern technology very often do so out of historical ignorance of the way technology works,' he says. 'Early in the eighteenth century there was a new kind of technology as hand presses and printing became cheaper and cheaper and cheaper. And it wasn't the full invention of printing, any more than Twitter is the full invention of the internet. The little development of the hand press led to magazines, journalism, political pamphlets. And do you know what? Oddly enough, many famous ones had names that were very like Twitter. They were called things like *The Rambler*, *The Idler*, *The Tattler*, *Spectator*. It was all very trivial. They weren't called *Earnest Debate*. They weren't called *Serious Penetration of Issues* or *The Philosopher*.'[66]

In short, we're often sold on the idea that the future is about the new, but sometimes it can be remarkably familiar. There is foolishness, I think, in focusing on objects and platforms and new modes of technology as though they themselves are somehow preeminent — as though they themselves represent the future. The future is actually about us; it's about human desires and frailties, just as the present is, and the past was. And most of our human traits never change. Or if they do, they change very slowly. Technology is just the dressing we as individuals and society wrap around ourselves at any given time: the rifle, the jet fighter and the atomic bomb — each altered the course of warfare, but they didn't create future conflict — people did that.

Belfiore, Michael, *The Department of Mad Scientists: How DARPA is Remaking Our World, from the Internet to Artificial Limbs*, HarperCollinsPublishers, 2010

Brand, Stewart, *Whole Earth Discipline: An Ecopragmatist Manifesto*, Viking Penguin, 2009

Brugmann, Jeb, *Welcome to the Urban Revolution: How cities are Changing the World*, Bloomsbury Publishing, 2010

Crawford, Matthew B., *Shop Class as Soulcraft*, Penguin Press, 2009

Cribb, Julian & Sari, Tjempaka, *Open Science: Sharing Knowledge in the Global Century*, CSIRO Publishing, 2010

Farivar, Cyrus, *The Internet of Elsewhere: The Emergent Effects of a Wired World*, Rutgers University Press, 2011

Fry, Tony, *Design Futuring: Sustainability, Ethics and New Practice*, UNSW Press, 2009

Honore, Carl, *In Praise of Slowness: How a Worldwide Movement is Challenging the Cult of Speed*, Orion Books, 2005

Kenny, Charles, *Getting Better: Why Global Development is Succeeding — and How We Can Improve the World Even More*, Basic Books, 2011

Kintisch, Eli, *Hack the Planet: Science's Best Hope — or Worst Nightmare — for Averting Climate Catastrophe*, Wiley, 2010

Lanier, Jaron, *You are Not a Gadget: a Manifesto,* Random House Digital 2010

Levy, Steve, *Hackers: Heroes of the Computer Revolution,* (25th Anniversary Edition), O'Reily Media, 2010

MacKinnon, Rebecca, *Consent of the Networked: The Worldwide Struggle for Internet Freedom,* Basic Books, 2012

Nair, Chandran, *Consumptionomics: Asia's Role in Reshaping Capitalism and Saving the Planet,* Infinite Ideas, 2011

Pariser, Eli, *The Filter Bubble*: *What the Internet Is Hiding From You*, Penguin, 2011

Ross, Carne, *Independent Diplomat,* Baker and Taylor, 2009

Rushkoff, Douglas, *Program or Be Programmed: Ten Commands for a Digital Age,* OR Books, 2010

Singer, PW, *Wired for War: The Robotics Revolution and 21st Century Conflict*, Penguin, 2009

Standage, Tom, *The Victorian Internet*: *The Remarkable Story of the Telegraph and the Nineteenth Century's On-Line Pioneers,* Walker and Co, 1997

Suzuki, David, *The Legacy: An Elder's Vision for Our Sustainable Future,* D & M Publishers, 2010

Thomson, Mark, *The Complete Blokes and Sheds: Stories for the Shed*, Harper Collins, 2002

Watson, Richard, *Future Files: 5 Trends That Will Shape the Next 50 Years*, Scribe, 2009

Watts, Duncan J, *Everything is Obvious*: How Common Sense Fails Us (*Once You Know the Answer)*, Atlantic Books (Random House) 2011

Zizek, Slavoj, *Living in the End Times*, Verso, 2010

NOTES

1   Tom Evans as quoted in the *Los Angeles Times*: 'In the end, rapture believers weren't going anywhere', 22 May 2011: http://articles. latimes.com/2011/may/22/local/la-me-rapture-20110522

2   David Morrison as quoted in *National Geographic News*, '2012: Six End-of-the-World Myths Debunked', 6 November 2009: http://news. nationalgeographic.com/news/2009/11/091106-2012-end-of-world-myths.html

3   Eric Schmidt, at the Washington Ideas forum, October 2010.

4   Brian David Johnson, The Tomorrow Project and Futurism at Intel: http//www.youtube.com/watch?v=Y0a40vp1Uyc&feature=related

5   Adam Connor as quoted inThe Telegraph, 21st April 2011:http//www. telegraph.co.uk/technology/facebook/8465401/Facebook-offers-too-much-free-speech-for-some-countries.html

6   Douglas Rushkoff's blog, August 1998: www.rushkoff.com/articles-individual/2008/5/9/why-futurists-suck/

7   *Forbes* magazine online, 'Facebook mints Six Billionaires. Zynga And Groupon Make Two', 9 March 2011: http://www.forbes.com/sites/ stevenbertoni/2011/03/09/facebook-mints-six-billionaires-zynga-and-groupon-make-two/

8   Figure as quoted in *The Economist*, 8th–14th January 2011 edition, p61, using figures from Thomson Reuters and 'press reports'.

9   Figure as quoted in *New Scientist*, 20 November 2010.

10   Rhett and Link, www.YouTube.com/watch?v=rSnXE2791yg.

11   FTC Chairman Jon Leibowitz, as quoted in *The Guardian* online, 29 November 2011: http://www.guardian.co.uk/technology/2011/nov/29/ facebook-ftc-privacy-settlement

12   Elmo Keep in an interview with Ian Townsend, 'The Privacy Paradox', Background Briefing, ABC Radio National, 16 May 2010.

13   Tim O'Reilly quoted in the *New York Times* online, 20 April 2011: http://www.nytimes.com/2011/04/21/business/21data.html

14   William Hague as quoted in *The Guardian Weekly*, 4 November 2011.

15   Brian Johnson in an interview with David Weber, PM, ABC Radio, 27 May 2011.

16   Jost Stollman in an interview with David Weber, PM, ABC Radio, 27 May 2011.

17 Katie Cincotta, 'The day my hard drive crashed', *Sydney Morning Herald*, 26 May 2011: http://www.smh.com.au/digital-life/digital-life-news/the-day-my-hard-drive-crashed-20110601-1ffrg.html

18 Data Transfer Techspert column, the *Courier-Mail*, 25 May 2011.

19 Avanade website: www.avanade.com/en-us/approach/research/Pages/Global-Research-Is-Cloud-Computing-Maturing.aspx

20 Howard Stringer as quoted in the *Wall Street Journal*, 18 May 2011: http://online.wsj.com/article/SB10001424052748703421204576328982377107892.html

21 Susan Wyndham, 'One click from Blog to Blah, Blah, Blah', in the *Sydney Morning Herald*, 13 April 2010: http://www.smh.com.au/entertainment/books/one-click-from-blog-to-blah-blah-blah-20100412-s44d.html

22 *Who* magazine (Australia), 13 December 2010, p11.

23 Nicholas Carr as interviewed by Fran Kelly, Radio National Breakfast, ABC Radio National, 23 September 2010

24 Ofcom's Communications Market Report 2011: www.ofcom.org.uk/research

25 John Kinsella, 'Neo-Luddism', The Drum, ABC online, 15 May 2009: http://www.abc.net.au/unleashed/30814.html

26 Duncan Watts as quoted in his online work profile: www.research.yahoo.com/node/2351

27 Jeff Howe, 'The Rise of Crowdsourcing', *Wired* Magazine, June 2006: www.wired.com/wired/archive/14.06/crowds.html

28 Frank Farrall as interviewed by Andrew Robertson, *Lateline Business*, ABC TV, 20 April 2011.

29 Thorvaldur Gylfason as quoted in 'Mob rule: Iceland crowdsources its next constitution', *The Guardian*, 9 June 2011: http://www.guardian.co.uk/world/2011/jun/09/iceland-crowdsourcing-constitution-facebook

30 Katharine Mieszowski, 'I make $1.45 a week and I love it', Salon.com, 24 July 2006: http://www.salon.com/2006/07/24/turks_3/

31 Australian Government Declaration of Open Government: www.agimo.govspace.gov.au/2010/07/16/declaration-of-open-government

32 Fred Wilson, Musings of a VC in NYC, 30 January 2011: www.avc.com/a_vc/2011/01/a-frightening-week.html

33 As quoted in an article by Cyrus Farivar, 'Iran's Answer to Stuxnet', *Technology Review*, 25 April 2011: http://www.technologyreview.com/blog/guest/26692/

34 Ethan Zuckerman, 'The First Twitter Revolution?', Foreign Policy, 14 January 2011: http://www.foreignpolicy.com/articles/2011/01/14/the_first_twitter_revolution

35 Eberhard Lauth, 'Twittering the Revolution', *The European* magazine, 24 January 2011: http://theeuropean-magazine.com/180-lauth-eberhard/181-political-upheaval-in-tunisia

36 Peter Eckersely as quoted in an interview with Stan Corey, Background Briefing, ABC Radio National, 15 May 2011.

37 Rebecca McKinnon as quoted in an interview with Stan Corey, Background Briefing, ABC Radio National, 15 May 2011.

38 Anupam Chander as quoted in an interview with Stan Corey, Background Briefing, ABC Radio National, 15 May 2011.

39 Nicolas Sarkozy as quoted in *The Telegraph*, 26 May 2011.

40 Mark Zuckerberg as quoted by Reuters, Reuters website, 25 May 2011: http://www.reuters.com/article/2011/05/25/us-eg-idUSTRE74O72L20110525

41 David Suzuki interviewed by Leigh Sales, *Lateline*, ABC TV, 15 October 2010.

42 Figures from Endarta research: www.enerdata.net/enerdatauk/press-and-publication/publications/g-20-2010-strongly-energy-demand-increase.php

43 David Suzuki, ibid.

44 The Bible, 1st Corinthians 13:11, King James version.

45 The Bible, Deuteronomy 14:6-7, King James version.

46 The Avalon Project: www.avalonlearning.eu

47 Latitude study, 'Children's 'Future Requests' for Computers and the Internet': www.life-connected.com/42-kids_internet

48 Stilgherrian, 'Gamification: Hot, new, unethical?' *Technology Spectator*, 2 May 2011: http://technologyspectator.com.au/emerging-tech/applications/Gamification-unethical

49 Sam Doust, 'Why "Gamification" is as stupid as it sounds', The Drum, ABC online, 18 March 2011: http://www.abc.net.au/news/2011-03-18/why-gamification-is-as-stupid-as-it-sounds/2652370

50 Eric Schmidt in a television interview with CNBC, 'Inside the Mind of Google', documentary aired December 2009.

51 As quoted in the *Sydney Morning Herald*, 8 November 2010.

52 Stephen Fry interviewed by Mark Colvin, PM, ABC Radio, 26 July 2010.

53 'Using technology to control intimate partners: an exploration study of college undergraduates', East Carolina University, 2011.

54 Sci-fi writer Robert J Sawyer , 'The Purpose of Science Fiction', *Slate* magazine, 27 January 2011: http://www.slate.com/articles/technology/future_tense/2011/01/the_purpose_of_science_fiction.html

55 As in SIGMA website: www.sigmaforum.org

56 www.en.wikipedia.org/wiki/Terraforming

57 Benjamin Donato, 'Fair is Foul, and Foul is Fair', Green Party of Canada website, 12 April 2011: http://greenparty.ca/blogs/16756/2011-04-12/and-foul-fair-debate-geoengineering

58 As quoted in a story by Candace Lombardi, 'Report: Geoengineering an option to limit climate change', cnet.com: www.news.cnet.com/8301-11128_3-10333596-54.html

59 Ridgewell, Andy, Freeman, Chris and Lampitt, Richard, 'Geoengineering', The Royal Society website: www.royalsociety.org/further/geoengineering

60 Alessio Rastani in an interview with the BBC's Maxine Croxall, 30 September 2011.

61 Singularity Institute website: www.singinst.org/overview/whatisthesingularity

62 The blogger 'Singularity Utopia' as quoted in the blog post 'Will the "Geek Rapture" Nonsense Ever Stop?', 25 October 2011, www.singularityweblog.com/will-the-geek-rapture-nonsense-ever-stop/

63 Ray Kurzweil interviewed by Steve Cannane, *Lateline*, ABC TV, 29 April 2011.

64 Steve Wozniak as quoted in 'Machines will be superior: Apple founder', *Business Spectator*, 3 June 2011.

65 Douglas Adams, 'DNA: How to Stop Worrying and Learn to Love the Internet', *The Sunday Times*, 29th August 1999: http://www.douglasadams.com/dna/19990901-00-a.html

66 Stephen Fry, op. cit.

ACKNOWLEDGEMENTS

A big thanks to Andrew Davies, my co-producer on the *Future Tense* program at the ABC. And also to Kerri Klumpp for the use of her discerning eye, which I promise to return shortly.